MICRO-CLUSTERS AND NETWORKS

THE GROWTH OF TOURISM

ADVANCES IN TOURISM RESEARCH

Series Editor: **Professor Stephen J. Page**
University of Stirling, UK
s.j.page@stir.ac.uk

Advances in Tourism Research series publishes monographs and edited volumes that comprise state-of-the-art research findings, written and edited by leading researchers working in the wider field of tourism studies. The series has been designed to provide a cutting edge focus for researchers interested in tourism, particularly the management issues now facing decision-makers, policy analysts and the public sector. The audience is much wider than just academics and each book seeks to make a significant contribution to the literature in the field of study by not only reviewing the state of knowledge relating to each topic but also questioning some of the prevailing assumptions and research paradigms which currently exist in tourism research. The series also aims to provide a platform for further studies in each area by highlighting key research agendas, which will stimulate further debate and interest in the expanding area of tourism research. The series is always willing to consider new ideas for innovative and scholarly books, inquiries should be made directly to the Series Editor.

Published:

Taking Tourism to the Limits
RYAN, PAGE AND AICKEN

Tourism in Turbulent Times
WILKS, PENDERGAST & LEGGAT

An International Handbook of Tourism Education
AIREY & TRIBE

Indigenous Tourism
PAGE AND AICKEN

Tourism Local Systems and Networking
LAZZERETTI & PETRILLO

Progress in Tourism Marketing
KOZAK & ANDREU

Extreme Tourism: Lessons from the World's Cold Water Islands
BALDACCHINO

Benchmarking National Tourism Organisations and Agencies
LENNON, SMITH, COCKEREL & TREW

Tourism and Social Identities
BURNS & NOVELLI

Forthcoming:

Tourism and Politics
BURNS & NOVELLI

Tourism and Small Businesses in the New Europe
THOMAS

Hospitality: A Social Lens
LASHLEY, LYNCH & MORRISON

For other titles in the series visit: www.elsevier.com/locate/series/aitr

Related Elsevier Journals — sample copies available on request
Annals of Tourism Research
International Journal of Hospitality Management
Tourism Management

MICRO-CLUSTERS AND NETWORKS

THE GROWTH OF TOURISM

by

EWEN J. MICHAEL
La Trobe University, Victoria, Australia

WITH CONTRIBUTIONS FROM

LAILA GIBSON
Karlstad University, Karlstad, Sweden

C. MICHAEL HALL
Otaga University, Dunedin, New Zealand

PAUL LYNCH
Strathclyde University, Glasgow, Scotland

RICHARD MITCHELL
Otaga University, Dunedin, New Zealand

ALISON MORRISON
Strathclyde University, Glasgow, Scotland

and

CHRISSY SCHREIBER
Otaga University, Dunedin, New Zealand

ELSEVIER

Amsterdam • Boston • Heidelberg • London • New York • Oxford
Paris • San Diego • San Francisco • Singapore • Sydney • Tokyo

Elsevier
The Boulevard, Langford Lane, Kidlington, Oxford OX5 1GB, UK
Radarweg 29, PO Box 211, 1000 AE Amsterdam, The Netherlands

First edition 2007

British Library Cataloguing in Publication Data
A catalogue record for this book is available from the British Library

Library of Congress Cataloging-in-Publication Data
A catalog record for this book is available from the Library of Congress

ISBN-13: 978-0-08-045096-4
ISBN-10: 0-08-045096-2

For information on all Elsevier publications
visit our website at books.elsevier.com

Printed and bound in The Netherlands

07 08 09 10 11 10 9 8 7 6 5 4 3 2 1

Working together to grow
libraries in developing countries

www.elsevier.com | www.bookaid.org | www.sabre.org

ELSEVIER   BOOK AID International   Sabre Foundation

Contents

List of Figures

List of Tables

Contributors

Laila Gibson Karlstad University, Karlstad, Sweden.

C. Michael Hall Department of Tourism, School of Business, University of Otago, Dunedin, New Zealand and visitor to Department of Economic and Social Geography, Umeå University, Umeå, Sweden.

Paul Lynch Department of Hospitality and Tourism Management, Strathclyde Business School, University of Strathclyde, Glasgow, Scotland.

Ewen J. Michael School of Sport, Tourism & Hospitality Management, Faculty of Law & Management, La Trobe University, Victoria 3086, Australia.

Richard Mitchell Department of Tourism, School of Business, University of Otago, Dunedin, New Zealand.

Alison Morrison Department of Hospitality and Tourism Management, Strathclyde Business School, University of Strathclyde, Glasgow, Scotland.

Chrissy Schreiber Department of Tourism, School of Business, University of Otago, Dunedin, New Zealand.

Acknowledgements

As the lead author and editor of this book, I remain deeply indebted to my co-contributors for their support and encouragement and for the ideas they have contributed. Indeed, it is more than flattering that individuals of the calibre of Laila Gibson, Paul Lynch and Allison Morrison, from The Scottish Hotel School, Strathclyde University in Glasgow, and C. Michael Hall, Richard Mitchell and Chrissy Schreiber, from Otago University in Dunedin, should have wished to participate in this task, let alone in a spirit of such active co-operation. This book is truly an international effort that in its own way demonstrates the effectiveness, and what can be achieved, in the expanding global network for researchers. Of course, none of this would have been possible without their dedication, time and effort.

The origins for this book lie in the outcomes from a project that started in 1998 as a simple study of niche markets in tourism. The purpose of research and inquiry is to find what is new, and to explain what has not been explained before. Like so many projects before it, the tangential findings in that earlier study exposed a pattern of relationships between the effective organisation of firms and their impacts on small communities that challenged the existing theory on clustering and location, which clearly warranted further investigation. While it is probably inappropriate to single out individuals, I would like to thank Ken Hopkins in particular, for he started on this exercise with me and his ideas and criticisms continue to lie buried in the sub-text here.

A book of this nature is never written quickly, and can never be done without the help and support of a highly professional editorial team. In this case, that support has come from the dedicated staff at Elsevier. The contributing authors and I are deeply grateful for the assistance provided by Stephen Page, the series editor, and by Mary Malin, our publishing editor whose exuberance and confidence has kept this project going. We are also grateful to her supporting staff, Hannah Collett and Joanna Scott, who have each contributed immeasurably to this production. In their own individual ways, each has demonstrated that it really is possible to conquer distance — for we have had to communicate with each other from the opposite sides of the planet to make this book possible.

Ewen J. Michael PhD,
La Trobe University,
Victoria, Australia

April, 2006

Preface

This book has been written to introduce a new approach to the growth of small tourism markets in regional and rural locations, based on the formation of *micro-clusters* in specialized niche activities. It has been written not just for those who seek to analyze the mechanisms for growth and the location of industry, but for those who work and operate their businesses within small community settings, where a long-term co-operative partnership between commerce and residents is the ultimate determinant for a sustainable future. Its central premise is that myriad small-scale clusters can provide an effective means to establish a local competitive advantage in tourism, based on the resources available to existing communities.

The analysis that is presented in the chapters that follow brings together contemporary views of the potential of *clustering theory* to promote development with considerations of how micro-markets operate within the paradigm of competition. It seeks to create a framework for regional development that might serve to contribute to the growth of small-scale tourism destinations, but this alone does not provide a guide for business development. Hence, this book examines how individuals can participate in the clustering process to build the networks that lead to a co-operative community environment that shares the gains from growth and expansion. The concept of micro-clustering clearly has applications for many industries beyond the development of rural and regional tourism destinations, but the intent and purpose here is to demonstrate an optimal strategy for these particular circumstances.

Rural decline, the diminution of economic opportunity and regional inequity are evident in many parts of the developed world, including Australia, New Zealand, and in some of the more peripheral regions of North America and Europe, including Ireland, Scandinavia and the smaller Mediterranean states. In the same vein, the lack of economic opportunity in the rural areas of emerging states, like many in Asia, in South Africa, in South and Central America and in a host of other places, is creating a need for new forms of growth that are compatible with the needs of the existing communities that live in these environments. As a consequence, any opportunities that might enhance or expand regional growth have become compelling issues for policy analysts to address, but they become even more critical when those opportunities suggest the potential to increase local employment levels in ways that can maintain community values and regional lifestyles.

This book presents one response to these issues; recognising, of course, that it suggests only one option among the many that may provide a basket of solutions for future policy practices. The following chapters outline an approach for building small-scale sources for growth in a myriad of regional economies through tourism clusters. This framework sits inside the conservative assumptions of mainstream economics, recognising that a range of small-scale activities will deliver a wider range of benefits that are perhaps more suited to meeting local community interests than occasional large-scale icon projects that are often practiced as the panacea in regional politics. The concept of micro-clusters reaffirms the principle that economic benefits derive essentially from multiplier effects, while social benefits usually stem from externalities; but, in this interpretation, the approach is driven by local community actions, with a product that reflects that community's interests and values. The novelty, here, lies in the development of a holistic model for application to micro-scale economic environments, where small communities create their own regional competitive advantage while retaining control of the development process.

The genesis of this book stems from an unlikely source. A study of Antiques dealers in regional Australia, which had originally been designed to evaluate their role in generating domestic travel, observed that the more successful operators exhibited patterns of geographic co-location or clustering (Michael, 2002). What was only a tangential finding in that study, quickly proved to be remarkably similar to the empirical observations by researchers in other micro-markets in other countries. More importantly, these researchers were implicitly commenting on observations about the same patterns of growth and expansion as these new *clusters* built their markets by attracting new streams of visitors to their regions. The outcome, then, was a consistent pattern of observations in different countries and in different segments of the tourism market about the behaviour of firms in localized micro-clusters, where these firms were creating and building their commercial success by establishing new tourism functions (or destinations) with their own unique competitive advantages. There is interest, of course, in explaining how this happens, but there is more value in determining whether or not this pattern of growth is amenable to policy manipulation and to deliberate interventions by public sector planners to promote community development.

Part of the explanation of the success of clustering strategies for business firms can be drawn from Porter's (1991, 1998) analyses of the impacts of co-location in strategic national economic development. Porter's approach is not entirely suited to micro-scale development, for it is concerned with larger regions within a national context, but it provides a lead for an effective answer. More is gained, however, by significantly revising Porter's *Diamond* model to allow for the critical role of firms that provide *complementary* products, for it would appear that these are the dynamic that initiates and enhances clustering in micro-environments. This approach also incorporates the effects of new multiplier and externality impacts (both positive and negative) on the host community.

The framework for developing micro-clusters in regional community environments provides an integrated and operational theory for public decision-makers and analysts alike. Explaining why clusters are effective is one thing, but what is needed is an explanation of how people can engage in the process, and here the role of networks in establishing co-operative business practices is demonstrated. The context for these discussions has been cast in the differing experiences and circumstances of regional communities from around the world, with examples drawn from Australia, New Zealand, Scotland, Sweden and elsewhere.

The intention is to explain the concepts of clustering in a model for micro-markets that is consistent with the global demands for competition, but in a way that makes the argument relevant for business planning by those who are faced with such locational choices. The argument is extended, however, to provide a rationale for the active intervention of government, for it is the regional and local agencies of public sector management that are confronted directly with the task of creating economic and social opportunity in small communities. The alternative that is offered here provides a model to develop clusters of complementary firms able to collectively deliver bundles of attributes to make up a specialized regional product. Micro-market clustering theory built around networks of business and community interests offers one alternative for government to enhance regional economic growth, and one that seems aptly suited to tourism development where the regional product requires a combination of many services to deliver the single experience the tourist seeks.

Chapter 1

Introduction

Ewen J. Michael

There has been a renaissance of interest among those concerned with regional development in the use of *Cluster Theory* over the past decade. This may be, in part, because the concept of clustering appears to have a particular application for the development of new industries in regional and peripheral areas. Intuitively, it suggests a mechanism to deliver new economic opportunities for communities that otherwise struggle to keep pace in a world that favours the concentration of large corporations and *capital* for the creation of a competitive edge. The practice of clustering, and particularly its practice at a micro-scale, has yet to prove itself as a dynamic strategy for regional development policy, and its costs and benefits are still subject to conjecture. Nevertheless, in the right circumstances, the potential benefits of micro-clustering may offer a new economic path to restore the prospects of some rural communities, with new avenues to stimulate *wealth* creation, *employment*, population growth, service provision and the restoration of civil *infrastructure*.

Tourism can be seen as an industrial function that produces a vast array of highly differentiated *outputs*. In fact, tourism is not one industry but many, for tourism outputs come from a range of different *production* processes. Part of the quantum of the tourism product is undeniably rural, where consumers seek the attributes that only visits to a regional location can provide. The regional tourism product itself is also highly differentiated — indeed some would argue that it is unique in every location – but, as an industrial activity, it can only be delivered in specific circumstances. Where a tourism function is possible, however, it may offer substantial economic and social benefits for the host community in circumstances where there are sometimes few alternatives. In this context, micro-clustering may offer an approach that helps create new tourism destinations, or expand existing ones, in a framework that could channel the benefits to meet the needs and values of the existing (or should that be *remaining*) population.

Some might suggest that there is an interconnection between the concepts of *tourism* and *clusters* that has been linked by historical commentators for centuries — in the sense that somehow this relationship is supposed to be obvious to the casual observer, and so can be treated as if it were assumed knowledge in some way. Hudson (1993) makes the point by accident in an intriguing description of the 'Grand Tour' in seventeenth and eighteenth century Europe. For over 200 years, until the French revolution undid the European aristocracy, it was not uncommon for the wealthy sons of the nobility to be sent, along with their accompanying entourage of tutors, servants and guards, on tours of intellectual discovery. For months, if not years at a time, the young aristocrats would journey from their northern European citadels to discover the wonders of the *new enlightenment* in Paris and the classical origins of Roman culture and the *renaissance* by visiting Florence, Rome, Naples and Venice, where they could view concentrations of antiquities and collections of art and heritage in clearly identified precincts. Indeed, the contemporary use of the word "tourist" stems from this time, as a means to describe those who undertook the journey and the places they would visit. Tourism has always been about *the journey* and *the place*, but the more attractive destinations have always been those that provide bundles of values for the visitor to consume.

In the contemporary world, of course, tourism is an international activity with broad appeal — there are now many more ways to undertake *the journey* and there are an infinite variety of *places* available for the tourist to visit. Some destinations offer singular attractions and some offer collections of different activities in the same location. The scale of activity in some destinations can be very large, and might even encompass whole cities, like London or Paris, while others can be so small that only a handful of visitors will travel there in any given period of time. The differences between destinations are profound, and call for quite different forms of analysis, interpretation, policy and business operation. The interest here, however, is confined to those smaller destinations in rural and peripheral regions.

The consideration of tourism in micro-clusters, of course, has a very contemporary origin. It stems from a series of tangential findings in a number of studies towards the end of the twentieth century into niche markets in tourism — including, for example, antique retailing in Southwestern Pennsylvania (Grado, Strauss, & Lord,1997); antiques as a tourism market in Australia (Michael, 2002), and Seaton's (1996, 1999) analyses of *Book Towns* in the United Kingdom and Europe. Collectively, these studies and many others point to the possibility that some of these markets, particularly those that generate a demand for travel, are amenable to clustering in regional areas. The Australian study (Michael, 2002) went so far as to suggest that the **co-location** of like firms exhibited the capacity to draw visitors to regional areas, effectively acting as a generator of domestic tourism (detailed in Chapter 6). The results were not conclusive but they suggested, or at least implied, the possibility that successful firms in non-metropolitan areas were more likely to be found operating in small co-located clusters, and sometimes these clusters created a visitor destination in their own right. During this time, of course, Porter (1991) had rekindled interest in the concept of industrial clustering with a revised approach that he and subsequent analysts could demonstrate was relevant for large-scale or macro regions, raising a debate about the potential for clustering theory to contribute to new approaches to development policy. For tourism analysts, however, the problems and issues do not concern large-scale regions but rather their focus is on smaller localities and their communities; and, hence, the new theoretical views seem an imperfect match with the emerging coincidence of empirical data for clustering in **niche markets**.

In this context, the term "*micro-cluster*" was coined to refer to the geographic concentration of a small number of firms in a cohesive local environment (Michael, 2003), where the complementary interaction between those firms contributed to an enhanced level of local specialisation. A micro-cluster, then, is defined by its local context, and the unique identification of its product, rather than by artificial perceptions of regionality or production processes. As a concept, this is not new, but it serves to shift the focus of analysis in economic development from the broader and more general issues that dominate larger regions or States, to the specific problems of individual localities, towns and villages and the people who live in these environments.

From this earlier work there now emerges a hypothesis to suggest the possibility that some niche markets, and particularly those that generate a demand for travel, are both amenable to clustering in regional areas and more successful when they do. The implication from this proposition is that micro-markets of this type, when operating in a cluster formation, are capable of creating a tourism function (or destination) in their own right. The inherent value in this argument rests in its intriguing consequence, for if a locality can establish a micro-cluster, then it may well be able to generate a range of accelerated economic and social benefits for that community. The development process, however, is driven by and embedded in its *micro* scale, where small communities remain in control of the structure and the nature of growth — it will be their choices which determine the form of development that takes place and it will be their decisions that will control the management of the *externalities* that arise as a result. More importantly, if the dynamics that deliver micro-clustering can be harnessed through a policy process, it suggests the prospect for a new pathway for regional tourism development that remains entirely consistent with community demands. In this sense, the micro-clusters approach may well incorporate a political dimension to the resolution of local development possibilities that many other policy frameworks lack.

If micro-cluster theory can contribute to the practice of regional development policy, and to regional tourism in particular, it will be because it allows local communities to engage in the process of growth on terms that are acceptable to them. Given the problems of rural decline, the diminution of economic opportunity and regional inequity in parts of Australia, New Zealand, South Africa and many of the peripheral regions of Europe and North America, any potential to expand regional growth warrants further exploration. The need is more compelling where that potential offers both employment growth and economic opportunity in ways that are consistent with the maintenance of community values and lifestyles.

While the notions of location and clustering are well understood in strategic planning, the same cannot be said about the forces that initiate and enhance the process of clustering in micro-environments. Arguably, even less is known about the nature and scale of the costs and benefits that successful clustering might impose on regional communities, and no work at all appears to have been done on the effects of de-clustering! The concepts of location concentration and clustering can be seen as *core knowledge* within the literature of strategic planning, geography and microeconomics; but they do not necessarily explain the dynamics that initiate and enhance clustering in truly micro-environments. Likewise, there are several contemporary studies of commercial *alliances* between firms (e.g., Dyer, Kale, & Singh, 2001), and of the effects these alliances have on operations and costs, but the benefits from these relationships are intended to be internalised for the advantage of the member firms, and so have little to do with the range of social and economic impacts that successful clustering might bring to a small community. In short, without a comprehensive understanding of the forces that apply in these circumstances, the potential for any form of policy application remains constrained.

For public sector and social planners with an interest in regional tourism development, the problem is still how to identify those dynamics that lead to successful clustering, and how to assess the social impacts that such a process might generate. This is *not* to suggest that micro-clusters are *the* panacea for regional development policy, but rather where particular market conditions favour the practice of cluster formation, as appears the case in many small rural destinations, this approach may create another *opportunity* for local growth. This rather generous statement, however, presupposes that micro-cluster formation is amenable to public sector intervention; and, as a corollary, that there exists both a role for government and a theoretical pretext for taking such actions.

These then are the issues that this book addresses. The approach that has been taken looks first at the issues exposed by the concept of *rural decline*, in part to explain the urgency in the need to identify new approaches to regional development. Rural decline is not so much an economic phenomenon as it is a social one: where the loss of opportunity and the perceived diminution of infrastructure in rural areas is failing to deliver new prospects for growth and, hence, is seen by the residents in those communities as the critical issue confronting the framework of the future policies that will affect them. Rural decline takes many forms, with many consequences for the people who are affected — although it is doubtful that anyone has expressed this so eloquently as Michael Sanders (2004) in his commentary on the changes to life in rural France:

> "*Les Arques* in 1900," she told me, "had nearly eight hundred people, today less than two hundred. Then, one hundred and twenty were of school age, today not twenty. Then, the village had four working mills, two cabarets [small bars], and a brickworks. *Cazals* had four hotels, eight cabarets, and six cafés! And have you seen *St Caprais*? ... The village is in ruins!" she exclaimed. "On dirait qu'il y a eu une guerre!" You would think there had been a war there.
> If, perhaps, Madame Delon had exaggerated the degree of *St Caprais'* dilapidation, her words struck home all the same. Caught in a downward spiral of eroding population and declining agriculture, it showed what time and the elements will do, in the space of just two generations, to stone and tile without the attentions of the hand of man. Without trade. Without, in short, a life.
>
> Michael Sanders (2004): *From Here You Can't See Paris*, Bantam, London, (p. 18).

Over the past decade, throughout the developed world, there has been a steady increase in the demands for new approaches to rekindle regional growth and create new opportunities for the **sustainability** of regional communities (see Prosser, 2001). Combining the perceptions of rural decline and regional inequity with the reactions of an increasingly volatile electorate creates a compelling argument for seeking out new mechanisms for development policies that are capable of bringing real benefits to regional residents. The task is made more difficult, of course, for any new direction must also conform to national growth strategies, the global demands of competition policy and the often conflicting expectations of local residents to deliver employment growth while maintaining community values and lifestyles.

As Chapter 2 notes, there are many approaches to regional development that might appropriately contribute to the reconstruction of opportunity for regional communities, but as yet no single approach or basket of choices has found a consensus of support in the policy domain. The potential for micro-cluster theory to make even a small contribution to the enhancement of these options remains only as one possibility, but one that seems particularly relevant where a community identifies a tourism function as part of its set of economic and social choices. The notion of growth through a *tourism cluster* is not an innovation in itself, for it simply recycles the principle that *economic benefits* normally stem from multiplier and accelerator effects, while *social benefits* are the consequences of its positive externalities. In small communities, however, clustering can be directed by local choices to optimise the consequences from growth, rather than being its victim.

Nevertheless, the issue of concern remains with the ways and means that the sources for reviving regional opportunities can be identified. To establish the background for this discussion, Chapters 3 and 4 consider the principles behind a model of successful micro-market clustering based on tourism. They serve to revise and re-evaluate the traditional approaches to cluster theory by incorporating contemporary analyses of the new economic approaches to *complementarities* — an interpretation that introduces the notion of *diagonal clustering* as the *agent provocateur* for accelerating growth. While this explains the economic dynamics inherent in the formation and maintenance of micro-clusters, more is needed to explain how individuals, businesses and communities can benefit from the process. The answer, perhaps, lies in Chapter 5, which applies the concepts of *network theory* to expose the human mechanisms that make the clustering model a viable strategy for growth.

All of this might seem quite abstract and theoretical, if it were not based on some empirical reality. To this end, Chapters 6, 7 and 8 seek to provide some illustration of real micro-clusters in operation, and of the networking processes that occur within them. The approach adopted here helps point to the key success factors for clustering that are relevant to an existing market's niche industries and community structures. It assumes the pre-existence of a community and its resources and lifestyle, for these are the factors that set the parameters for building any new level of activity. These examples seek to illustrate the dynamic alignment of complementary economic activities between firms and communities that add value to the final local product, where the intention is to deliver a *package of attributes* to targeted groups of *new* consumers.

Regional development, of course, is haphazard by nature as communities respond to the vagaries of their environment and of market forces in their own terms. While the prevailing policy paradigm of competition eschews a role for government as the paternalistic director of industrial development, rural communities still expect their choices to be supported by public action. Many of the issues and problems that have arisen among some regional communities over the past 20 years or so have contributed to a political environment where the approaches of government are now being questioned and social change is being demanded. It is in this context that new models for development are being sought, but contemporary experience suggests that any such approaches must necessarily incorporate the affected communities in the decision-making mechanism. Chapters 9 and 10 deal specifically with the economic and political issues surrounding the role for government and for public sector intervention in regional development, albeit with a particular focus on the potential to support the initiation of clustering processes by local host communities in ways that enable them to drive the key resource allocation decisions.

Among other things, these chapters look particularly at the need for equity and transparency in any of the actions of government that might facilitate or sponsor the development of business opportunities, irrespective of whether that be at the national, regional or local levels. Micro-clusters can form successfully in small communities in unstructured ways and without the specific policy support of the public sector, but this discussion suggests a new role for government as the agent that serves to support and optimise the collective gains from the community's own choices. There may well be tasks that are best served by government, including acting as the arbiter on the mutual assurances that new entrants to a cluster might require; thus positioning the appropriate agencies as the catalysts to stimulate tourism growth in regional and rural environments. The intent of this book, after all, is to suggest ways in which the public decision-making system can support and enhance the growth of these cluster formations, and to identify the ways that development decisions can be devolved effectively to the communities that will have to live with their consequent costs and benefits.

References

Dyer, J. H., Kale, P., & Singh, H. (2001). How to make strategic alliances work. *Sloan Management Review, 42*(1), 37–43.

Grado, S. C., Strauss, C. H., & Lord, B. E. (1997). Antiquing as a tourism recreational activity in Southwestern Pennsylvania. *Journal of Travel Research, 35*(3), 52–56.

Hudson, R. (Ed.) (1993). *The grand tour, 1592—1796.* London: Folio Society.

Michael, E. J. (2002). Antiques and tourism in Australia. *Tourism Management, 23*(2), 117–125.

Michael, E. J. (2003). Tourism micro-clusters, *Tourism Economics, 9*(2), 133–146.

Porter, M. E. (1991). *The competitive advantage of nations.* London: Macmillan.

Prosser, G. (2001). Regional tourism'. As Chapter 4. In: N. Douglas, N. Douglas, & R. Derrett (Eds), *Special interest tourism.* Milton (Qld.): Wiley .

M. Sanders (2004). *From here you can't see Paris* (p. 18). London: Bantam..

Seaton, A. V. (1996). Hay on wye, the mouse that roared, book towns and rural tourism. *Tourism Management, 17*(5), 379–382.

Seaton, A. V. (1999). 'Book towns as tourism developments in peripheral areas *International Journal of Tourism Research, 1*, 389–399.

Chapter 2

Issues in Regional Development

C. Michael Hall and Ewen J. Michael

Objectives

This chapter identifies some of the issues confronting rural and regional communities – in particular, those that affect their prospects for economic development and their capacity to maintain employment, opportunity and lifestyle for future generations.

- It explores some of the arguments that seek to explain why many rural populations are in decline, noting in particular the impacts of globalization and deregulation in agricultural markets and their consequent impacts on rural populations.
- The chapter explores the need for new forms of production to retain employment that enhances the sustainability of these communities in ways that are consistent with their needs and values.
- Tourism is defined as an economic activity, but, as this chapter notes, it is sometimes treated as a panacea for regional development policies when in reality it is only one among many possible options that might contribute to a basket of solutions for development in rural areas.
- The development of small-scale tourism destinations within regional areas offers one such possibility to revitalize rural growth, but it is identified as a very specific form of activity that will suit the needs of some communities but not others.
- The approach taken to examine the role of government highlights the schism between the role of national governments, and their commitment to broad economic approaches to competition, with the role of municipal and local authorities, who must meet the needs of communities in a changing environment.

Micro-Clusters and Networks: The Growth of Tourism
Copyright © 2007 by Elsevier Ltd.
All rights of reproduction in any form reserved.
ISBN: 0-08-045096-2

The changing nature of the issues that now confront regional development are largely a consequence of the global drive towards a more competitive or *free market* environment. Much of this process, which began to take shape over 30 years ago, seeks to liberalize trade and reduce costs in the *production* of agricultural and other commodities, but as these products often form the industrial base for regional and rural communities, it has been inevitable that these same communities have had to bear the brunt of change.

A Changing Environment

For some analysts and commentators, these changes reflect part of the agenda of the political project of *neo-liberalism*. Tickell and Peck (2003, p. 166) define neo-liberalism in process-based terms, 'as the mobilization of state power in the contradictory extension and reproduction of market (like) rule' (emphasis in the original). A more descriptive explanation is offered by Standing (2002, p. 26), who suggests there is a basic series of policy measures through which neo-liberalism is projected, and that this can be characterized in terms of policies in support of:

1. trade liberalisation,
2. financial market liberalisation,
3. *privatization* of production,
4. *deregulation*,
5. foreign capital liberalization through the elimination of barriers to foreign direct *investment*,
6. secure *property rights*,
7. unified and competitive *exchange rates*,
8. diminished public spending through 'fiscal discipline',
9. switching in public expenditure to education, health, *infrastructure* and security,
10. development of a more narrowly targeted 'social safety net' in contrast to the wider notion of the welfare state, and
11. the creation and support of flexible *labour markets*.

However, as with *globalization* the impact of neo-liberal ideas, although significant, is not evenly distributed around the world. Different states have adopted elements of neo-liberalism, in different ways and to different degrees.

> "… the concrete shape of the 'project' itself has always been institutionally variable, both across space and through time. In other words, the project has evolved, and it has evolved unevenly." (Tickell & Peck, p. 168)

There is no exception for tourism in this process, for it too has been bound up in neoliberal policy-making in a variety of ways. This includes the restructuring of the role of the state in tourism development and the framework for tourism governance. However, neoliberalism's impact on economic production has also affected the way within which tourism is seen as a policy tool, in part as a response to the economic restructuring that has occurred because of the changed regulatory regime in which markets and economic production now operate. For example, tourism is now an integral component for *place* competition and for regeneration strategies (Hall, 1997; Malecki, 2004), with such effects being felt throughout much of the developed world – in urban and rural areas alike.

Much of the attention to tourism's role in regional development has its grounding in the substantial economic change that has been brought about in rural regions, which are due, at least in part, to the neo-liberal influences on the nature and structure of international trade regimes and the role of the state in managing the domestic dimensions of trade within such regimes. In accord with this agenda, many of the world's leading exporting nations have acted in concert since the 1970s to begin a process that would reduce the *subsidies* provided for rural industries involved in agricultural, mining and forest production. In part, their intention was to ensure they would be positioned to compete equitably on the basis of their own *comparative advantage* in the contest for future *markets*. Such an intention, perhaps, reflects the neoliberal principle, 'that the absence of state intervention *is* the market' (O'Neil, 1997, p. 291).

In theory, and arguably sometimes in practice, the elimination of rural subsidy programmes was supposed to encourage a higher level of specialized production, where costs would be lowered, global output levels would be increased and *consumer* prices would be reduced. Again, in principle, these *efficiency* gains were supposed to enhance the opportunities for trade among the agricultural exporters, giving them a capacity to import more sophisticated manufactures from the developed industrial states. Despite the efforts since, many of these exporting nations, including Argentina, Australia, Brazil and New Zealand, have found it difficult to compete fairly on the basis of costs, and many of the benefits that were promised as the consequence from these reforms have failed to realize those earlier expectations – at least, in a form that is visible for the rural communities in these states. In great part this has been because of the enormous variations between countries in the extent to which state subsidies have been reduced. Indeed, this has become a major issue in negotiations in *north–south trade*, and the role of agricultural subsidies in the developed world remains as a contributing factor in the underdevelopment of the agricultural economies in Africa in particular. However, these issues are not isolated to north–south relations alone, but also constitute a major stress within the European Union between countries that seek to maintain current levels of agricultural subsidy, such as France and Poland, and those that seek to shift the European Union's expenditure into new industrial development and innovation, such as the United Kingdom and Sweden (Daugbjerg, 1997; Lowe, Buller, & Ward, 2002).

It may be that this also reflects a broader failure to understand the political consequences of deregulation, especially in those countries where subsidies have been reduced. As O'Neil (1997, p. 292) observed:

> "... the neo-liberalist vision of 'less state' is entirely illusory. Neo-liberalism is a self-contradicting theory of the state. The geographies of product, finance and labour markets that it seeks to construct require *qualitatively* different, not less, state action. Neo-liberalism is a political discourse which impels rather than reduces state action."

While the global agenda to liberalize trade continues, the impacts from changing interregional migration, changing market conditions, the growth of *technological change*, and the continuing practices of the United States and the European Union to protect their rural producers through *quotas* and other restrictions, have combined inexorably to alter the potential pathways for economic development in the rural areas of many of these states. It is within this global context that the paradox of 'rural decline' appears, for it refers not to the increasing quantity and value of agricultural production but to the consequent impact of change on the resident communities in rural areas.

Concepts of Rural Decline

As a broad assertion, there exists in many of the world's developed and developing states, which have or still retain a strong agricultural sector, a consistent and visible pattern of increasing agricultural efficiency and *productivity*, growing farm incomes and improving rates of return on agricultural investments. Simultaneously, however, this pattern of economic growth has been accompanied by a paradoxical decline in the levels of employment within the agricultural sector and, often, by reduced opportunities for employment in alternate sectors as the diversity of regional industries contracts: a circumstance that has forced many residents to seek their economic opportunities elsewhere by migration to the major urban centres. The decline in rural residency has reduced local levels of *consumption*, and in the face of falling *demand* there has been a contraction in the provision of infrastructure and *services*, which further accelerates the loss of social and economic amenity and opportunity for the remaining rural population. This situation has been further exacerbated in those states where governments have sought to corporatize or privatize many of the services they once owned, including banking, posts and telecommunications, health and education, which now necessitates that their operators respond primarily to market forces rather than to social need.

This has meant, for example, that while many rural areas of the developed world exhibit regional economic data that appears to be relatively strong, these same areas still suffer substantial problems from population decline and service loss, which may well accelerate still further should the global agricultural sector be subject to 'free trade'. This apparent contradiction warrants further consideration. It lies at the heart of the social demands on government for a range of responses to promote new forms of economic opportunity in regional areas, where tourism and other forms of amenity-related mobility – such as second homes – are regarded as key mechanisms in the process of reinvigorating rural and regional economies (Hall, 2006).

One way to illustrate the 'paradox of rural decline' is to investigate the issues that have arisen in specific states – and the changes that have occurred in Australia and New Zealand can serve this purpose. Australia's circumstances are not unique and are mirrored for example in the social consequences of the radical reforms that were introduced in New Zealand in the 1980s. Arguably, they are also visible, perhaps to an even greater extent, in some of the South American states, like Brazil and Argentina. The same patterns of social change also exist in North America and Western Europe, if ameliorated to some extent by government programmes to support and maintain the viability of rural communities. Indeed, the maintenance of rural and peripheral area populations and economies, through policy mechanisms such as the 'Common Agricultural Programme', is a cornerstone of European regional policy. Nevertheless, the Australian and New Zealand narratives serve to highlight the impacts of change on rural communities and the nature of the new demands for economic growth that have emerged, and which many western governments now confront.

The dynamics for change in Australia, for example, originate with the shift of government policy (1972–1975) that first reduced rural production subsidies, and subsequently eliminated them over the following two decades. New Zealand followed suit in the 1980s, but with a policy agenda under Prime Minister Lange's Labor government (1984–1989) that reversed an extensive program of agricultural and rural region protection schemes in less than three years. To date, neither country has shown the slightest inclination to return to these prescriptions. For many in regional Australia and rural New Zealand, the impacts that stemmed from these policy adjustments were not necessarily perceived as the consequences that might normally flow from the incremental variations that usually arise from changes in public administration, but rather were seen as fundamental reductions in the economic opportunities that affect their livelihoods and social well-being.

'Rural decline' is a vexed issue in this context for both countries, for the proponents of change had argued that the actions necessary to make the agricultural sector more sustainable in the long term, and more competitive in future global markets, required an increasing level of specialization and efficiency to improve rural productivity and the level of investment in new technologies. Today, the same proponents of change can now point to the commercial viability of many of the industries that make up the agricultural sectors in both Australia and New Zealand, to the increasing volumes of output and to its increasing value, and to the accelerating rates of return from investments in farms (Hopkins, 2005, p. 17). However, for many rural communities the contra argument is also visible in clinical economic data: as the reduced number of small agricultural-holdings; the falling share of small farm product; the declining level of total rural employment, particularly in the agricultural sector; the drift of population to larger cities and urban areas, and, depending on the region, the loss or diminishing quality of social infrastructure, including communication, financial, postal, fuel and other services.

To return to the Australian example, the rural economy has grown substantially in a macro sense over the last 15 years or so, despite the extensive droughts across the eastern States throughout the period from 1997 to 2006. Total agricultural production (measured as an index of the wholesale value of crops, livestock and livestock products) increased by 40.7% in the 10 years between 1987 and 1997, substantially more than *real Gross Domestic Product* which increased by only 30.3% over the same period (ABS, 2000). Growth has been driven by the increase in the number of large farms: where the total number of establishments engaged in rural activity increased by 11% in this time, but their average size increased by 15%, and their average acreage under cultivation increased still further. On the other hand, the number of employed persons did not increase at all (ABS, 2000; Hopkins, 2005, p. 17). In short, the quantity of output and the value of output have been steadily rising, but through a process that has seen farms consolidate to reduce both their labour costs and overheads. Despite these substantial gains in productivity, a more revealing perception of the rural crisis is demonstrated by the narrowing of the gap in the Farmers' Terms of Trade Index, between total farm receipts and expenditures, which fell by 15% in the decade to 1997 (ABARE, 2000).

The issue, as it is perceived from the perspective of many rural communities, is that the increases in output and productivity have not translated to increases in visible growth, employment or economic welfare. Where gains have been made, they have accrued to the operators of large farms or to the corporations that control the new, intensive production systems, where *profits* and margins leak back to urban-based shareholders. Agricultural producers, however, constitute only a minority of regional residents. For some years analysts have observed that Australia's rural development policy is "... *fatally flawed...*" confusing *farm* and *rural* as synonymous terms, and consequently ignoring the needs of the four out of five rural Australians who are not farmers (Sher & Sher, 1994, p. 13). While successive governments have sought to make the farm sector more competitive in a global market (with some success at a macro level), their approaches to regional development, which affect most of the resident population, have been piecemeal and dilettante, often driven by the needs of central bureaucracies for short-term, cost-based outcomes.

Similar issues to those experienced in Australia emerge in the case of New Zealand. Within 12 months of the initial deregulation of the New Zealand economy in 1984 all production subsidies had been removed, including those for fertilizers, and guaranteed funding for disaster relief. At the start of 1984, subsidies were estimated to represent as much as 33% of farm income; but, by 2003 this had fallen to less than 2%, and most of this comprised spending on agricultural research (Smith & Montgomery, 2004). Indeed, it is significant to note that the 'New Zealand Experiment' (Kelsey, 1995) has been described as the most comprehensive and sweeping economic restructuring undertaken by any OECD country (Bray & Walsh, 1998) in order to increase competitiveness (Crocombe, Enright, & Porter, 1991).

At a superficial level, rural New Zealand appears to have made substantial gains as a result of the changes to government policy that have occurred since the mid-1980s, particularly with respect to agricultural and rural protectionism, industrial relations and public sector management. Despite the growth of international tourism, the agricultural sector is still the mainstay of the country's export earnings. The dramatic restructuring that the agricultural sector underwent led to the development of not only a more corporate approach to the business of farming, in terms of its structure, but also a greater focus on what the market actually wants in terms of its outputs. This has meant that agricultural production is now more diverse in New Zealand than it was at the start of the 1980s. While beef, lamb, dairy and wool production remain significant, there is now far more adding of value to these production processes through increased specialisation. In addition, new markets have been opened up in horticulture, deer farming and wine. While more agricultural products are being exported than ever before, they are being produced on larger farms utilising more technology and with correspondingly less employment (Smith & Montgomery, 2004), with the consequence that there are significant flow-on affects for the rural regions within which farm enterprises are embedded (Johnsen, 2003).

The results of the restructuring process now means that many New Zealand rural and peripheral regions exhibit the classic signs of rural decline, such as service and population loss, even though they exhibit significantly better economic returns than before. For example, Statistics New Zealand (2005) report that the estimated resident population of highly rural/remote areas fell by 1.1 percent between 2001 and 2003, while the national population increased by 3.3 percent. The same pattern is apparent in the declining commencement rate for new building construction per 1,000 households, which was below the national average in 2002 and 2003. As Statistics New Zealand (2005) note:

'In the future, it seems likely that the proportion of New Zealand's population living in these areas will decline. Yet they will remain of great importance as a vital part of New Zealand's economic production, as a tourist attraction, and in parts of the North Island as a centre for Maori culture'.

With respect to the changes in rural economy and society, the Australian and New Zealand situation can be seen as broadly representative of the rural and peripheral areas in other developed countries (Jenkins, Hall, & Troughton, 1998; Hall, 2006). The consequence of over 30 years of neo-liberal policy settings and economic restructuring in such countries has seen a steady decline in rural services and infrastructure, resulting in increased social externalities and, what is proving to be more important, a decreased potential for long-term regional growth. The cycle of decline in regional areas is an old story, but perhaps exacerbated by the pace of improving technology: where fewer employees are required to deliver many services, including health, transport, finance and communications, reducing demand and employment, thus causing still further reductions in economic activity in both the short and long term. As the social and economic infrastructure declines, still more rural residents are forced to seek their opportunities elsewhere. In this environment, rural youth is particularly at risk, for there are fewer and fewer prospects for gainful employment; and, as they migrate to the towns and cities, the very nature of community lifestyles is changed. The social costs are compounded, of course, when the platform for growth, regeneration and innovation becomes so diminished that new opportunities cannot be exploited in the absence of human or entrepreneurial capital.

A summary of some of the attributes usually associated with rural and peripheral areas that emerge in the tourism literature are listed in Table 2.1, although it should be noted that the extent to which these attributes apply to regions is highly variable and in some cases substantially contested (Hall, 2005b).

The Policy Gap

One of the consequences of economic globalisation and restructuring that is now manifest in regional and rural communities is an increasing level of political and social volatility. Rural electorates no longer seem 'rusted-on' to conservative political agendas and their expectations for public-sector support appear to be changing — and changing rapidly. Consequently, there are also new demands for approaches to policy to rekindle regional growth and to create new opportunities for the sustainability of rural communities (see also Prosser, 2001). The concept of *rural decline*, as expressed in the politics of the developed world at least, is not so much an economic phenomenon as it is a social and cultural one, where the loss of opportunity and the failure to deliver new prospects for growth in population, services and amenities are seen as the critical issues that confront the development of future policy. In addition, there is often considerable policy confusion between the use of farm or agricultural policy and the need for more general rural development policy. For example, Potter and Lobley (2004) have noted that in the UK the growing diversification of the income base of many farm households to non-farm income sources, including tourism, is leading to the emergence of a community of land managers that is more diverse and decoupled from agricultural policy support than it has ever been before.

Table 2.1: The characteristics of peripheral areas identified in tourism literature.

- Peripheral areas, by definition, are geographically remote from mass markets, therefore implying increased transportation and communication costs for suppliers and consumers
- Peripheral areas tend to lack political and economic control over major decisions affecting their economic and social well-being
- Internal economic linkages normally tend to be weaker at the periphery than at the core, potentially limiting the ability to achieve high multiplier effects where development relies on a substantial degree of importation of goods and services, but income multipliers can be higher where development relies on human resources and labour supply, as can be the case with tourism
- Peripheral areas tend to have reduced access to educational, communication, health, social and financial services than core regions
- Migration flows tend to be from the periphery to the core representing a loss of tangible and intangible human capital
- Some peripheral areas can attract new forms of in-migration with respect to retirement and second home development, although this trend is often confined to older age groups
- Peripheries may be characterized by a comparative lack of innovation as new products tend to be imported rather than developed locally
- The national state and local administrative authorities may seek to play a relatively greater interventionist role in rural and peripheral areas than in core regions in terms of influencing industrial location decision-making
- Information flows within the periphery and from the periphery to the core tend to be weaker than those from the core to the periphery
- Peripheral regions often retain high aesthetic amenity values because their resource base remains relatively underdeveloped in comparison to the core areas

(Sources: Grado, Strauss, & Lord, 1997; Hall, 1997; Botterill et al., 1997; Hall & Müller, 2004; Hall, 2005a, 2006; Hall & Boyd, 2005; Jansson & Müller, 2006.)

The problem is well recognized, but the solutions are not. Transnational associations of states, such as the OECD or the European Union, along with national governments and provincial administrations seem caught in a hiatus between recognizing the need for action and the conflict it would create with the competitive market paradigm in which they work (Hugonnier, 1999; Hall, 2005a), while local and municipal authorities have been left to grapple with its realities (Ward, Lowe, & Bridges, 2003; Goodman, 2004; Lamine, 2005). In the meantime, the response from regional voters has been to demonstrate their frustration with an escalating pattern of vote switching and support for more extreme viewpoints in the search for sympathetic change. The emergence of rural-based right wing political groups in the 1990s, such as *One Nation* in Australia or, to a lesser extent, *New Zealand First* in New Zealand, is symptomatic of the disillusionment experienced by many regional voters with the traditional mechanisms for communicating disaffection through mainstream party politics and the electoral choices available to them. Increasingly, it would appear that rural voters in particular have become more willing to switch their preferences away from old party allegiances, and are using the ballot box to impact on regional, State or national governments to impose short-term demands for immediate relief.

The core of the theme running through these demands is the reconstruction of the prospects for economic growth – through the provision of new infrastructure and services, including telecommunications and information technology, and the maintenance of critical health, welfare and education services that directly impact on local communities perceptions' about their 'quality of life'. The demand is not for handouts or public *welfare* benefits, but for the retention of a viable social base that offers the potential for individuals and communities to pursue their own economic opportunities and wellbeing. Within this explosive mix of social and economic conflicts, there has emerged a new and different set of expectations for *public sector* support. The problem, of course, is that the governments in Australia, New Zealand and elsewhere, have yet to build a consistent understanding of how to meet these needs in ways that might satisfy this increasingly cantankerous electorate at a time where many localities are facing an increasing level of competition for capital and people (Malecki, 2004; Hall, 2005b).

These problems are not distinctly Antipodean, and are mirrored to some extent in other developed countries, particularly in the smaller peripheral nations of Europe. Nevertheless, some countries appear to have recognized the issues and responded much earlier to the impacts of change. OECD data suggest that many of the governments, including the USA and those in the core of Western Europe, have substantially switched the direction of their rural policies over the past two decades to deliberately rebuild the infrastructure and development base of regional communities, in an attempt to reverse the trend of declining employment and economic and social opportunity (Hugonnier, 1999). Consequently, there now exists an expanding gap between the growth capacities of many regional communities in Australia, New Zealand and other countries where rural social and economic infrastructure has been neglected, when compared to the opportunities that are available to many communities in those economies where governments have intervened more directly, such as within the European Union.

The argument, in essence, is that the older approaches to policy, based on subsidized agricultural production, regional equalization and sporadic *icon* developments, have given way to new concepts derived from the competitive paradigm (Hall, 2005a; Michael, 2006). In this context, the macro-economic policies of governments are designed to support the comparative advantage of regions to better pursue the gains that are possible from the globalization of trade. On the other side of the ledger, however, the same competitive model envisages that regional communities will be able to exercise greater local autonomy, particularly in terms of the choices they make about resource allocation decisions. While this is the rhetoric of international politics, its practise has been limited. There is therefore a clear need for a consistent framework for contemporary policy that can continue to maintain the expansion in rural economic efficiency; but, which simultaneously returns some of those gains to the regional communities that deliver it, in ways that expand their social *opportunities* by creating new pathways for growth with positive outcomes that are consistent with the existing needs and values of the resident population.

Tourism and Tourism Development

It is within this context that *Tourism* emerges as an issue. Perhaps, somewhat ironically, the same forces of globalization that have contributed to the economic restructuring of rural and peripheral regions in the developed world are also some of the same forces that have contributed to the growth in international tourism (Hall, 2005b). The rapid growth of the global tourism industry, and perhaps arguably the growing preference of travellers to participate in niche markets, has been perceived by many rural communities as an opportunity to develop a new range of economic activities that fits well with their exist-ing resources and needs (Hall & Boyd, 2005a; Novelli, 2005). The potential to expand new tourism business opportunities is almost universally perceived by regional commu-nities as part of the solution, even though the prospects for development are often more imagined than they are real. Indeed, many of the arguments put forward in favour of tourism development suffer from the misconception that "...when all else fails, there's always tourism..." (Killion, 2001, p. 170). In reality, however, tourism development policies are most economically relevant to regional communities only in those circum-stances where a competitive product can be created (Hall, 2005a, 2005b). Nevertheless, some forms of tourism development might well contribute to the basket of solutions that will revitalize some communities, and hence the opportunity to engage in these activi-ties has evolved as an integral part of the political demands that are now being placed on public sector planners.

The issues surrounding tourism development in regional areas are complex (Butler, Hall, & Jenkins, 1998). The analysis of any industry, from a social, economic or financial perspective, requires a careful delineation of its borders and limits, to establish a degree of certainty or definition for the entity under examination — the analyst needs to know exactly what activities characterize that particular production process. Flow-on and *spillover effects* are part of what the business analyst wants to identify. However, when an industry is said to come under the *tourism* label there is instant confusion and ambiguity; for, in reality, it is defined by misnomer. An *industry*, as an economic entity, is defined by the commonality of its production process for a group of similar firms, but the tourism industry is defined by the activity of consumers when they travel (Hall, 2005b; Michael, 2002). The process of travelling, however, is not always connected with leisure or recre-ation, which, from lay perceptions of what constitutes tourism, is normally assumed to make up the tourism experience. Part of a business activity may therefore involve tourism and part of it may not, or worse, the same product or activity may be a tourism experience for one consumer but not for another (as any travel agent can attest). In truth, the issues associated with assessing travel demand have always been ambiguous.

Certainly, tourism industry researchers have been contributing to the refinement of these issues as each new problem is identified and addressed, but, in matters of definition, precision often remains a matter of perception. Nevertheless, there is value in rehearsing the arguments about what constitutes *tourism* to clarify what is at stake when policymak-ers seek to promote its development in this field rather than in some other. The intention here is not to redefine tourism, but simply to distinguish its characteristics. In essence, a clear identification of the key elements of tourism will open the way to a sufficient insight about the activity that leads, perhaps, to a better understanding of its functions and policy implications.

The traditional approaches to *tourism* analysis originated almost entirely from stud-ies of travel, in that they recognized the movement of people for reasons that were unre-lated to commerce or migration. Transport economists and statisticians clearly needed to separate classes of travellers and travel markets for broad industry studies, but defining tourism solely by travel over arbitrary distances or for convenient time-periods did not prove particularly helpful for detailed industry analyses (Michael, 2002). In more recent times, the emphasis has switched to the behaviour and motivation of travellers, bringing the purpose for travel into the assessment. This helps to identify a particular group of consumers with particular attributes as the defining focus of the industry. In this approach, the notion of tourism appears as a leisure or non-working activity, which, when coupled to the idea that "… a person chooses to perform…" the particular behaviour, serves to identify the individual's own motivation as a determining factor (Aronsson, 1994, p. 79). While not sufficient as a concept in itself (it does not distinguish, for example, some social activities like *sport* from tourism) it still delivers a reliable enough bases for categorizing what is or is not *tourism*. This interpretation, of course, still assumes "… that the economic consequences of these activities are not forgotten: the *tourist*, when all is said and done, is still a consumer, albeit in some sort of specific market" (Michael, 2002, p. 118).

It seems difficult to be more precise without recourse to particular examples, industry cases or segments of more general tourism activities. To illustrate the point, *heritage tourism* might refer to those particular aspects of tourism generated by motivations associated with images of past cultural and social practices, real or otherwise (Stewart, 1990; Palmer, 1996). What distinguishes heritage or cultural tourism from any other market segment is not the nature of the activity so much as it is the delivery of specific socio-psychological needs for the visitor, focussed perhaps on interests that explore kinship, family, artistic expression and other visible aspects of human endeavour (Zeppel & Hall, 1991).

The problems of definition, of course, become more complex the more they are examined, and the issues are exposed wherever the borders between *travel* and *tourism* are challenged. With no easy resolution available, it makes sense to work with the key elements or characteristics of leisure tourism for which there is common acclaim. These might be summarized as:

- The existence of voluntary *travel* or *visitation* outside of the consumer's home area for reasons not associated with work or employment;
- *Motivation* based on an individual's own perceptions of leisure or recreational requirements; and
- *Consumption* or *expenditure* determined by those same travel and motivational requirements.

In this context, tourism *development* policies aim to establish tourism products and build appropriate consumer markets, while tourism *growth* policies aim to increase either or both the volume of visitation and the economic value of visitor activities. However, it is important to recognize that while leisure tourism may constitute the bulk of temporary human mobility, other categories of travel such as those related to health and education may also be important contributors to economic development, particularly as they often use much of the same infrastructure as the leisure tourist and may even lead to permanent relocation (Hall & Müller, 2004; Hall, 2005b). Tourism expenditure has the potential to bring a range of benefits to nations, and the growing propensity for people to travel implies that these gains might continue for some time. Among these benefits is the prospect that tourism can be dispersed into the regional areas of a state to create new markets and new experiences for consumers and new opportunities for resident populations. Consequently, tourism development policies are often perceived as one element of the package of solutions that may be relevant to rural communities to revitalize regional growth.

The problem, nevertheless, is that the current approach to tourism development in many countries is often framed within the much broader strategies that dictate a state's parameters for its own macroeconomic management. In this context, tourism development tends to be subsumed as a subset within the state's commitments to economic development, and so is cast in the same competitive paradigm. The business of tourism, however, is based on the existence of *destinations*, which by definition exist in particular locations and impose their effects on local communities and which are differentially accessible to the consumers of different source regions. National approaches to tourism development are often unable to recognize the impacts and externalities of tourism growth, and in particular lack the means to understand these effects on unique local and community values, with the consequence that much of the administration required for tourism's operational needs must necessarily fall to municipal and local authorities. The current structure of tourism development policies often provides little actual support for regional needs, even though tourism growth offers multiple *externalities* (both positive and negative) that might deliver multiple solutions in some local circumstances. More importantly, it might be noted, this approach leaves municipal and local authorities with the unenvied responsibility of acting as the initiators for regional tourism planning with no resources other than those the local communities can provide.

The issues are compounded further by the reluctance of many public sector planners to comprehend the object of 'tourism policy' as being about the means to enhance *visitations* to myriad localities rather than as a political excuse to sponsor *icon* activities or particular destinations. New models for development policy need to reverse this mindset to acknowledge the benefits and impacts from growth arising from a vast array of micro-economic sources, that often reflect regional intangible capital (Hall, 2005b), rather than from singular showcase activities.

Analysing the structure of tourism policy in this way emphasizes the schism between national policy directions and the contrary demands for action placed on administrators at the community level. It also emphasizes that this is a political process, where there is an interconnection between the dynamic impacts of economic change and the needs of stakeholders and interest groups who have demands for outcomes that affect their welfare (see Hall, Jenkins, & Kearsley, 1997; Michael, 2001). It needs to be noted, of course, that tourism is only one component of a much broader approach to *development*, and that tourism is only relevant in those localities for which a competitive advantage exists.

References

ABARE. (2000). *Indexes of prices received and paid by farmers*. Canberra: Australian Bureau of Agricultural and Resource Economics.

ABS. (2000). *1999 yearbook Australia*, Cat. No. 1301.0. Canberra: Australian Bureau of Statistics.

Aronsson, L. (1994). Sustainable tourism systems: The example of sustainable rural tourism in Sweden. *Journal of Sustainable Tourism*, 2(1–2), 77–92.

Botterill, D., Owen, R.E., Emanuel, L., Foster, N., Gale, T., Nelson, C., & Selby, M. (1997). Perceptions from the periphery: The experience of Wales. In peripheral area tourism: International tourism research conference, 8–12 September 1997, Unit of Tourism Research at the Research Centre of Bornholm, Bornholm.

Bray, M., & Walsh, P. (1998). Different paths to neo-liberalism? Comparing Australia and New Zealand. *Industrial Relations, 37*, 358–387.

Butler, R.W., Hall, C.M., & Jenkins, J. (Eds). (1998). *Tourism and recreation in rural areas.* Chichester: Wiley.

Crocombe, G.T., Enright, M.J., & Porter, M.E. (1991). *Upgrading New Zealand's competitive advantage.* Auckland: Oxford University Press.

Daugbjerg, C. (1997). Policy networks and agricultural policy reforms: Explaining deregulation in Sweden and re-regulation in the European Community. *Governance, 10*(2), 123–141.

Goodman, D. (2004). Rural Europe redux? Reflections on alternative agro-food networks and paradigm change. *Sociologia Ruralis, 44*(1), 3–16.

Grado, S.C., Strauss, C.H., & Lord, B.E. (1997). Antiquing as a tourism recreational activity in southwestern Pennsylvania. *Journal of Travel Research, 35*(3), 52–56.

Hall, C.M. (1997). Geography, marketing and the selling of places. *Journal of Travel and Tourism Marketing, 6*(3/4), 61–84.

Hall, C.M. (2005a). *Competing from the periphery: Mobility, tourism and regional development,* UOWP2005.3 University of Otago Working Papers in competition, School of Business, University of Otago, Dunedin.

Hall, C.M. (2005b). *Tourism: Rethinking the social science of mobility.* Harlow: Prentice-Hall.

Hall, C.M. (2006). Tourism, regional development and peripheral areas. In B. Jansson, & D. Müller (Eds), *Tourism in high latitude peripheries: Space, place and environment.* Wallingford: CABI.

Hall, C.M., & Boyd, S. (Eds). (2005a). *Nature-based tourism in peripheral areas: Development or disaster.* Clevedon: Channelview Publications.

Hall, C.M., Jenkins, J., & Kearsley, G. (Eds). (1997). *Tourism planning and policy in Australia and New Zealand: Cases, issues and practice.* Sydney: Irwin.

Hall, C.M., & Müller, D. (Eds). (2004). *Tourism, mobility and second homes: Between elite landscape and common ground.* Clevedon: Channelview Publications.

Hall, D. (1997). Sustaining tourism development in the fragile Balkan periphery of Europe. In peripheral area tourism: International tourism research conference, 8–12 September 1997, unit of tourism research at the Research Centre of Bornholm, Bornholm.

Hopkins, P. (2005). Huge farms drive more production. *The Age,* 13 June, p. 17.

Hugonnier, B. (1999). Regional development tendencies in OECD countries. Regional Australia summit, keynote presentation, Canberra, 26–29 October 1999, 14pp.

Jansson, B., & Müller, D. (Eds). (2006). *Tourism in high latitude peripheries: Space, place and environment.* Wallingford: CABI.

Jenkins, J., Hall, C.M., & Troughton, M. (1998). The restructuring of rural economies: Rural tourism and recreation as a government response (pp. 43–68). In: R. Butler, C.M. Hall, & J. Jenkins (Eds), *Tourism and recreation in rural areas.* Chichester: Wiley.

Johnsen, S. (2003). Contingency revealed: New Zealand farmers experiences of agricultural restructuring. *Sociologia Ruralis, 43*(2), 128–153.

Kelsey, J. (1995). *The New Zealand experiment: A world model for structural adjustment?* Auckland: Pluto Press.

Killion, L. (2001). Rural tourism. As Chapter 7 In: N. Douglas, N. Douglas, & R. Derrett (Eds). (2001) *Special interest tourism.* Milton (Qld.): Wiley.

Lamine, C. (2005). Settling shared uncertainties: Local partnerships between producers and consumers. *Sociologia Ruralis, 45*(4), 324–345.

Lowe, P., Buller, H., & Ward, N. (2002). Setting the next agenda? British and french approaches to the second pillar of the common agricultural policy. *Journal of Rural Studies, 18*(1), 1–17.

Malecki, E.J. (2004). Jockeying for position: What it means and why it matters to regional development policy when places compete. *Regional Studies, 38*(9), 1101–1120.

Michael, E.J. (2001). Public choice and tourism analysis. *Current Issues in Tourism, 4*(2–4), 308–330.

Michael, E.J. (2002). Antiques and tourism in Australia. *Tourism Management, 23*(2), 117–125.

Michael, E.J. (2006). *Public policy — the competitive framework.* Melbourne: Oxford University Press.

Novelli, M. (Ed.). (2005) *Niche tourism: Contemporary issues, trends and cases.* Oxford: Butterworth Heinemann.

O'Neill, P.M. (1997). Bringing the qualitative state into economic geopgraphy. In: R. Lee, & J. Wills (Eds), *Geographies of economies* (pp. 290–301). London: Edward Arnold.

Palmer, C.A. (1996). The making of a nation: Heritage tourism and the British national Identity *1996 Australian Tourism and Hospitality Research Conference,* Canberra: Bureau of Tourism Research (pp. 481–488).

Potter, C., & Lobley, M. (2004). Agricultural restructuring and state assistance: Competing or complementary rural policy paradigms. *Journal of Environmental Policy & Planning. 6*(1), 3–18.

Prosser, G. (2001). Regional tourism. As Chapter 4 In: N. Douglas, N. Douglas, & R. Derrett, (Eds), *Special interest tourism.* Milton (Qld.): Wiley.

Sher J., & Sher K. (1994). Beyond the conventional wisdom: Rural development as if Australia's rural people and communities really mattered. *Journal of Research in Rural Education. 10*(1), 2–43.

Smith, W. & Montgomery, H. (2004). Revolution or evolution? New Zealand agriculture since 1984. *Geojournal, 59*(2), 107–118.

Standing, G. (2002). *Beyond the new paternalism.* London: Verso.

Statistics New Zealand. (2005). New Zealand: An urban/rural profile, www.stats.govt.nz/urban-rural-profiles/highly-rural-remote-areas/economic-development.htm (accessed 18 September 2005).

Stewart, J.K. (1990). Heritage attractions and tourism: Myths and issues. *Tourism research: Meeting the needs of industry — conference proceedings,* T.T.R.A.-Canada (pp. 91–98).

Tickell, A., & Peck, J. (2003). Making global rules: Globalization or neoliberalization. In: J. Peck, & H.W. Yeung (Eds), *Remaking the global economy* (pp. 163–181). London: Sage.

Ward, N., Lowe, P., & Bridges, T. (2003). Rural and regional development: The role of the regional development agencies in England. *Regional Studies, 37*(2), 201–214.

Zeppel, H., & Hall, C.M. (1991). Selling art and history: Cultural heritage and tourism. *The Journal of Tourism Studies, 2*(1), 29–45.

Chapter 3

Development and Cluster Theory

Ewen J. Michael

Objectives

- This chapter explores the concepts of clustering and co-location from an economic perspective.
- It seeks to explain how firms can extract greater commercial benefits by operating in ways that utilize and extract the synergies that are generated from the co-incidence of their co-location, so providing a rationale for clustering as both a *business strategy* and as a *policy tool* for enhancing economic growth.
- The chapter provides an explanation of the different forms or types of clustering that can occur between firms at different levels of the production process, but notes that in small-scale or regional environments it is often the case that the benefits from clustering are optimized by combining different types of firms at different levels of production.
- The complementarity that exists between different types of goods and services is used to revise the concept of *diagonal clustering*, which seems particularly relevant for tourism clusters where consumers are seeking not to purchase a single product but rather a *bundle of attributes* that makes up their travel experience.
- Clusters require some degree of co-operative practice to occur between firms, but, as this chapter notes, this does not imply collusion or some threat to the prevailing competitive paradigm, but rather provides a means for small communities to contest for a place in a broader market.
- This analysis of cluster formation allows small-scale or micro-cluster effects to be identified and their relevance to tourism in rural and regional areas to be further explored (in subsequent chapters).

Micro-Clusters and Networks: The Growth of Tourism
Copyright © 2007 by Elsevier Ltd.
All rights of reproduction in any form reserved.
ISBN: 0-08-045096-2

Arguably, there are many approaches that might be considered to be feasible as policy options to enhance the level of economic and social opportunity for regional communities, though none as yet appear to have found a consensus of support among national policy-makers. Clustering theory is explored here as one such possibility, for it seems particularly relevant for those communities that seek to build or expand a tourism function as part of their gamut of economic and social choices.

The Concept of Clustering

The principles of cluster analysis have their origins in traditional location theories that were established over 40 years ago. Over the last decade or so, however, they have been substantially revised, with the initiative stemming largely as a consequence of Porter's (1991, 1998) work to analyse the success factors for firms operating in very large regional associations. At this level, at least, Porter has demonstrated the value of clustering and location theory as effective tools for analysing economic growth and for drawing the concomitant links to business development strategy. By inference, this analysis also serves to identify many of the factors that critically impact on the opportunities that are available for regional communities. Today, clustering theories take a variety of forms to meet a range of different applications in regional analysis (see Karlsson, 2007).

The general assumption behind the clustering models is a step beyond the simple benefits to firms and communities that can be explained by economic specialization. Clustering is predicated by the notion that the co-location of like firms will produce a range of synergies, which if captured, may enhance the growth of market size, employment and product. Porter (1991, 2003), and others since, has demonstrated these approaches in macro-regional analyses, but little has been done to apply these concepts in small localized environments. Indeed, it remains supposition that cluster theory is applicable at all to micro development, but it would seem, at the very least, to offer one means to enunciate those economic success factors that are amenable to policy actions and processes relevant to industry and to regional communities.

The intuitive value that stems from the clustering approach is that it suggests a policy tool or mechanism as an option for accelerating growth. The *Porterian* model relies on the conventional notion that a co-location of like industries in a geographic concentration can produce multiplier effects (economic) and consequent social impacts (externalities), but adds to the argument by noting that the rate of regional growth may be accelerated by the co-location of symbiotic industries. The additional step identified in Porter's argument is important, for those policies that foster mere competition through location concentration (if effective at all) lead only to marginal economic gains based on economies-of-scale, while those cluster formations that actually generate an interactive synthesis between firms can lead to a cumulative gain in benefits — most obviously in the form of both increased output and lower cost structures. In this approach, the rate of regional growth can accelerate as new symbiotic industries are drawn in to share those benefits.

The clustering of firms is not in itself a recipe for economic growth, for it implies only that the co-located firms can exploit the synergies between them to lower production costs. However, it is the creation of an environment of shared synergies and common resources that can prove attractive to other firms in the right circumstances that acts as the catalyst for new investment, the entry of new firms and the expansion of production.

For tourism the proposition is intriguing. Clusters formation, as a catalyst for growth, can be effective in many environments where firms are focussed on a particular segment of the production process. Markets are not an amorphous entity, rather they comprise sets of related activity with distinct consumption attributes (Michael, 2006, ch. 7), hence there is the potential for firms to cluster in any particular segment — and each of these segments may be as different as a retailing precinct for high fashion clothing is from a cluster in aeronautic engineering (Lublinski, 2003). However, clustering might well be at its most effective in non-metropolitan environments when the activities of the co-located industries are based on *visitation*, in that increases in the demand for travel enhance the need for the complementary growth of the support industries that deliver visitor services. This is not to suggest that other forms of industrial clustering do not encourage economic growth, but rather that tourism clusters are premised on creating a bundle of complementary attributes that serve to satisfy consumer needs, creating more and more opportunities for firms that choose to co-locate with each other. Hence, the proposition, that tourism-based cluster formations might add to multiplier and externality effects, and serve to *accelerate* the opportunities for new forms of economic wealth by creating a demand for a host of complementary activities which in turn generate their own effects.

Increasing visitation, of course, simultaneously brings new impacts and externalities to the host community, not all of which may be welcomed. The social impact of clustering remains a new field of research, although Seaton (1996, 1999) provides some guide for observing these effects with his analyses of six specialized 'Book Towns' in north-western Europe, where growth has been fostered around micro market clusters. The key to controlling social externalities in these environments appears to lie in the small scale of the development process, allowing local interests to stay in control of the choices being made.

Clusters or Alliances

There are real issues in recognising clusters as a distinct form of industrial organisation, separate from other forms of commercial alliance. By empirical example, clusters have emerged, grown and sustained themselves; but, equally, there are instances where deliberate attempts at cluster formation have failed, though perhaps none so spectacularly as the attempt in the 1990s to establish the 'Multi-Function Polis' as a technology-based satellite city in Adelaide, South Australia (Parker, 1998). Equally, there are many other small-scale examples where local or municipal authorities and planning agencies have aspired to establish industrial theme parks under the umbrella of 'clustering'; but these are frequently mislabelled, for their reality is little more than a commercial tryst at land development. In truth, genuine cluster formations are often quite difficult to perceive.

There are, of course, other forms of commercial alliances that also offer substantial rewards for their participants. However, their success is not automatic either, with Dyer, Kale, and Singh (2001, p. 37) reporting "... almost half fail", although their case-studies suggest that those based on a geographic co-location fare better (Dyer et al., 2001, p. 42). On occasion, the terms *'cluster'* and *'alliance'* are sometimes used interchangeably, and while there are circumstances where this is understandable, there is a need to separate these concepts for policy interpretation and the formation of development strategies. The term *'alliance'* has a practical application in discussions of business strategy, as part of the normal commercial arrangements firms make with each other; and, put simply, refers to the institutionalisation of arrangements that firms develop among themselves "... to access complementary resources and skills that reside in other companies" (Dyer et al., 2001, p. 37). In this sense, an alliance provides the means for a firm to share any of its information, production or distribution resources with one or more other firms on a cost-effective basis, so long as it does not lead to collusion in the market behaviour of the allied firms. The range of alliances between firms is almost infinite, from simple cost sharing strategies to joint research for new products, from agreements to access patents and copyrights to establishing common procedures for compliance regulation. The scale of such arrangements is similarly variable, and can range from a single one-off contract between two small businesses to an embedded relationship between groups of multi-national corporations, as is visible in the global partnerships between airlines in the 'Oneworld' or 'Star Alliance' networks.

A cluster, on the other hand, is a concept that implies a sense of co-operative exchange between both the firms and the community where they are in geographic co-location or close proximity to each other. The common location necessarily implies some level of interaction between firms, but in itself this may not translate to any recognizable benefit for those firms. However, where those firms create and exploit the advantages of their common location, the concept of clustering starts to emerge as an entity with some merit of its own. Firms with similar production processes or common markets can develop synergies in the supply of resources and infrastructure, marketing, information and the pooling of labour skills and distribution systems, which serve to lower costs and improve the competitive advantage of the clustered firms. A common location may also serve to pool the customer base, attracting buyers who know they will have a range of choices available, so reducing their search costs.

Of course, it is quite feasible for firms within a cluster to also enter into alliance relationships, perhaps with other firms within the cluster or with firms outside it. The difference, however, remains: for the benefits of clustering are available to all the cluster's member firms and spill-over to its host community, driven by the economic dynamics of the synergies that proximity and co-operative practice brings, and so can be analysed in the context of regional and local development. The benefits of alliances, however, are designed to be extracted only by those firms that make the individual commercial choice to belong to that association, and so become part of the strategic process for a firm's own growth and commercial gain.

Forms of Clustering

The traditional approaches to cluster analysis focussed on two distinct types of formation, based loosely around the analogy that a production process is likened to a series of links in a chain — where each link adds value in a sequence of steps to produce a final product for consumer use. In this model, clusters of firms can form around one link in the chain or can co-locate to facilitate a series of links in the same *value chain*. Singularly, each type appears as a form of economic co-location liable to enhance the market benefits for participating firms by creating sets of operational synergies that reduce costs and improve revenues through a pooled customer base.

In effect, clustering permits a group of firms to capture the external economic benefits from their association, which might be supposed to lead to lower cost structures and to enhance the opportunities for market growth. These gains, of course, have some impact on each firms' internal economies, but how they are applied within each firm remains as part of its own autonomous decision-making. This understanding from clustering theory, which evolved from post-war economic analyses, continues as an entrenched part of the contemporary approaches:

> "... Generally, the more industries that are located in a given area the greater
> the external economies that become possible." (Mountjoy, 1966, p. 107).

More recent explanations of cluster types have posited a third form of cluster formation. Here, the argument is not based on a grouping of firms within a value chain, but rather on the co-location of firms that provide dissimilar but complementary products and services that expand the scope of the cluster's outputs. How firms access the alleged benefits from clustering, however, has often proved more problematic to explain, for the distribution may well be asymmetric. The answer may well reside in the notion that it is not simple co-location that matters; rather, it is the *structure* of the cluster, and the way it brings firms and their host communities together, for it is this interaction that generates the synthesis to enhance production synergies and to increase the collective market size. In other words, it is the relational dynamics that are created between firms that leads to their further commercial success, and to the growth of community wealth.

As each type of clustering exposes a different linkage between firms, with differing economic and social impacts, there is merit in explaining each separately (from Michael, 2003).

Horizontal Clustering

Horizontal clustering is the most common and most easily recognised type of cluster formation. It occurs where similar or like firms from the stage in the value chain for the same industry co-locate in a geographic area. These firms are *competitors*, selling like products using similar productive resources. However, their co-location pools the potential customer base to increase total sales, and may sometimes create other advantages in terms of product availability, labour supply, shared information and infrastructure, to reduce costs or the effects of externalities. Simple examples can be identified in the distinct precincts of retail and manufacturing activity that can be found in every sizeable city. (The arrow, above, demonstrates an increasing number of firms in a horizontal cluster as it grows from the left to the right.)

Vertical Clustering

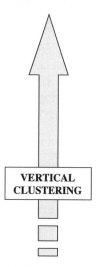

The co-location of firms operating at different stages in an industry's supply chain is referred to as vertical clustering. Here, there is an integrated linkage between production stages and consumers that enhances specialization. The close proximity between firms minimizes logistics and distributional costs, and may help to concentrate labour supply, workforce skills and market information. Rudimentary examples are visible in every viticultural region, where independent grape-growers supply the local wineries, and where there are often co-located warehousing, distribution and specialist transport firms — a complete production chain from grower to retail delivery. (The arrow, here, serves to illustrate this relationship as an increasing level of integration between firms as it rises.)

Diagonal Clustering

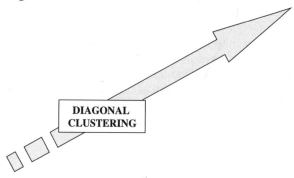

The clustering typology is expanded to recognize *diagonal* clustering, to identify an increasing concentration of *complementary* (or symbiotic) firms. Here, each firm adds value to the activities of others, even though their products may be quite distinct and clearly belong to other industry classifications. Diagonal clustering occurs where firms working together create a bundle of separate products and services that the consumer effectively purchases as a single item. The situation is common in many tourism destinations, where separate firms with separate production processes supply activities, transport, hospitality, accommodation, etc. The co-location of complementary providers adds value to the tourism experience; while, conversely, the absence of key services will probably limit the growth of existing firms. (This arrow implies a growing concentration of complementary activity providers as it moves from the lower left to the upper right.)

In the framework stylized in Figure 3.1, it is possible to envisage an optimal outcome for an industry-based cluster, where a variety of firms operate across all three dimensions to maximize the gains from their co-location. As an abstract model, this appears to have

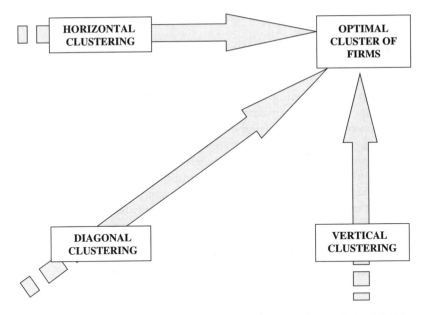

Figure 3.1: Optimizing cluster formations in micro industries (from Michael, 2003, p. 137).

some merit in applications for smaller communities seeking to optimize the outcomes from a clustering process, even if the total level of activity is on a micro scale. All elements of production, distribution and complementarity are brought together to reduce costs and enhance that locality's particular competitive advantage. If the cluster is able to exploit these advantages, then the community's outcomes will have been optimized. Over time, of course, there is still the potential for further gains, for member firms or the host community, if the cluster's scale and scope can continue to expand.

Complementarity and Diagonal Clusters

The inclusion of the concept of diagonal clustering stems in part from the renewed emphasis in strategic business planning of the critical role that complementary firms play in the consumers' decision process. Since Adam Smith wrote the Wealth of Nations (1776), economists have simply assumed that all firms are in competition with each other, but this is not exactly true. As Brandenburger and Nalebuff (1997) have explained, if one firm is the producer of any particular product, then another firm producing a complementary product or service cannot and should not be regarded as a competitor. The reason is obvious, because the activities of the complementary producer actually serve to add more value to the original product than it has alone. The true competitor, of course, is a firm that seeks to sell a substitute product or whose activities detract from the value of the original product in some way. This helps explain how a firm gains from the growth of complementary activities and why it is in those firms' self-interest to seek to co-operate with each other, without challenging the normal assumptions of competitive behaviour.

The corollary from this argument also helps to explain that most firms, in the context of the broader market, actually have no competitive relationship with most other firms, for they are neither the providers of complements or substitutes to them. The reality of competition, then, is confined to specific market segments where only the activities of some firms can affect the outcomes for other similar producers. Complementary providers, however, have every reason to co-operate to build their businesses for long-term sustainability.

This clarification led Brandenburger and Nalebuff (1997) to suggest a strategy for business growth by groups of firms, or for firms in particular regional associations, to create a new focus around building the alignment of complementary activities between compatible firms. While not new in itself, it leads to the obvious strategy that business growth is more about expanding complementary activities than it is about competition:

> "Thinking complements is a different way of thinking about business. It's about finding ways to make the pie bigger rather than fighting with competitors over a fixed pie. To benefit from this insight, think about how to expand the pie by developing new complements or making existing complements more affordable." Brandenburger & Nalebuff (1997, pp. 14–15).

For tourism development, perhaps, this maxim might be amended to include thinking about how to make complements more "accessible", which is precisely the role that diagonal clustering fulfils.

Diagonal clustering (the co-location of complementary firms) and diagonal integration (the operation of complementary activities within one firm) are relatively new approaches for both tourism business and regional development strategists. Poon's (1994) analysis of the tourism and hospitality industries established the existence of strong diagonal value chain relationships arising from the expansion of information technology that accelerated the capacity of firms to interact, permitting them to benefit from economies-of-scope, system gains and communication synergies. In these circumstances, firms add value to each other's activities by integrating or bundling complementary services into a *total* product for sale; in effect, allowing firms to diversify their marketable products to meet the needs of a target group of consumers (Poon, 1994, p. 224). However, the principles explored initially by Poon are not confined solely to the consequences of the information revolution, but rather can be applied more broadly to the capacity of firms to align themselves with each other to manipulate their complementarities to deliver an integrated product — at one location or another. This allows firms to tap the economies-of-scope and the synergies between products, rather than focus simply on the pursuit of economies-of-scale, which are the intended gains from both horizontal and vertical clustering.

The concept that collections of firms can improve their economic outcomes by aligning themselves with each other to deliver an integrated product has a particular application for small-scale regional tourism development. An obvious illustration of such a relationship occurs where a firm creates tour packages for a destination; where the saleable package combines the discrete products of a number of clustered or co-located firms, perhaps providing transport, accommodation, hospitality, tour guides, destinations and venues, for purchase as one entity by consumers. While larger firms might seek to integrate many of these separable functions within their own production process, the likelihood is that in a small tourism destination the range of services will be provided by a number of firms.

The test for a diagonal value chain lies in the consumer's perception of the bundling of attributes of the products or services they consume, and so dissimilar products in terms of production requirements can blend together as an entity for consumption purposes. As Lancaster (1966a, 1966b) noted, each good or service has separate characteristics and a unique sets of attributes, which is what the consumer wants. Hence, consumer behaviour is driven not so much by the demand for goods per se, but for the characteristics possessed by those goods:

> "Goods, as such, are not the immediate objects of preference or utility or welfare, but have associated with them characteristics which are directly relevant to the consumer." (Lancaster, 1966b, p. 14).

Where complementary activities, goods or services can be packaged or bundled in some way, the range of attributes is increased and consumer satisfaction is enhanced. In tourism, this process is essential because it is the compilation of the values to be gained from the *experience* of the visit that the consumer seeks to purchase. For example, a local gift shop or souvenir stall might well provide an integral service for consumers who visit a nearby heritage tourism attraction, adding value to their experience because they are able to purchase some memento of their visit. There is no reason, of course, why the gift shop should be connected to the core attraction, other than that it serves as a complementary provider. Hence, in the context of tourism development, it is the growth of complementary activities (or the breadth of product offerings) that generates economies-of-scope and accelerates wealth and employment opportunities.

The strategic focus of cluster analysis is to provide industry participants and regional communities with information associated with positive forms of clustering, rather than traditional analyses of market competition, that might meet their individual local needs. This approach, if applied to tourism development, requires a full assessment of the customer base (demand behaviour) and the mechanisms for producing the local tourism product (whatever form that may take). It also requires, as Porter (1991) dictates, an assessment of a region's *related and supporting* industries and an investigation into the strategies and rivalry patterns of existing firms, to determine whether geographic concentration can be converted into more strategically sophisticated clustering relationships. More importantly, it must establish any symbiosis between clusters of like firms and the alignments for complementarity that will affect the growth of firms that co-locate with them. Cluster formation, as a policy approach, appears possible in limited circumstances, but where those circumstances apply, the benefits to be derived may be substantial. Politically, it offers the singular advantage that growth will be shaped and driven in accord with the needs of the community that hosts the cluster.

The shared externalities that are generated from horizontal and vertical clustering deliver benefits to member firms from the accumulated economies-of-scale that increased co-location brings. In essence, it is supposed that a cluster formation will generate economic gains through economies-of-scale and the synergies that arise from a growth pole to expand the market. As the cluster grows, the more it is possible for member firms to access common infrastructure, specialized labour and information to lower total costs, and the greater the capacity of the collected group of firms to increase and access the market's pool of customers. Diagonal clustering adds yet another dimension by increasing the economies-of-scope to widen the market base and diversify the range of *production possibilities*. In short, the cluster moves to a new growth paradigm by building on the existing base of complementarities to generate both new levels of output and new types of output within the existing economic and social structure. Diagonal clustering optimizes the opportunity for expansion within a community's existing resource base.

Clusters and Competition

In the past, economists and public sector planners have been suspicious of the use of cluster theory for policy applications. By empirical example, clusters of co-located firms, both large and small, have emerged and grown successfully around the world; but, equally, there are instances where deliberate attempts to plan and foster cluster formations have failed. It is not surprising, then, to find that there is some reluctance on the part of public sector planners to revisit the concept, but part of the reason might well lie in the apparent contradiction between the principles behind clustering with the paradigm of competition.

One approach to explaining this problem is to illustrate it in terms of principles and the conflict a government agency would face if it chose to expend its resources fostering a cluster formation. If a cluster is established in a dynamically competitive market (rather than a co-operative one), the clustered firms may well seek to capture the benefits of its externalities for themselves. Indeed, this is what is supposed to happen in a perfectly competitive market. The initial benefits promised by the cluster's formation will attract entrants, but competition within the cluster will eventually drive each firm to produce where their marginal cost is equal to their average cost (MC = AC), and so compete away the gains made through the cluster's formation until economic profit is reduced to zero. Again, this is what is supposed to happen in a competitive market environment; and, in itself, may be acceptable to the public sector policy-makers. The problem, however, is that the synergies between firms will be left unattended, for their exploitation would imply benefits not just for the initiating firm but for all other (competing) firms. The possibilities for growth in these circumstances can come only from a successful firm's expansion of its individual market. The incentives for further new entrants to join the cluster are now eliminated, perhaps along with the rationale for establishing the cluster in the first place. As a policy for growth, this kind of cluster development might accord with concepts for establishing new entities but not necessarily for expanding them; so while it may fit macro-economic objectives it is doomed to self-destruction as a sustainable mechanism for enhancing regional needs. If cluster theory is to be operationalized, a better response than this is required for regional growth.

The new economics of complementarity, labelled by Brandenburger and Nalebuff (1997) as *co-opetition*, has an application to cluster theory by helping to explain why some cluster developments succeed where others do not. As noted, clusters form to create or take advantage of economic specialization through shared externalities and enhanced market size; but, the notion of *co-opetition* provides a rationale to explain why it is in the self-interest of firms to build upon their alignment of complementary production. In this sense, effective clustering positions the member firms to compete more effectively, not with each other but with those outside the cluster that deliver a similar economic product.

The assumption, of course, is that the additional gains attributable to the cluster's formation can *actually* be captured as reductions to the average costs of the member firms and that the potential to expand its market opportunities is actually shared somehow among those firms — even if those outcomes fall asymmetrically within the cluster. Nonetheless, it is the existence of complementarities between the firms that generates the synergies that provides the cluster with its competitive advantage. The more synergies that exist between the member firms the greater the benefits that can accrue to them; and, hence, their competitive position (with firms outside the cluster) should improve.

References

Brandenburger, A. M., & Nalebuff, B. J. (1997). *Co-opetition* (Foreword ed.). New York: Currency Doubleday.

Dyer, J. H., Kale, P., & Singh, H. (2001). 'How to make strategic alliances work. *Sloan Management Review*, *42*(1), 37–43.

Karlsson, C. (Ed.). (2006). *Handbook of research on clusters: Theories, policies and case studies.* Cheltenham: Edward Elgar. [forthcoming 2007].

Lancaster, K. J. (1966a). A new approach to consumer theory. *Journal of Political Economy*, *LXXIV*(Feb–Dec), 132–157.

Lancaster, K. J. (1966b). Change and nnovation in the technology of consumption. *American Economic Review*, *LVI*(2), 14–23.

Lublinski, A. E. (2003). Does geographic proximity matter? Evidence from clustered and non-clustered aeronautic firms in Germany. *Regional Studies*, *37*(5), 453–467.

Michael, E. J. (2003). Tourism micro-clusters. *Tourism Economics*, *9*(2), 133–146.

Michael, E. J. (2006). *Public Policy — the competitive framework.* Melbourne: Oxford University Press.

Mountjoy, A. B. (1966). *Industrialization and under-developed countries* (2nd ed.). London: Hutchinson.

Parker, P. (1998). The multi-function polis 1987–1997: An international failure or innovative local project?' *Pacific Economic Papers.* Technical Report no. 283, Australia-Japan research centre, Australian National University, Canberra.

Poon, A. (1994). *Tourism, technology and competitive strategies.* Wallingford, UK: CAB International.

Porter, M. E. (1991). *The competitive advantage of nations.* London: Macmillan.

Porter, M. E. (1998). Clusters and the new economics of competition. *Harvard Business Review*, *6*(November–December), 77–90.

Porter, M. E. (2003). The economic performance of regions. *Regional Studies*, *37*(6 & 7), 549–578.

Seaton, A. V. (1996) Hay on wye, the mouse that roared, book towns and rural tourism. *Tourism Management*, *17*(5), 379–382.

Seaton, A. V. (1999). Book towns as tourism developments in peripheral areas. *International Journal of Tourism Research*, *1*, 389–399.

Smith, A. E. (1776). *An inquiry into the nature and causes of the wealth of nations*, Sir John Lubbock's Hundred Books Ed. 1892, London: Routledge.

Chapter 4

Micro-Clusters in Tourism

Ewen J. Michael

Objectives

- This chapter continues the economic exploration of clustering and co-location, but now focuses particularly on small-scale tourism development.
- Tourism is considered in the context of regional development policy and the prevailing paradigm of competition to establish the role it can play in diversifying the production choices that are available for small communities.
- The discussion reflects on the size of regional populations as a constraint of scale that predetermines the nature of the industry's potential solutions, mitigated still further by the significance local communities place on maintaining values and lifestyles as part of their social dynamics, which in turn establishes the conditions for their responses to development.
- Within the constraints imposed by the *paradigm of competition*, micro-clusters are identified as a development mechanism that fosters the ability to build a local level of specialisation and a competitive advantage for a small tourism destination.
- The chapter defines micro-clusters as small concentrations of firms in close geographic proximity, bound by a single community of social and economic interest.
- The analysis of cluster formations in tourism focuses on the need to identify the dynamic alignment of complementary activities that can be brought together to expand *economies-of-scope* and the breadth of product offerings to meet the consumers' needs.
- This chapter also defines and explains the role of *multipliers* and *externalities* in enhancing the benefits that can be extracted from successful micro-cluster formations in tourism.

Micro-Clusters and Networks: The Growth of Tourism
Copyright © 2007 by Elsevier Ltd.
All rights of reproduction in any form reserved.
ISBN: 0-08-045096-2

The extension to the traditional approach to clustering analysis developed in Chapter 3 arises from the inclusion of the concept of *diagonal* clustering. This identifies the concentration of complementary (or symbiotic) firms, where each additional firm adds value to the products and services produced by the existing firms. In the context of regional development, it is the growth of complementary activities (or the breadth of product offerings) that generates economies-of-scope and accelerates wealth and employment opportunities, while for tourism development it is often the range of product choice that helps determine a destination's sustainability.

The issue at stake is the relevance of this approach for applications in small rural communities, where the social and economic dynamics of a micro-environment may well impose a different set of needs or constraints on any policy framework that seeks to contribute to the development of new opportunities and social well-being.

Problems of Scale and Community

The local communities in regional Australia, rural New Zealand and the peripheral areas of western Europe and North America share similar problems to some extent in their search for economic security. These environments are distinctive and diverse in their own settings, but each is equally familiar with the impacts of technological change and the declining base for rural employment. The effects have been particularly severe on younger residents faced with fewer and fewer options for longer-term employment. The loss of jobs and economic opportunity has been mirrored by declining populations and an increase in social costs both for the remaining residents and for those who embark on inter-regional migration paths. Over the past decade, there has been a vocal call by rural residents for action to rekindle the growth of economic opportunity, to restore the potential for income generation and reaffirm the base for community values and lifestyle: a call that has been answered in part by some governments, in Ireland, Scandinavia and some of the states in Canada and USA, but not so effectively in other areas.

Governments, in the face of political demand, are now engaged in a desperate search for new forms of economic activity to take up some of the ***opportunity cost*** imposed by the macro benefits of contemporary agricultural production processes. The competitive paradigm that pervades the thinking of the policymakers in the developed states calls for regions and localities to exploit their own production advantages, but the mechanisms that are supposed to make this process possible remain to be determined.

> ... the very notion of regional competitiveness is itself complex and contentious, and even though policy-makers everywhere have jumped onto the regional and urban competitiveness bandwagon, we are far from a consensus on what is meant by the term and how it can be measured: as is often the case, policy has raced ahead of conceptual understanding and empirical analysis
>
> (Kitson, Martin, & Tyler, 2004, p. 991).

In this environment, the approaches to regional development policy must necessarily remain fluid. However, in any particular region or locality and in the absence of some new staple form of production, the probability is that the emergence of new opportunities will arise only through a plethora of new and expanded *micro*forms of economic activity — which, at best, can only deliver incremental benefits to regional communities. Nevertheless, it is an approach that is consistent with the *competition paradigm*, for it is based on regions pursuing their own competitive advantages and carries with it the added gains from diversification, which — marginal as they may be — help to shore up the stabilisation of the macro economy. One such possibility in these circumstances comes from the expansion of tourism and visitation to those regions that can devise the appropriate products to meet the market's needs.

Tourism, as an industrial activity in regional areas, is not the panacea that many local politicians would like to think it is, but rather is a contender for growth if the appropriate circumstances exist or can be created. Creating a tourism function in a local environment requires a product, innovation and human resources — all of which are scarce. Of course, if a tourism function can be created, it offers further opportunities for accelerated growth; hence, it is attractive to local planning authorities because it stimulates the development or expansion of a range of supporting industries, including accommodation, hospitality, motor vehicle services, etc. to service the demands of visitors, but which also add to the amenity of the incumbent residents. The prospects for growth, however, are confronted by issues of scale where the size of small rural communities becomes the critical determining factor. As a matter of definition, these small communities, in any given locality, exist with a separate identity, yet the smaller ones might contain less than a hundred residents while even the larger ones number only a few thousand. Communities of this size simply cannot support the range of skills and infrastructure to foster new industrial processes. The problems are compounded because, even when entrepreneurs are willing to work within these constraints of scale, the small population base makes it difficult to raise and maintain capital from the community's own internal sources, forcing them to seek external support from public resources or from a disassociated national or international capital market.

The spillover effects from tourism are not all positive, and the social impacts that arise from visitation, even from small numbers of tourists, can significantly disrupt local community values and lifestyles (Hall, Jenkins, & Kearsley, 1997). To create a tourism function requires a degree of community support, or at least a recognition among the community's members of the contribution that the new activities make to local wealth. New small-scale tourism developments may impose only minor impacts, but in rural environments already depressed by changing employment practices and declining populations, the new activities may well challenge local values for those that remain. For example, a declining fishing village may well see a new venture in maritime tourism as a competitor for the few remaining resources that maintains the *status quo*, rather than as an opportunity for growth. Given that small resident populations have their own social dynamics, and given that visitors must inevitably interact with those community members, it remains axiomatic that any new or expanded ventures will need the endorsement of the communities they will affect.

The issues of scale also have a political dimension that mitigates against the development of tourism in small communities. National and regional planning agencies lack the bureaucratic resources to work in local environments, focussing their attention instead on icon developments or activities likely to generate substantial flows of visitors, rather than attempting to operate with hundreds (if not thousands) of very small tourism business ventures. Local development, particularly in rural areas, becomes the bailiwick of municipal authorities with little influence on the broader strategic processes of government, and where they are often without access to sufficient capital to sponsor or support local initiatives even when they promise good returns on investment. In Australia, as an illustration of the way the policy environment works in many similar jurisdictions, the State of Victoria's agency responsible for tourism (Tourism Victoria) in its *strategic plan* calls for government to manage only those tourism activities that will *significantly* affect the State's capacity to attract domestic and international visitors, or contribute to "... community renewal in regional centres" (Tourism Victoria, 2002, p. 2). While Tourism Victoria does support industry-based liaison councils and regional tourism associations to provide some degree of industry communication and co-operation, there are no public structures to facilitate the interests of small-scale operators or communities. In effect, while small communities may well have public sector sympathy, there is little real support on offer, other than that which communities have built for themselves at the municipal level.

Tourism Micro-Clusters

In the context of a small community and a market limited by scale, the development of a new or expanded tourism product in a regional environment is never going to be easy. Access to capital, human resources, marketing and commercial infrastructure are constrained by the physical difficulties of a locality's distance and relative isolation from the main centres of economic activity, serving to increase cost structures even if there exists an attractive tourism activity at that particular locality. As Lublinski (2003, p. 453) observes, in an era of globalisation "... where distance seems to be no longer an obstacle ..." for the movement of capital, knowledge and other resources "... we would expect economic activity to be spread over space ..." but instead there is a global pattern in many industries of spatial concentration. While Kitson et al. (2004) lament the policymakers adherence to the "credo of competitiveness" as the framework for regional development; it is the reality of the economic benefits that can be extracted by firms from co-location that enables regions to jostle for a place in a market where costs must reflect some level of global parity. These same dynamics apply to tourism developments and to tourism regions, irrespective of whether they are large or small.

It is at this point that the concept or theory of *micro-clusters* can be seen to offer real benefits as a development model. At a minimum, it provides one alternative to enhance the competitive advantage of a region through specialisation, and, as such, may be relevant in many local environments. The concept of a micro-cluster can be applied to identify a concentration of firms in close geographic proximity: where, in sociological terms, they are bounded by a single community of social and economic interests. Although the number of firms and the size of those firms may be very small, they are effectively contributing to a local specialisation and engaged in servicing a common clientele. A simple example from the tourism industry, which might not be unusual in many countries, can be found perhaps in a location endowed with fishing resources where local shops and artisans produce and supply the gear for visitors. Where the existing operators develop co-operative and complementary interactions to service this market, they are doing so within the context of the community's own needs and values, and so start to exploit the synergies between them. The interaction between them enhances their specialisation, improves their market potential and generates the opportunities for others to add adjacent and symbiotic activities — fishing guides and tour operators, hospitality and accommodation services, rod and fly crafts or a host of other possibilities. The micro-cluster emerges with a uniquely identified local product that is clearly defined by its own context, and determined in accord with the values of its own community.

At a qualitative level, there are descriptive analyses of tourism destinations growing initially from a cluster of firms based on a common economic theme. The most obvious is Seaton's (1996, 1999) documented studies of the emergence of Book Towns in the United Kingdom and Europe, which clearly illustrate the capacity of a tourism niche market to stimulate complementary growth in a local environment. In another account, Nilsson (2001) narrates the 200-year history of the Åre Valley, Sweden, where small clusters of hospitality providers have expanded continuously by repositioning and revitalizing the region's nature-based activities as competitive products. However, it is the strength of anecdotal data that seems compelling, and the examples seem evident in countries around the world. Just for the purposes of illustration, in Victoria, Australia, there are many small regional tourism destinations that have emerged, where each is based on a local specialisation. Former fishing villages have repositioned themselves as maritime leisure centres (Lakes Entrance) or commercialised their focus on marine heritage and music (Port Fairy): some viticulture regions remain as centres for wine, while others specialise in food and local produce to meet visitor needs. The list goes on, and more detailed examples are given in Chapters 5–8. Put succinctly, however, the common theme is one where local communities and groups of operators have selected and built their own comparative advantages. Collectively, these observations add weight to the view that successful clustering in a tourism niche market is able to capture some of the benefits from both economies-of-scale and of-scope, and as the build up of complementary activities continues in a successful cluster, may even deliver some *accelerator* impacts through induced investment.

The critical function to initiate a small cluster's formation in any area of industrial specialisation is to find the mechanisms that bring a set of complementary activities together in a co-operative manner that accords with community values. The outcome, while still small scale, is that the synthesis and synergy between the co-located firms extracts economies-of-scale that help to lower local cost structures, enhance the points of access to capital and marketing and the availability of a wider range of infrastructure. In most types of industry formation, the improvement in cost efficiency that stems from economies-of-scale will serve to enhance the competitiveness of individual firms and enhance the cluster's growth, but where a cluster's specialisation is based on the provision of human services — as is the case with tourism — there is a concomitant demand to diversify to meet a range of consumer needs in the one location. For these industries, even at a small scale, this stimulates the call for the added dynamic of complementarities to expand the economies-of-scope that increase the breadth of product offerings and new opportunities for diversification. Both effects in combination establish a new growth function, but still on a scale that an existing community can comprehend, while still remaining in control of the fundamental choices to be made.

This assumes that any such approach must be inclusive of community needs and its application determined by local interests and values — for to assume otherwise would be to ignore the tenor of democratic demands and serve simply to aggravate regional disaffection with the political process (see also, Hugonnier, 1999). The intent, for policy purposes, is to build upon any existing symbiosis between compatible firms and community resources to exploit the potential complementarities that will affect the growth of firms that choose to co-locate. While, cluster formation, as a strategic tool, appears possible in tourism applications; it perhaps more importantly offers another advantage, which may be important in regional politics, if the mechanisms are found to incorporate the host community in shaping the pattern of cluster growth so that the outcomes match local values and local perceptions of lifestyle needs.

Although micro-market clustering theory offers an alternative for enhancing the competitive advantage of a region through specialisation, there are still problems with the hypothesis. The tenets of successful clustering are said to stem from the existence of co-operative and mutually supportive linkages among co-located firms, although it remains the ability to exploit them that drives the emergence of a sustainable competitive advantage. However, the empirical evidence comes only from testing areas that are already regionally successful, such as Silicon Valley or Boston Massachusetts (Porter, 1998, 2003). Indeed, the Porterian model, which is the basis of many contemporary analyses, may not be entirely appropriate for micro-market applications. First, it is concerned with large-scale regions and industry sectors, rather than with the forces that effect local environments and small-scale groupings of firms. In reality, no argument has been proposed to suggest that the dynamics that pertain to a local environment have the same impacts on small-scale groups of firms as those that drive location and concentration in larger regions. While the Porterian analysis may well be applicable to broad-scale evaluations of economic development, it is not necessarily a prescription for enhancing opportunities in micro-environments.

The approach adopted here is made proactive for regional policy purposes by inverting the original methodological structure. It uses existing market niche industries and existing community structures to identify key clustering success factors that apply in specific local circumstances. It assumes the pre-existence of a community and its resources and lifestyle, which will set the parameters for building any new level of activity. Indeed, this approach is built around the needs of a community for economic sustainability and, hence, is not designed or intended for any *greenfield* application. The task is to search for a dynamic alignment of the complementary economic and social activities among the existing firms and the existing community with the potential complementarities that new firms might bring. The aim is to identify the need for new producers, or the ways in which existing producers can modify their outputs, to add value to the total regional product, with the intention of delivering a *package of attributes* for a targeted group of (new) consumers.

The critical function to initialise the cluster effects, however, still resides in the mechanisms that bring this set of complementary activities together in a co-operative manner that accords with community values. In this sense, the operators and the community that makes up the cluster depend for their long-term sustainability on the degree of co-operative practice that can be established between them (see Chapter 5). The key for policy, then, is to find ways to bring this set of complementary activities together in a co-operative process. The outcome, while small scale, is that the synthesis and synergy between the co-located firms extracts economies-of-scale that service growth, but with the added dimension of economies-of-scope to increase opportunity and diversification. Growth brings its own externalities, but on a scale that still allows the existing community to direct the fundamental choices that need to be made.

Multipliers and Externalities

Multiplier, accelerator and externality effects are important attributes of growth policies, but their impacts are often poorly understood. The term *multiplier* implies a rapid change in economic well-being. Consequently, multiplier effects are often confused with positive *externality* effects and so are sometimes treated as policy goals in themselves. In truth, multipliers are merely the means to explain the cause of economic change where the level of domestic production and wealth is altered as a result of some new expenditure being injected into, or leaking out of, a relatively self-contained economic system. (The related notion of an *accelerator* effect occurs where the expansion of one new economic activity immediately leads to the requirement for further activities and further investment and expansion.)

It is often easier to illustrate the *multiplier* effect by example. Consider what happens when a new economic activity commences, such as the construction of a new tourist resort in a relatively isolated location. This project will cost many millions of dollars (or the local currency equivalent). In normal circumstances, the funds will be raised through the global financial market and injected into the local economy to pay for the construction, including the importation of equipment, technology and the like. The building phase will utilise local labour and equipment, which increases current domestic production and income, but this is *new* production and *new* income that is unrelated to, or *autonomous* from, the previously existing level of economic activity. Much of the money invested in the construction of this new resort is now effectively transferred to the local suppliers and workers as a new source of disposable income that they did not have before. This is not the end of the process, rather it is the beginning of the multiplier effect, for those who receive an increase in income in turn purchase consumer goods and services, increasing the demand to create domestic output and so creating more income for others. More income leads to more demand, more demand leads to more production and more production leads to more income — so that the total sum of expenditure will have a value several times greater than the original investment. When the resort opens, there will be new jobs created and another round of multiplier effects will begin. An *accelerator* effect might arise as a consequence if the new resort opens successfully, by stimulating the creation of a number of new activities in support of this new tourism market.

Multiplier effects at the national level are moderated by a range of other factors that adjust income and spending, like taxation and imports, and in reality rarely have impacts greater than 1.5–1.8 times the initial increase (or decrease) in new spending. The multiplier effects from changes in a macro-economic environment are well understood; as they are for particular industries, such as tourism, where the effects are measurable in visitor numbers and expenditures (e.g., Bull, 1995, p. 148), but these same presumptions are not so safe in small markets or regions. Local multipliers are difficult to measure and often vary significantly between regions; depending on how self-contained the particular local economy happens to be. The normal presumption is that local regional multipliers will have a lesser impact than those for metropolitan areas or other major economic centres, because payments will need to be made for the services and resources that have necessarily come from outside the region. However, as has been argued before (Michael, 2006), the multiplier impacts or flow-on effects from growth in small communities are probably more significant than conventional wisdom recognises, in part because the consequences of growth, and the positive and negative externalities it creates, are more obvious among smaller populations. Where local growth occurs in labour intensive industries, it generates higher multiplier effects because new spending is drawn to a region and a new workforce becomes part of the resident population, while local growth based on capital-intensive industries delivers lower multiplier effects because much of the income that is generated leaks back to the originating source.

In part, the interest in enhancing regional tourism development stems from this logic. The probability is that local tourism growth generates quite high value multiplier outcomes because most tourism activities are destination based, and so, necessarily, much of the tourism workforce needs to be resident in the locality, enabling the growth in incomes to be captured within the local sub-system. Moreover, increased visitation brings with it changes to the structure of the local area's demand for the provision of goods and services, including new demands for a range of visible complementary services in hospitality, accommodation and other traveller needs beyond the immediate tourism product. This kind of change may well accelerate the need for new investment in the provision of these kinds of services.

As yet, the evidence to test this hypothesis is not entirely conclusive, and often derives by implication from studies that were not configured to test it. Nevertheless, there are examples where micro-clusters of tourism-related firms have contributed to strong local growth patterns. A study of clusters of antique traders in Pennsylvania (Grado, Strauss, & Lord, 1997) found their activities to be the source of the local domestic tourist trade (see also Chapter 6). Here, the increase in visitation generated a surprising and very high local income multiplier effect greater than three (i.e., each dollar of expenditure on the local antique industry generated more than three dollars of flow-on income in the local economy). While this result seemed unusual, a similar pattern of effects from domestic visitation was identified with clusters of antique dealers in rural Victoria, Australia, but with the caveat that these clusters appeared to have stimulated the growth of other firms delivering complementary products and services (Michael, 2002, p. 122). For policy analysis, the lesson to note is that where these clusters were successful they also served to stimulate, or *accelerate*, the growth of other firms delivering complementary products or services, further enhancing the opportunities for wealth creation in those communities.

Another issue of interest in the development of micro-cluster formations concerns the enhanced ability of the host community to control the *externality* impacts that growth will necessarily bring. Externalities can be defined as the spillover effects that result from those economic activities that impose costs or benefits on people, firms or communities who are unrelated to the transaction taking place (Michael, 2006, p. 61). The efficiency generated by an effective market system relies on the notion that the equilibrium price paid for any good or service is supposed to reflect the full costs of all the resources that have been used in the production process. When externalities occur, there are costs or benefits created that are not reflected in this price, but which raise or lower costs in other production processes and will be unfairly attributed in the final price that consumers pay for those other products. More often than not, however, these costs or benefits transfer to the public and appear in a disguised form as social issues that are ultimately addressed through public expenditures.

Tourism generates more than its fair share of externalities. This is largely because tourism generates visitors to any particular destination, and they bring with them not just an increase in the demand for goods and services but also a whole range of social impacts for the host community. Many of these can be minor and perhaps of little public debate, say when traffic congestion increases in a country town at weekends, but they can range out to transnational flow-on effects where the social order in one state is disrupted by visitors from another, as might be demonstrated occasionally by the antics of travelling "soccer hooligans". Externalities are described as *negative* when they impose costs on others, but they can be *positive* where they produce benefits or lower costs for third parties, or, indeed, for whole communities. Economists tend to view externalities as cost effects, but communities see them as visible impacts that are the consequence from some activity; say for example as incremental increases in environmental degradation that stems from the increasing numbers of visitors. Hall and McArthur (1993), for example, point to the "paradox of heritage management" that arises when a heritage-based attraction is successfully marketed but where the flow-on effects from this exposure also serves to denigrate the attraction's value.

In the context of small tourism clusters, there are opportunities here for the host community to make development choices that will partly condition the nature of the externality effects that will arise. While there is scant discussion in the literature on regional development that considers the significance of this proposition, the reality remains that the type of tourism niche market that a community chooses to specialise in will impose different types of externality — not all of which will be positive. For example, if a community encourages a cluster of firms with a focus on festivals or event activities, in anticipation of the positive externalities from economic growth, it will also experience new issues in managing the effects of sudden peak load increases in visitor numbers and, perhaps, some of the impacts from crowd behaviour that will not necessarily match the existing community's lifestyle and values. Wherever a community chooses to specialise in some niche market there occurs a consequent set of flow-on outcomes — some activities are seasonal, some call for the community to integrate itself with the tourism activity, some appeal to particular classes of consumer that necessarily excludes others, some impose social costs that may or may not be acceptable to the resident population, and so the list continues. However, the distinct advantage of cluster formations for small communities is that it is a model for development that requires the community's involvement in the economic choices to be made. While the externality effects of any particular set of choices are not entirely predictable, they are by and large *recognisable*, and so make up part of the opportunity cost that determines the community outcome.

References

Bull, A. (1995). *The economics of travel and tourism* (second ed.). Melbourne: Longmans.

Grado, S. C., Strauss, C. H., & Lord, B. E. (1997). Antiquing as a tourism recreational activity in southwestern Pennsylvania. *Journal of Travel Research, 35*(3), 52–56.

Hall, C. M., Jenkins, J., & Kearsley, G. (Eds). (1997). *Tourism planning and policy in Australia and New Zealand: Cases, issues and practice.* Sydney: Irwin.

Hall, C. M., & McArthur, S. (1993). *Heritage management in Australia and New Zealand.* Auckland: Oxford University Press.

Hugonnier, B. (1999). Regional development tendencies in OECD countries. *Regional Australia Summit, Keynote Presentation,* Canberra, 26–29 October 1999, (14 pp.).

Kitson, M., Martin, R., & Tyler, P. (2004). Regional competitiveness: An elusive yet key concept? *Regional Studies, 38*(9), 991–999.

Lublinski, A. E. (2003). Does geographic proximity matter? Evidence from clustered and non-clustered aeronautic firms in Germany. *Regional Studies, 37*(5), 453–467.

Michael, E. J. (2002). Antiques and tourism in Australia. *Tourism Management, 23*(2), 117–125.

Michael, E. J. (2006). *Public policy — the competitive framework.* Melbourne: Oxford University Press.

Nilsson, P. A. (2001). Tourist destination development: The Åre valley. *Scandinavian Journal of Hospitality and Tourism, 1*(1), 54–67.

Porter, M. E. (1998). Clusters and the new economics of competition. *Harvard Business Review, 6*(November–December), 77–90.

Porter, M. E. (2003). The economic performance of regions. *Regional Studies, 37*(6 and 7), 549–578.

Seaton, A. V. (1996). Hay on Wye, the mouse that roared, book towns and rural tourism. *Tourism Management, 17*(5), 379–382.

Seaton, A. V. (1999). Book towns as tourism developments in peripheral areas. *International Journal of Tourism Research, 1,* 389–399.

Tourism Victoria. (2002). *Victoria's tourism industry strategic plan summary 2002–2006.* Melbourne.

Chapter 5

The Role of Networks

Paul Lynch and Alison Morrison

Objectives

- This chapter introduces another dimension to the analysis of micro-clusters: the role of networks and the process of networking as mechanisms that enhance the ability of small business operators to offer competitive products within a local region.
- 'Networks' are carefully defined as social structures that enable the operators of small firms to build the level of trust necessary for them to share in the development of the local tourism product, while 'networking' is best appreciated as the process used by the members of the network to mobilize relationships and learn from each other.
- The discussion suggests that networks can be structured in different ways with different degrees of formality in their arrangements, and, as a consequence, each type of network will engage in a different networking process.
- The importance of 'social analysis' is emphasised to explain the nature and the significance of the relationships that are established in different kinds of networks.
- Social analysis serves to explain how 'trust' is created within a network, thus providing a sociological dimension to better explain the co-operative behaviour of small firms' operators that was first noted in Chapter 4.
- The chapter provides a review of five different network formations in four countries to illustrate some of the differences in how networks operate in practice.

Micro-Clusters and Networks: The Growth of Tourism
Copyright © 2007 by Elsevier Ltd.
All rights of reproduction in any form reserved.
ISBN: 0-08-045096-2

The point of departure for this chapter is to challenge any assumption that small tourism firms operate in a unitary vacuum, trading within an impersonal market place. In the contemporary world, a more accurate view is one perhaps that is depicted by linkages and connections, with firms and their owner-managers embedded in networks of social, professional and exchange relationships. From a strategic management perspective, Van Laere and Heene (2003) argue that the capacity to collaborate with other actors is becoming a core competence of organisations, as many of the skills and resources essential to small firm prosperity lie outside the firm's own boundaries. This is supported from a tourism perspective where Morrison and Thomas (1999) suggest the common issues faced by the small firms include a shortage of funds, and a lack of marketing and management skills. In addition, the development of the small firm in tourism is hindered by a lack of knowledge of other businesses in the sector and of the ways to work together or to link with them (Andriotis, 2002; Page et al., 1999). One way for tourism firms to overcome this weakness is to establish *networks* (Copp & Ivy, 2001), as part of a clustering process linked in a value chain composed of vertical and/or lateral networks (OECD, 1999).

This chapter aims to establish and define networks as mechanisms that enable those involved in tourism operation and management to build the trust necessary to create a beneficial clustering effect. This necessarily involves engaging in a definitional debate, but with the intention of contributing to an understanding of the distinction between *networks* and *networking*, and the place of social analysis in the development of knowledge about their nature, dynamics and role in local tourism environments. Case study material is introduced to illustrate key characteristics and dimensions associated with such tourism networks, and to emphasise the impact of environmental conditions and facilitators, and the outcomes in various international contexts.

Networks or Networking — Definitions and Debate

Shaw (1997) notes that the term 'network' has been loosely applied in entrepreneurial research, and, as a consequence, suggests there has been a general failure to recognise that *networks* and *networking* are different constructs. Curran, Jarvis, Blackburn, and Black (1993, p. 13) criticise: "… much of the theorising and research using the notions of 'network' and 'networking' as conceptually and methodologically poorly realised." They found that the term *network* has been used as everyday speech rather than as an academic description of a particular phenomenon with a precise meaning. According to O'Donnell, Gilmore, Cummins, and Carson (2001), the popularity of the network construct has, in some instances, led to misapplication and inconsistency; consequently, findings pertaining to entrepreneurs' networks are often confusing and contradictory. In reviewing previous research into the process of networking, O'Donnell (2004) found it to be disparate, inconsistent in terms of terminology and the concepts adopted, and suggested that their findings were often inconclusive as a result.

The elusiveness of definitional precision is in part explained by Gummesson (1994), who uses the term 'imaginary organisation' to refer to the fact that networks are not tangible objects, but rather are social constructs comprising people, activities and thoughts that are not spatially limited to one specific location. The same argument is endorsed by Taylor and Thorpe (2004), for they suggest that the use of the term 'network' is not to represent a definable spatial entity made up of a finite, identifiable set of individuals, such as a physical

Table 5.1: Rosenfeld's distinctions between a cluster and a network (with authors' commentary).

Feature	Cluster	Network	Authors' Commentary
Specialised services	Attract needed specialised services to a region	Allow firms to access specialised services at lower cost	Agree
Membership	Open	Restricted	The reality of clusters is that there is no membership in a strict sense as it is an artificial construction. Technically formal and informal networks need to be joined but tend to be open to all interested
Cohesion	Based on social values that foster trust and encourage reciprocity	Based on contractual agreement	Network descriptive feature ignores informal social networks. Cluster descriptive feature could equally be applied to successful networks
Function	Generate demand for more firms with similar values and related capabilities	Make it easier for firms to engage in complex production	Agree
Cooperation/ competition	Require both cooperation and competition	Based on cooperation	Broadly agree
Aims	Have collective visions	Have common business goals	Networks require collective visions as well as goals. Difficult to see how a cluster can really have a collective vision given it is an artificial construction

Source: Adapted from Rosenfeld (2001).

business unit, but that it should be seen as a fluid entity with permeable boundaries. The semantics of definition are taken still further when Rosenfeld (2001) and Nordin (2003) seek to distinguish *networks* from *clusters* (see Table 5.1); but, in so doing, they rely on restricted definitions of a 'network', which perhaps simply emphasises the difficulties of definitional precision. Some of this confusion and contradiction can be tracked to the academic *home* from which this research emanates. For example, Taylor and Thorpe (2004) use social network analysis to explore the content, texture and meanings associated with the social dynamic of networking relationships, while Halme (2001) identifies the main body of evidence about inter-organisational learning as stemming from the *business network* setting, underpinned by **transaction cost economics**. From a resource-based and value-creating perspective, Van Laere and Heene (2003) emphasise the relevance of networks to small firms drawing on strategic management theories and principles.

A more consistent interpretation, however, can be gleaned from *social network* theory, for it informs investigation into the networks in which small firms are socially embedded (O'Donnell et al., 2001). Curran et al. (1993, p. 13) argue that 'networks' are best seen as "... primarily cultural phenomena ...", that is "... as sets of meanings, norms and expectations usually linked with behavioural correlates of various kinds": but they suggest it is "... the meanings, norms and expectations which are important ..." and that the behaviour correlates serve largely to indicate the kinds of social relations that are worth investigating.

Such varied conceptual starting points inevitably shape the different ways of knowing 'networks' and 'networking' and impact on how they are defined. Nevertheless, there seems to be a level of agreement that it is not the existence of a *network* that in itself has the potential to generate benefits, but rather it is the use of that network through the process of *networking* that actually brings about the gains for the network's membership. The critical element to this distinction rests on an understanding of how the ideas and patterns of action develop among groups and individuals (Halme, 2001) — a view supported by Taylor and Thorpe (2004), whose studies suggest the significance of the social dimensions to entrepreneur decision-making. In short, a *network* might simplistically be viewed as the structure and scaffolding that supports and contains *networking*, but this is rich in social meaning, texture and the relationships involved in the process of networking.

The lazy and imprecise labelling of the two concepts seems to lead many analysts to a 'safer' route, where they avoid the terms *networks* and *networking* simply to sidestep the associated terminology debates. Regrettably, this often results in them using related but separate terms such as *partnerships*, *alliances* and *collaboration* — causing still more confusion for each of these has their own more precise meanings in their given contexts. Despite these difficulties, it is possible to identify a significant body of literature focusing on networks, which reveals their "structural imperative" (O'Donnell, 2004). There is a mixed approach to what might constitute an appropriate definition of a *network*: for example, they have been described as an organized system (Szarka, 1990), or as a specific type of casual alliance (Knoke & Kuklinski, 1983), or as just an informal association (Thompson, Frances, & Mitchell, 1991). Thus, while there appears to be agreement that *networks* consist of a series of direct and indirect ties from one actor to a collection of others (Smith-Ring, 1999), the level of agreement about the formality required to bind these ties is at variance. There is a consensus that the network ties represent co-operative conduits linking firms to a set of persons, objects or events (Knoke & Kuklinski, 1983), or to other business firms, governmental bodies or organisations, persons or others (Smith-Ring, 1999), and that it is essentially these ties which lubricate the social relations between the network's actors. This also helps in the co-ordination of the network participants' political and economic lives (Thompson et al., 1993) for the exchange of ideas and information to their mutual benefit (Knoke & Kuklinski, 1983).

Lynch (2000, p. 95) observes that, "... the term (networks) describes the interactions of the firm with the external environment, and offers potential insights into such areas as business relations, industrial organisation, regional agglomeration, strategic management of small firms and the culturally induced outlooks and behaviours of small firms." To this can be added O'Donnell's (2004) conclusion that *networking* is an activity that varies according to the individual owner-manager and according to the person with whom the interaction takes place. The process of networking, then, can be defined as the activation of the actors, relationships, ties, inter-connections, conduits and content that has been framed within a network structure. It is possible to identify dimensions of networking to include: level of networking, networking proactivity and the strength of network ties. The reality, however, remains that it is not the existence of a network *per se* from which the benefits will accrue, but rather the use of that network through the *process* of networking that generates the desired outcomes (Shaw, 1997).

Small Firm Networks and Tourism

Networks are a phenomenon which is being given increasing attention in the management literature on small business development (see reference list at the end of the chapter). At a generic level, a range of different types of networks are easily identified, and these may be classified in various ways. For example, Conway (1998 cited in Shaw & Conway, 2000, p. 376) devised a network classification, which is provided in Table 5.2 . This particular classification is useful as a means for conceptualising and analysing networks. While it is comprehensive, it does neglect the concept of the virtual network that exists only through cyber-technology, for example, via the Internet or e-mail; and, as a further omission, Halme (2001) notes that networks may also vary according to the type of organisational configuration that pertains. For example, O'Donnell et al. (2001) observe that frequently in the literature networks are categorised as vertical networks and as horizontal networks,

Table 5.2: Network classifications.

Classification	Description
Network membership	Diversity of actors (professional, user, social)
Nature of linkages	Formal versus informal
Type of exchange or transaction	Information, goods, friendship or power
Network function or role	Problem-solving or idea generation
Network morphology	Size, diversity, density, stability of links
Geographical distribution of network	Balance between local, national and international members

Source: Conway (1998) in Shaw and Conway (2000, p. 376).

but it should be noted that relying on this distinction often does not capture the full range of possible inter-organisational network arrangements.

Inter-firm networks have become a popular form of organisational cooperative relationship, and increasing attention is being given to them by academics, analysts, planners and operators alike in the fields of hospitality and tourism (Petrillo & Swarbrooke, 2005). Within the context of the tourism sector, while it is recognised that networks serve multipurposes, one such function is their role in assisting the formation of alliances to facilitate the packaging of a series of related products or services at specific destinations. The cooperation required for a network to operate successfully is perceived as essential for any tourist destination (Soisalon-Soinnen & Lindroth, 2005). For example, Tinsley and Lynch (2001) provide an empirical example of informal tourism-related networking in a rural destination on the west coast of Scotland. They investigated the networking process between the destination's small tourism businesses — including hotels, bed and breakfasts, gift shop, art and craft shop and grocery store — to demonstrate the role that co-operation played in the destination's development. Palmer (1996) offers a public–private sector network example in findings from English district councils, driven by the rationale that attracting more tourists to regional tourist destinations can benefit not only the narrow financial objectives of tourism operators, but also the more diverse social objectives of the public sector.

Social Analysis

O'Donnell et al. (2001) recognise that a deeper appreciation of the content of network relationships would increase understanding of the process of networking. While this is not a new finding, as is evidenced in the work of Mitchell (1969), who conceptualised networks as social entities; he describes a social network as a set of *morphological* dimensions that consider both the pattern and structure of the network, with its interactional dimensions, which are based on considerations of networks as a process. Thus, it has been argued that network analysis considers both the structure and the process of the relationships that join individuals, groups and organisations (Granovetter, 1973), while it is the content of those relations that actually captures the meanings people attach to the relationships that are formed (Mitchell, 1969). These meanings incorporate the individual's motivations, expectations and the outcomes they anticipate from participation in a network (Curran et al., 1993). More recent work (Halme, 2001; Van Laere & Heene, 2003) supports this view, but also points to the relative neglect of the dimensions pertaining to the interaction that occurs between network actors themselves.

According to Lynch (2000), network analysis has provided a mechanism by which one can explore aspects of both the nature and function of social and business networks, as well as the meanings, norms and expectations supporting those relationships, with evidence to highlight the importance of social relationships in small hospitality enterprises and those which may be considered as 'minority firms' (Ram, 1994). Thus, the application of social analysis to the structuring of networks and the process of networking aims at identifying the pattern, content, meanings, motivations, expectations, norms, and nature of interactional relationships. This contributes to an improved understanding of socially embedded relationships, which is of particular significance as it has been demonstrated that market exchanges are embedded in, and defined by, larger and more complex social processes (Van Laere & Heene, 2003).

Lazaretti and Capone (2005) point to the *embeddedness* of tourism firms within the local community and the significance of interactions between local non-economic and economic community members. Some analysts, such as Michael (2006), of course, would argue that this is not a distinction based on economics, because a community and its economy are interdependent, but rather it is an attempt to draw out the differences that separate community interests according to the priority they give to their roles in commerce and trade or to other aspects of social engagement.

Nonetheless, it remains important to differentiate between the levels of intensity of *social embeddedness* or engagement that will be exhibited by different kinds of network structures. Szarka (1990, pp. 11–12) provides evidence of this, offering three categories of network to embrace the economic and social determinants of small firm networks as follows:

- *Exchange networks*: comprise the companies and organisations with which a small firm has commercial transactions, where the unit of analysis is the firm; (these networks are sustained by their communication and social networks, as below);
- *Communication networks*: comprise the collection of organisations and individuals with which a small firm has non-trading links that inform its business activities — such as consultants and advisors, local and central government and its agents — where relationships are characterised by official and semi-official information flows;
- *Social networks*: comprise the linkages between family, friends and acquaintances — they have two components: the personal network involving concrete contacts with specific individuals, and secondly, the wider cultural dimension in which the actors operate.

O'Donnell et al. (2001) present a different approach to network categorisation. They suggest instead that the research into entrepreneurial networks falls into two principal categories: inter-organisational networks and the entrepreneur's personal or social network — which, alternatively, might be labelled as *formal* and *informal* networks. The *social* network is defined as comprising family and friends with two elements: "... the personal network which the small firm owner has with specific individuals, and the cultural dimension in which the actors are immersed" (Saker, 1992, p. 4). Dodd (1997) reconsiders the implications of social networking in terms of the interrelated sets of pairings that are inherent in the concept of any relationship, which directly or indirectly includes the owner-manager of a small firm. The stronger and deeper the ties an owner-manager has with the group, the more likely their core attitudes and aims are to be shaped and influenced by social (informal) rather than commercial (formal) networks.

Gibson, Lynch, and Morrison (2005) augment this debate by adding further categories to the analysis of networks as *formal, semi-formal* and *informal*. These are expanded as follows:

- Formal: a formalised set of actors who interact in the context of identified aims, for example, a regional tourism organisation. While social interactions may be valued, these are subordinate to the formalised aims.
- *Semi-formal*: a formalised set of actors who interact in the context of identified aims, for example, a local business marketing consortium. Social interactions may be perceived as of equal importance to the formalised aims.

- *Informal*: a set of actors who meet mainly for social purposes but also exchange information which has instrumental (business) value. No formal membership or clear goals exist, as occurs, for example, in a neighbourhood host families 'network' (see the *Scotland: host families* case-study later in this chapter).

Networks — The Mechanism for Trust

'Social capital theory', according to Leana and Van Buren (1999), emphasises the importance of relational capabilities in the management of the connections to the community in which a firm is embedded; and, hence is of particular importance to the smaller tourism firm given the central role played by its owner-manager. These authors use the term 'associability' to indicate an organisation's ability to participate in collective goals and actions while subordinating their own individual goals and actions. They also refer to the propensity to 'trust' another party. As pointed out by Buoncore and Metallo (2005), the presence of high-trust relationships leads to higher levels of social exchange and cooperative behaviours. Associability and trust are identified by Leana and Van Buren (1999) as affective and skills-based dimensions of relational competencies.

As noted in Chapter 4, individual businesses engage in competition within a local economy, but they are also very much a part of the local social fabric that creates the sense of identity as a *community*. This relationship, combined with the notion of 'embeddedness' within the community, has concerned a number of analysts in the tourism organisational literature, (see, e.g., Altejevic & Doorne, 2000; Lazaretti & Capone, 2005). However, it is the work of Brandenburger and Nalebuff (1997) that explains why businesses which compete might also need to cooperate with one another in order to achieve success (see the discussion of *co-opetition* in Chapter 4). The reality remains that working in a network alongside other businesses with which one is in competition requires a degree of *trust*, a kind of relationship glue (Buoncore & Metallo, 2005), for it is *trust* that engenders the kind of cooperation that is for the general as well as the individual good. Hence, from the perspective of social analysis, the importance of relational competencies is evident.

It is possible to identify certain environmental conditions and facilitators of *trust*. According to some analysts these include: geographical isolation; organically 'grown' networks; high social density; co-location within a locality (Walton, 1978); person familiarity; frequency of communication; dependency of relationships over time (Van Laere & Heene, 2003); development of inter-organisation norms of behaviour (Palmer 1996). Working together successfully in a network is an evolutionary process, but one that nonetheless may be facilitated with public sector support (Gibson et al., 2005). The role for the owner-managers of small tourism firms is to marshal their social capital in order to develop and exploit their networks of social, professional and exchange relationships. It is too simplistic to say that such relationships are purely instrumental, for *trust* is an essential ingredient in the development of relationships to the level where cooperation for business purposes can occur. Such trust is frequently dependent upon the strength of the social relationship. Networking is a process that acts as the structure or mechanism that permits owner-managers to develop that level of trust. Hence, *networks* can be seen as developing as a result of the *networking* process; and it might even be argued that it is the coalescence of organisational networks within a locality that leads to the creation of a business cluster.

Networks in Action

In the following case studies, examples are given of tourism networks internationally that embrace a range of different network types. They illustrate the nature of networks, their aims and some of the contributions they make as models for other applications. These cases also serve to illustrate some of the limitations to the effectiveness of networks and to the challenges that they face.

South Africa —— The Highlands Meander Project

This *formal,* private sector led network is located in South Africa (and the following description of its activities is adapted from Rogerson, 2002). This network is focussed on linking the tourism resources in a number of small interconnected localities, and marketing them as a single destination. This involves facilities such as accommodation, trout farms, restaurants, and crafts centres. Its goal, simply stated, is to increase the flow of tourists and create new jobs and businesses.

Here, several local authorities supported the private operator's network in order to collectively enhance the enterprises' base for competitiveness through tourism derived economic development. Established in 1998, its key aims are to achieve greater marketing effectiveness through collaboration, and to build *capacity* within the tourism destination area. Funding is drawn from membership fees and sponsorship. The tangible achievements of the network include the development of a detailed route map for the region, and a book on its history, cultural and eco-tourism sites, and with appropriate information on other hospitality and tourism-related services. Other outputs can be evidenced in terms of:

- Market development relative to conference, meetings and adventure tourism;
- Inter-network collaboration, co-operation and the forging of synergistic partnership across all sectors of the regional tourism industry; and
- Innovation and new product generation to capitalise on growth and niche markets.

The network is centralised, organised by private sector 'volunteers' at a local level, meets on a regular basis, with meetings that are open to non-members. It is not without its weaknesses, of course, but in this region they are partly a reflection of the current socio-economic composition of the membership. The network's benefits, for example, have not figured prominently in the empowerment of poorer local communities, nor is there much evidence that the spread of economic benefits has reached them. Local politics act as a barrier to participation and attendance at network meetings is low. There is a need perhaps for stronger local authority involvement and for those authorities to better ensure adherence to South Africa's social policies as a pre-condition for their support of the network. Further work is also needed to reduce the economic leakages from the gains being made by the tourism operators to optimise the benefits for local communities.

It would appear that this network provides an example of good intentions, alongside fundamental difficulties in its management and sustenance. Potentially, the benefits that could arise from the network's functions include the following although their realisation may be more problematic:

- The network can serve as a powerful mechanism to stimulate learning and exchange, contributing to the development of new cultural values and to accelerating the speed with which supporting agencies can implement new development initiatives;
- The network can promote business activity and capacity building within the tourism destination, encouraging the best use of small enterprises' and support agencies' resources, inter-trading within the network and the opportunities for market development; and
- The network can contribute to addressing some of the significant social and economic problems within impoverished communities, by better engaging small and micro-enterprises, community groups, government officials and local authorities.

Scotland — The Ayrshire Food Network

The Ayrshire Food Network is located in south-west Scotland. It presents itself as an example of an innovation championed through the efforts of an individual — Howard Wilkinson, who in 2006 still serves as the network's Chairman. It grew out of a Culture and Heritage Project set up by a regional tourism forum that had a sub-focus on Food/Gastronomy. The Ayrshire Food Network describes itself as an *informal* network involving artisan food producers and fine food providers, who use the best of the local produce from Ayrshire. Analysts, however, might prefer to describe it as a *formal* network, for its structure better meets the earlier definition. Its purpose is to promote the creation and production within Ayrshire of artisan food and beverages, and their usage and consumption by way of a network of businesses in Ayrshire and the surrounding environs.

The Ayrshire Food Network has 35 members, the majority of which are small- or micro-sized enterprises. The membership consists of restaurants, primary producers, coffee shops, specialist suppliers and shops, and hotels and bed and breakfast tourist accommodation. In some ways, it could be described as an anti-response to the globalization issues raised in Chapter 2, for the membership believes in the need to preserve biodiversity, encourage food supply traceability and the reduction of *food miles* (which is the distance fresh food products are required to travel from point of production to the point of consumption). It forms part of a geographic, business and tourism cluster that is concerned with sustainability across economic, social, environmental and tourism criteria. Cohesion and consolidation within the cluster allows the coming together of complementarities in food, culture and heritage — optimised by the beautiful natural environment, fertile farming and a colourful historical legacy that includes the fact that Scotland's best-loved poet, Robert Burns, was born in Ayrshire.

The Ayrshire Food Network is supported by private enterprises and public sector agencies at the local, regional, national and European levels. In addition, it engages in a networking process with other institutions and networks, including:

- A local further education college that has access to objective 3 European funding — SME learning networks;
- An associated network that shares similar network aims and configurations in Finland and Sweden;

- The Ayrshire farmers market, a co-operative of primary producers (noting that some of its membership is shared with the Ayrshire Food Network);
- Lobbyist organisations, such as the 'Slow Food Movement' established in Italy in 1986 with 83,000 members internationally that promotes food and wine culture, and defends food and agricultural biodiversity worldwide.

The Ayrshire Food Network set up in 2003, primarily as a distribution and marketing network. There is a commitment among members to deliver a total quality customer/tourist experience as manifested through their small- and micro-enterprises, their products and traditions. This has been enhanced through customer service training for members and other training initiatives. Joint marketing activity takes the form of the production of a multi-lingual brochure that is distributed at Prestwick Airport and to 4,500 hotel bedrooms in Ayrshire. The Ayrshire Food Network exhibited at the 'Slow Food's' 2004 Terra Madre Conference in Turin that brought together 5,000 food producers from approximately 130 different countries.

The Ayrshire Food Network has created significant outputs in its own right. For example, it has established a sophisticated e-business portal that facilitates an on-line community, encouraging and maximising business-to-business opportunities and promotion to consumers (*www.inandaroundayrshire.com* and *www.ayrshirefarmersmarket.co.uk*). The portal also promotes inter-supplier trading arrangements, provides links to the individual web pages of other Ayrshire Food Network members, and to the complementary regional food and drink offerings provided by other consolidators (including: *www.scottishgourmetfood.co.uk* and *www.scottishgourmethampers.co.uk*). As another example, with the assistance of the 'Scottish Enterprise Tourism Innovation Toolkit', which seeks to provide a range of practical tips, techniques and tools to enable businesses to be more creative, more innovative and more successful, the Network has developed the *Ayrshire Experience Box* — made up of a selection of food, information about Robert Burns, a music CD, maps and details of Ayrshire food producers and the Food Trail.

At a regional level, the network seeks to enhance business activity to provide attractive employment opportunities for the young to remain in the locality rather than to migrate to the cities. The Ayrshire Food Network's chairman, Howard Wilkinson, as the owner of a micro-business that specialises in Vegetarian and Vegan produce, has observed from his own experience that: "… you don't have to be big to do something rather special. It's about thinking collaboratively. On our own we're nothing. Working with other people we are rather special". To this he adds an Olympic ring analogy, where significant innovations and business performance achievements are secured by the individual members of the network, because they collectively engineer the composition of interlinked, overlapping, complementary networks of networks.

Canada — The Niagara Wine Route

The Niagara Wine Route network is another example that is primarily driven by the private sector (and the following description of its activities is adapted from Telfer, 2001). However, it represents a network of a range of private and public sector organisations aiming to improve the reputation over time of Niagara, Canada, as a wine region and to increase the level of wine tourism in that region. It was established in the 1990s and draws funding from private and public sources. Membership includes 52 wineries in the

Region and includes sub-networks, such as Niagara-on-the-Lakes wineries. It can be classified as both a *formal* and an *informal* network, as the wineries collaborate across a range of vertical and horizontal linkages. The Wine Council of Ontario, a non-profit trade association, serves in the role as the network's central management, even though its core tasks are to develop and implement industry marketing and research programmes, the setting of regional standards, and the policy and future directions for the wine industry, as well as to act as the liaison body between wineries, grape growers and government organisations in Ontario. It also works closely with the Vintners Quality Alliance, the national organisation responsible for introducing and maintaining standards for Canadian wines.

Transactions within the formal network take the form of exchanges directed at quality and product development and marketing. Within the network, transactions are represented by:

- the development of joint initiatives, primarily related to association memberships, advertising, and festivals;
- at an operational level, facilitating the organisation of wine production, as occurs where the larger wineries can bottle and store the wine from the smaller wine-makers, along with other examples of shared expertise and resources; and
- encouraging partnerships with specialist oenology and viticulture education institutes to support research and product development.

In this sense, the Niagara Wine Route network represents a collaborative knowledge sharing, problem-solving and idea generation association built around individual enterprise, agency and collective enhancements. Its benefits stem from its geographical distribution, which is both local and state wide, and include:

- *Learning and exchange*: through peer learning contributing to knowledge transfer, tourism education processes, communication, acceleration of the speed of implementation of support agency initiatives, and the facilitation of small business development;
- *Business activity*: stimulated by co-operative activities that foster innovation, new product development and the extraction of marketing synergies, which in combination serve to enhance the reputation of the region for wine tourism, increasing visitor numbers, extending the visitor season, and increasing the level of entrepreneurial activity; and
- *Community values*: fostered through the network's common purpose and focus, engaging support for small enterprises in the destination's development, and the retention of more of the income earned by these developments within the destination.

Malaysia — Small chalet owner-managers

An investigation undertaken by Ahmad and Morrison (2004) into the networking practices of small châlet owner-managers, who provide tourist accommodation in coastal and island destinations in Malaysia, provides yet another insight into the ways that networks operate. The owner-managers of 37 small châlets and resorts along the east coast of the Malayan peninsula were interviewed to explore their networking practices. The criteria for selection were that the châlets operated within the selected geographic areas; that they were located near the coast or the beach; that they were small in size (less than 50 rooms); and that they were owned by an individual and managed in a personalised manner by the owner or manager.

Despite the supposed business purpose of the networks that Ahmad and Morrison (2004) examined, they were found to have two strong social dimensions to them. First, the networks were composed of family and ethnic linkages that made use of personal and family contacts embedded in a close-knit community; and, second, that the concept of *place* or *locality* is important in that the owner-managers have developed relationships with business contacts within a specific geographic area, mainly bounded by the 'village'. Most enterprises represent family businesses utilising family members as their source of labour. In this region, the communities are geographically remote, which imposes time and cost factors that may restrict regular communications and meetings with contacts further afield. Nevertheless, most of the households in these destinations rely on tourism and hospitality related activities for their business survival, which intrinsically leads them to networking with people with the same interests, for they share a similar life-style and confront the same problems that may not be appreciated in the same way by outsiders.

These networks are male-dominated, but this is an obvious reflection of the local culture. A strong preference is demonstrated for informal networks composed of a close network of actors, the majority of which can be classified as family, friends and/or acquaintances. For the analyst, they present as close-knit and dense networks, with information travelling and spreading through them fast and easily. There appears to be a minimal inclusion of government officials as contacts within these networks, and any more formalised network arrangements tended to comprise professionals, such as, accountants, bank managers, or lawyers, rather than bureaucrats or public sector officials.

Despite the social structure of these networks, their core role remains with business-related matters. The benefits from networking given by the châlet owners included: the enhancement of management and operational capabilities; the stimulation of ideas that could result in innovation; the formation of alliances to assist in the co-ordination of products and services at different tourist destinations; and the sharing of advice and knowledge — where the owner-managers use their networks as platforms to discuss their problems in running their business. Indeed, the analysts found that the owner-managers tended to discuss different business aspects with different network contacts. They were willing to invest their time and money in maintaining and sustaining the network's relationship ties and connections, meeting regularly in predominately social venues, and/or within their business premises; however, these networks are still perceived as low cost and low maintenance. This is hardly surprising given that the networks' members live close to each other in the same communities and that many are family relations, which contributes a positive social dimension to the routine of meetings to offset the low material expectations and gains from each network activity. While the network members generally considered the cost/benefit of participation to be worthwhile, the ability to demonstrate tangible benefits appears to be low; with the singular exception of knowledge sharing that was perceived as the strongest benefit from the networking process. Those owner-managers who found this aspect the most beneficial were those who participated in networks that were built on friendship and strong personal relationships, where the *trust* factor is implicit, and the knowledge shared had resulted in enhanced business capabilities.

Scotland — Host Families

A different view of the significance of networks can be appreciated from a study of host families in the city of Edinburgh, Scotland (Lynch, 2000). In this environment, 'host families' comprise those households who contract with local English language schools to provide food and accommodation to students who have come to Edinburgh to study English as a foreign language.

The aim of the study at the outset was not to investigate networks and networking, rather it was to determine the significance of neighbourhood relationships, but the paramount role of *social networks* emerged as the critical finding during that research. The investigation involved four stages: first, in-depth interviews and a focus group with hosts; secondly, semi-structured interviews with 14 representatives from a structured sample of English language schools and others who were responsible or experienced in the organisation of such accommodation; and, as a third stage, interviews were conducted with 206 hosts to explore their characteristics and motivations. Finally, workshops were held with organisational representatives during the research to check the emerging findings and discuss the emerging themes.

The key relationship here is between the host/family and their guest, which it was found both sustains and is sustained by the quality of relationship between the host and the external organisation and between the guest and that external organisation. The hosts are invariably female. They identified 'liking the kind of students received' as the most important reason for valuing the organisation they would accept guests from. The hosts seemed to value those organisations that indicated a high understanding of their responsibilities towards the guest students, which can be described as a moral relationship that reflects a matching of values and expectations in the hosts' attitudes towards their role. The financial aspect of the relationship for the hosts could be described in terms used by Herzberg, Mausner, and Synderman (1959) as more of a *maintenance* factor than a *satisfier* — where the income received was important, but where the relationship that evolves between the host and the guest more critically determines the host's willingness to proceed. However, it is the *affective relationship* with the organisation, which represents the more important satisfiers from the host's perspective: indeed, some were inclined to judge an organisation by its ability to demonstrate the strength of its moral relationship with the guest. A strong emphasis by hosts was placed on the affective relationships between them and the organisation that sponsored their guests, with positive relationships being identified as those that could lead to referrals for new hosts. Such organisational relationships were occasionally supported by periodic social events.

The importance of social networks at a neighbourhood level was reflected in a number of ways, including geographic proximity, recruitment, communication and support. The *density* of networking among host families is reflected in the findings that 58% of hosts knew three or more other host families, and that 47% of host families known to other survey respondents lived within one mile (1.6 km) of each other. Postcode analysis indicated that certain neighbourhoods were favoured by the English language schools for recruitment purposes: and while part of the explanation for this location pattern included geographic proximity to the sponsoring organisation and the level of access to transportation, another part of the explanation lay in the density of the neighbouring host family network. The benefits of the neighbourhood social networking process appeared to include:

- learning and exchange — through peer learning and the contribution to knowledge transfer and communication;
- business activity — initiated and stimulated through personal relationships; and
- community values — fostered through shared hosting activity.

The study's results implied that most recruitment to any particular organisation was by 'word-of-mouth', but that certain hosts with particularly dense social networks were perceived more favourably as host *leaders* in certain neighbourhoods and as more able to serve the vital functions of communication and information. In short, at the neighbourhood level, it seemed that it was the *affective ties* that were the initiating force behind the decision to host.

Discussion

An overview of the case studies applying Conway's network classifications is provided in Table 5.3. These illustrate the use of networks and networking to develop and sustain tourism provider activities and thereby support the development and sustainability of tourist destinations. The results suggest a clear alignment of the interests of the individual service provider and the tourism destination as a whole. Each case study shares a geographical linkage with variously strong and weak ties (Granovetter, 1973) among the participants, and, to varying degrees, reflects the embedded nature of businesses in economic as well as non-economic communities. The importance of relational capabilities is seen most clearly through the Ayrshire Food Network's case study, where the founder may be likened to a network entrepreneur (Gibson et al., 2005) who serves a critical role in setting and encouraging the norms, values, and trusting behaviours for others within the network to follow. Within a tourism context, this role of the network entrepreneur is in need of further research.

The networks also reflect both the various stages of development as well as the formality of their structure. In this context, the informal networks might be viewed as potential formal networks-in-waiting as they contain the social glue of communication patterns and norms of behaviour that could form the foundations for more formal networks, which might perhaps contribute towards a more advanced stage of economic development. Arguably, the dynamic nature of networks, a concept illustrated well in the discussion of Buoncore and Metallo (2005), is not as well conveyed through case studies that tend to be 'snapshots' taken at a point in time, but nevertheless the Malaysian owner-managers and the Edinburgh host families studies illustrate the importance of physical proximity, frequency of contact, respect and personal friendship, as well demonstrating the restricted nature of the membership that may arise — for example, in relation to gender or socioeconomic grouping. In the Highlands Meander case, however, where the same phenomenon is observed, it is critical for the relevant public sector funding bodies to use their influence to ensure open membership within the terms of reference of the network.

Table 5.3: Case studies — network classifications.

Case Study	Network Membership	Nature of Linkages	Type of Exchange	Network Function or Role	Network Morphology	Geographical Distribution
Highlands Meander	Public and private sector organisations	Formal	Instrumental collaboration	Destination marketing; economic development	Medium — low density, narrow reach	Across several local authorities
Ayrshire Food Network	Primarily private sector organisations	Formal	Instrumental collaboration	Economic, social, environmental and tourism sustainability	Medium density, diverse reach	Primarily local but links to other local, regional, national and international networks
Niagara Wine Route	Public and private sector organisations	Formal and informal (a semi-formal network)	Instrumental and social exchange	Destination marketing; business and economic development; learning and exchange; community development	Medium-low density, diverse reach	Local and regional

| Malaysia; small chalet owner-managers | Community (male) business members | Primarily informal | Social and instrumental exchange | Strengthening of community; learning and exchange; business cooperation | High density, narrow reach | Local |
| Host families | (Female) neighbours | Informal | Social and instrumental exchange | Strengthening of community; learning and exchange; | High density, narrow reach | Local |

All the case studies reveal examples of wider linkages to other vertical and/or horizontal networks and, in this sense, one can see the formation of networks in clusters. Such networks individually and collectively provide value for the network participant by leveraging knowledge and resources they would not otherwise readily gain and thereby aiding their competitive capabilities and effectiveness. The cross-sectoral composition of the network memberships is a feature of the Highlands Meander, the Ayrshire Food Network and Niagara Wine Route networks, and serves more clearly to illustrate the attempts to develop a distinct sustainable tourist destination.

The more *formal* networks illustrate a greater concern with tangible outputs, and these are summarised in relation to learning and exchange, business activity and community values. Such outputs are not easily attained and, as a cautionary note, it should be observed that achieving a successful network is constrained by a variety of factors, including resources and the heterogeneity of the membership's aims and values (Gibson et al., 2005). Learning and exchange, and the development and reinforcement of community values, are key benefits of *informal* networking, which may on occasion lead to business activity benefits.

While this chapter has briefly reviewed the definitional debate concerning networks and networking, it has proposed a simplified analogy whereby a *network* represents a social structure and scaffolding while *networking* is the process employed to mobilise relationships for particular purposes. Various perspectives on networks have been identified, which arise from the particular interests and emphasis of academic disciplines. Networking is seen to be especially concerned with the activation of the network actors, and the relationships and ties between them. *Social network analysis*, of networks and networking, contributes to an understanding of how market exchanges are embedded in existing social processes. Within the tourism industry, inter-firm interaction has a special importance for tourism destination development where the level of *embeddedness* by small tourism organisations within their local communities has been demonstrated. The classification of networks as *formal*, *semi-formal* and *informal*, along with the emphasis on their social (as opposed to their organisational) aims, suggests that networks can operate as trust-building mechanisms for business purposes and that their coalescence serves to support the creation of a business cluster. The case studies have emphasised the contributions that networks have made to local processes that have enhanced learning and exchange, business activity and community development. The issue that remains unresolved by these studies, however, is how best such networks should be supported by public agencies as a component part of a region's broader economic development strategy.

References

Ahmad, G., & Morrison, A. (2004). Small firm social networking in tourism and hospitality. *Tourism: State of the Art II, refereed papers*. Glasgow: University of Strathclyde.

Altejevic, I., & Doorne, S. (2000). Staying within the Fence: Lifestyle entrepreneurship. *Journal of Sustainable Tourism, 8*(5), 378–392.

Andriotis, K. (2002). Scale of hospitality firms and local economic development: Evidence from Crete. *Tourism Management, 23*(4), 333–341.

Brandenburger, A., & Nalebuff, B. (1997). *Co-opetition*. New York: Currency Doubleday.

Buoncore, F., & Metallo, C. (2005). Tourist destination networks, relational competencies and "relationship builders" — the central role of information systems and human resource management. in: C. Petrillo, & J. Swarbrooke (Eds), *Networking and partnerships in destination development and management: Proceedings of the ATLAS annual conference 2004* (pp. 377–398). Arnhem: ATLAS.

Conway, S. (1998). Developing a classification of network typologies. cited in Shaw, E. & Conway, S. Networking and the small firm. In S. Carter, & D. Jones-Evans(Eds). (2000). *Enterprise and small business*. Harlow: Financial Times/Prentice Hall.

Copp, C., & Ivy, R. (2001). Networking trends of small tourism businesses in post-socialist Slovakia. *Journal of Small Business Management, 39*(4), 345–353.

Curran, J., Jarvis, R., Blackburn R., & Black, S. (1991). Small firms and networks: Methodological strategies and preliminary findings. In M. Ram (1994), unravelling social networks in ethnic minority firms. *International Small Business Journal, 12*(3), 42–53.

Curran, J., Jarvis, R., Blackburn, R., & Black S. (1993). Networks and small firms: Constructs, methodological strategies and some findings. *International Small Business Journal, 11*(2), 13–25.

Dodd, S. (1997). Social network membership and activity rates: Some comparative data. *International Small Business Journal, 15*(4), 80–87.

Gibson, L., Lynch, P., & Morrison, A. (2005). The local destination tourism network: Development issues. *Tourism and Hospitality Planning and Development, 2*(2), 87–99.

Granovetter, M. (1973). The strength of weak ties. *American Journal of Sociology, 78*(6), 1360–1380.

Gummesson, E. (1994). Making relationship marketing operational. *International Journal of Services Management, 5*(5), 5–20.

Halme, M. (2001). Learning for sustainable development in tourism networks. *Business Strategy and the Environment, 10*(2), 100–114.

Herzberg, F., Mausner, B., & Synderman, B. (1959). *The motivation to work*. New York: Wiley.

Knoke, D., & Kuklinski, J. (1983). *Network analysis*. Beverley Hills: Sage.

Lazaretti, L., & Capone, F. (2005). Networking in tourist local systems. In C. Petrillo, & J. Swarbrooke (Eds), *Networking and partnerships in destination development and management: Proceedings of the ATLAS annual conference 2004* (pp. 485–498). Arnhem: ATLAS..

Leana, C., & Van Buren, H. (1999). Organizational social capital and employment practices. *Academy of Management Review, 24*(3), 538–555.

Lynch, P. (2000). Networking in the homestay sector. *The Services Industries Journal, 20*(3), 95–116.

Michael, E.J. (2006). *Public Policy — the competitive framework* Melbourne: Oxford University Press.

Mitchell, J. (1969). The concept and use of social networks. In: J. Mitchell, (Ed.), *Social networks in urban situations* (pp. 1–50). Manchester: Manchester University Press.

Morrison, A., & Thomas, R. (1999). The future of small firms in the hospitality industry. *International Journal of Contemporary Hospitality Management, 11*(4), 148–154.

Nordin, S. (2003). *Tourism clustering & innovation: Paths to economic growth and development*. Mid-Sweden University : ETOUR.

O'Donnell, A. (2004). The nature of networking in small firms. *Qualitative Market Research: An International Journal 7*(3), 206–217.

O'Donnell, A., Gilmore, A., Cummins, D., & Carson, D. (2001). The network construct in entrepreneurship research: A review and critique. *Management Decision, 39*(9), 749–760.

OECD. (1999). Boosting innovation. The cluster approach', OECD proceedings, cited by Breda, Z., Costa, R., & Costa, C. Clustering and networking the tourism development process: A market driven approach for a small backwards tourist region located in central Portugal (Caramulo). In C. Petrillo, & J. Swarbrooke (Eds), *Networking and partnerships in destination development and management: Proceedings of the ATLAS annual conference 2004* (pp. 469–484). Arnhem: ATLAS.

Page, S., Forer, P., & Lawton, G. (1999). Small business development and tourism: Terra incognita? *Tourism Management, 20*(4), 435–459.

Palmer, A. (1996). Linking external and internal relationship building in networks of public and private sector organisations: A case study. *International Journal of Public Sector Management, 9*(3), 51–60.

Petrillo, C., & Swarbrooke, J. (Eds). (2004). *Networking and partnerships in destination development and management: Proceedings of the ATLAS annual conference 2004.* Arnhem: ATLAS.

Ram, M. (1994). Unravelling social networks in ethnic minority firms. *International Small Business Journal, 12*(3), 42–53.

Rogerson, C. (2002). Tourism and local economic development: The case of the highlands meander. *Development Southern Africa, 19*(1), 143–167.

Rosenfeld, S. (2001). Backing into clusters: Retrofitting public policies cited by Nordin, S. (2003). *Tourism clustering & innovation: Paths to economic growth and development,* Mid-Sweden University : ETOUR.

Shaw, E. (1997). *The impact which [sic] social networks have on the development of small professional service firms.* University of Glasgow, Glasgow, unpublished PhD thesis.

Smith-Ring, P. (1999). Processes facilitating reliance on trust in interorganisational networks. In: M. Ebers (Ed.), *The formation of inter-organisational networks* (pp. 113–145). Oxford: Oxford University Press.

Soisalon-Soinnen, T., & Lindroth, K. (2005). Regional tourism co-operation in progress. In: C. Petrillo, & J. Swarbrooke (Eds), *Networking and partnerships in destination development and management: Proceedings of the ATLAS annual conference 2004* (pp. 511–522), Arnhem: ATLAS.

Szarka, J. (1990). Networking and small firms. *International Small Business Journal, 8*(2), 10–21.

Taylor, D., & Thorpe, R. (2004). Entrepreneurial learning: A process of co-participation. *Journal of Small Business and Enterprise Development, 11*(2), 203–211.

Telfer, D. (2001). Strategic alliances along the Niagara wine route. *Tourism Management, 22*(1), 21–30.

Thompson, G., Frances, J. R., & Mitchell, J. (Eds). (1991). *Markets, hierarchies and networks: The co-ordination of social life.* London: Sage.

Tinsley, R., & Lynch, P. (2001). Small tourism business networks and destination development. *International Journal of Hospitality Management, 20*(4), 367–378.

Van Laere, K., & Heene, A. (2003). Social networks as a source of competitive advantage for the firm. *Journal of Workplace Learning, 15*(6), 248–258.

Walton, J. (1978). *The blackpool landlady: A social history.* Manchester: Manchester University Press.

www.ayrshirefarmersmarket.co.uk, accessed 23 October 2005.

www.inandaroundayrshire.com, accessed 23 October 2005.

www.scottishgourmetfood.co.uk, accessed 23 October 2005.

www.scottishgourmethampers.co.uk, accessed 23 October 2005.

www.scotexchange.net/businessdevelopment/innovation_2004-2/innovation_toolkit/ [Scottish Enterprise Innovation Toolkit (2004)], accessed 27 October 2005.

Chapter 6

Micro-Clusters: Antiques, Retailing and Business Practice

Ewen J. Michael

Objectives

- This chapter is the first of the three that illustrates the ways that micro-clusters form and operate within the tourism industry, based on examples in a variety of niche markets in Australia, New Zealand, Scandinavia and the United Kingdom.
- This chapter begins with an illustration based on antiques retailing as a tourism activity in Victoria, Australia, as a means to demonstrate both how micro-clusters form in small rural settings and how significant their impact can be for the host community.
- The discussion reflects on the role of micro-clusters as tourism generators, where the establishment of new destinations draws visitors into the local economy, and how the choices made by a local community can determine the nature of these developments.
- Within the constraints imposed by the *paradigm of competition*, micro-clusters are identified as a development mechanism.
- The chapter considers some of the practices that have led to successful cluster formations, which foster the ability to build a local level of specialization and a competitive advantage for a small destination, along with some of the causes that might contribute to *declustering*.
- The analysis of successful cluster formations in tourism serves to emphasize the role played by small business operators in building a level of mutual interaction and trust to create the dynamic alignment of complementary activities that expands the economies-of-scope and the breadth-of-product offerings within a local environment that better meets the consumers' needs.

Micro-Clusters and Networks: The Growth of Tourism
Copyright © 2007 by Elsevier Ltd.
All rights of reproduction in any form reserved.
ISBN: 0-08-045096-2

Micro-clusters are visible in many forms. They can be found in many locations and in many industries. They are visible, for example, in some forms of manufacturing, where groups of firms co-locate and interact to deliver particular kinds of outputs, such as metal fabrication or vehicle repairs and servicing. The same patterns of location are similarly apparent in many service industries, such as health care, where hospitals and specialist medical providers seek to co-locate, or in the legal system where law firms and associated providers choose to position themselves close to the courts and to the offices of the appro-priate bureaucracies. The retail precincts in every sizeable town and city serves as yet another reminder, and in larger metropolises these precincts may be sub-divided into even smaller districts where particular types of retailers congregate to provide specialist prod-ucts in clothing, jewellery, foodstuffs and the like. There are very good reasons for these forms of industrial co-location; but, clustering is not confined solely to metropolitan areas but occurs also in regional and rural environments.

These same observations also apply to tourism activities! Hence, this chapter sets out to illustrate the effects of micro-clustering and network formations in one of the myriad niche markets that contribute to the broader tourism industry. It uses the retailing of antiques in rural and regional areas as a case study of co-location by small firms, where successful clustering practices enhance the establishment of micro destinations. The fol-lowing two chapters continue this theme with illustrations of clustering and networking in other niche markets. Chapter 7 explores the formation of tourism wine clusters in the south island of New Zealand, while Chapter 8 compares tourism destinations in Scotland and the north of Sweden but with a more precise focus on the role of networks as the mechanisms that support these types of micro-clusters.

The Antiques Industry: An Illustration

The retailing of *antiques, collectables, memorabilia, oldwares* and other such products is a well-recognized trade throughout the western world. Coincidentally, this trade also forms part of the broad range of services offered at many identifiable tourism destinations, espe-cially where the tourism product is based on heritage or cultural pursuit. Examples of these activities are commonly found throughout western and northern Europe, North America, Australia and New Zealand, but are also increasingly to be found in the newer destinations in eastern Europe, and in the emerging destinations of Asia, including India and Bali.

Until the 1990s, however, there were few analysts who regarded the retailing trade in gen-eral to be part of the basket of activities that makes up tourism — despite the rather obvious connection between visitors and their purchases of goods and services — and there were even fewer who viewed the antique trade as a component part of the services provided under the umbrella of tourism in some destinations (for exceptions, see Zeppel & Hall, 1991; Grado, Strauss, & Lord, 1997; Michael, 2002). This is perhaps understandable, given the considerable difficulties of separating retailing for local consumption from tourism derived activities, but even the most cursory review produces clear illustrations in the regional areas of many coun-tries where clusters of antiques and oldwares traders deliver the entire commercial tourism function for small towns. In this sense, through simple observation, it is apparent that the antiques industry often creates its own tourism destinations, or serves as a significant sup-porting activity for the other attractions at the same location. More curious, perhaps, is

Michael's (2002) observation that it is rare to find an antiques firm operating in isolation from other elements of the tourism or hospitality industries — implying the existence of a complementary relationship that neither economists nor retail management analysts have yet to explore.

The *antique trades*, as a broad descriptor for this industry, can be found in most developed and developing economies. In most western countries, retail sites are often located in distinct precincts of the major cities or in specialist zones in suburban shopping strips, but they are also found in clusters in rural areas and country towns. As a market, the antique trade exists with its own local and regional dynamics, but its products are also exchanged globally and in cyberspace. It is a substantial global trade, although in the world context it is dominated by European and American interests. Few governments are actively involved in the industry's regulation, other than through normal commercial trading requirements, and many so-called oldwares products are in reality current production items. Some states restrict the export of genuine heritage items, but few go to the lengths that Thailand does to register and stamp every real antique item to assure buyers of its legitimacy. In short, it is essentially a private market where the consumers' own knowledge determines the value they place on authenticity: it is a trade where the old maxim — *buyer beware* — has meaning.

The way the antiques trade operates in Australia serves as a good illustration of the global pattern and of its connection with the tourism industry. It is a billion-dollar industry, operating in a private market with little government involvement. Michael (2002) estimated that there were more than 3000 individual retailers throughout Australia in 1998, ranging from small, single-operator stallholders in public markets to major commercial enterprises employing 100 people or more. Consumer demand for antiques and oldwares appears to have fallen in the period 1995–2003 as a result of escalating prices for genuine items, changing fashions and the emergence of new suppliers of quality furniture and furnishings in reproduction styles. The current estimates for the Australian industry would suggest that there has been little growth in total value or employment, but, given that some of the larger metropolitan dealerships have closed over the past 5–8 years, the only visible expansion has occurred in regional areas.

Antiques' trade fairs and commercial exhibitions are a persistent feature of this business and regularly draw tens of thousands of visitors to metropolitan and rural centres, with the *international* exhibitions in Melbourne and Sydney capable of drawing more than 100,000 visitors annually. This form of marketing reached its zenith in the late 1990s (Garmony-Burton & Russell, 1999), but there are still more than 20 such fairs held in Victoria alone each year. In this niche market, the distinctions between retailing, culture and leisure are often difficult to sustain, blurring instead into an amalgam of common behaviours that perhaps challenge the findings of some contemporary researchers (McHone & Rungeling, 1999) making it impractical to distinguish between a *cultural* or a *leisure* tourist and the special events they attend. In this context, they are one and the same.

While it is axiomatic that the *antiques trade*, like any other business, can be regarded as part of the overall *tourism industry* according to the functions of that business's location, there is little understanding of the role these firms play in generating particular types of demand for travel to particular locations. The hypothesis explored here is that the *antiques industry* exhibits a set of characteristics that seem appropriately matched to a *tourism* analysis. Viewed from this perspective, observations can be drawn from the operation of the Australian industry that shed new light on its role in support of tourism, and on its capacity to generate regional economic growth. For policymakers, this is yet another reminder of the significance of some retailing markets to the evolution of tourism demand. Regional development planners might note that, more importantly, this industry serves as an example of those niche markets that not only appear to generate a demand for travel, but one that is compatible with the social and economic needs of small communities. Harnessing the synergies between this industry and the broader tourism market, of course, remains the problem that confronts those with a responsibility for regional economic development.

Antiques — Defining a Niche Market

A precise definition for what constitutes the *antiques trade* is difficult to provide. The popular conception is that the selling of antiques, collectables, oldwares, etc. is simply a retail activity comparable to any other, with a separate identity only in the characteristics of the goods that are traded. In some situations, particularly in inner city areas with concentrated retail precincts, this approach may often be appropriate; but, in general there remains something very different about the way this industry operates — the unique nature of the trading goods and their manufacture (restoration) and distribution, the market's segmentation and stratification, the locational choices of retailers, the motivation of customers, the approaches to marketing, etc. — all point to an industrial activity that is distinct from simple retailing.

The distinction is confirmed by the attitudes of individual retailers and their representative industry associations. For them, it is obvious that they are not part of one single coherent industry, but rather are members of much smaller and highly specialised market segments. From the operator's point of view, the industry comprises several discrete sets of distinguishable retailing function, although each can be further sub-divided into more highly specialised segments. Most *antiques* dealers consider themselves to be specialists in a particular field, say period furniture from the Victorian era as an example, but will focus their commercial attentions on an even narrower sub-set of their field, such as early Victorian (1837–1860) dining room furniture. An individual firm, as another example, might concentrate on *collectables*, such as ceramic and porcelain products, but probably from a particular time-period by specific manufacturers. There are, of course, many situations where dealers bridge across market segments or trade across similar or related activities, such as with arts, crafts and hobbies, and may well include newly manufactured goods, like Moorcroft ceramics or hand-made reproduction furniture, as examples, as part of their trading stock. The degree of overlap between one or other of the various specialist antiques markets makes simple distinctions a hazardous exercise.

This pattern of specialisation and further micro segmentation, at one level or another, is visible across all categories of the industry's operation. Just to illustrate, the Australian Antique Dealers Association (1999) listed 125 separate fields in which their members claimed to specialise. While some segments are serviced by many dealers, others are specialised in such unrelated rarities as Egyptian relics or iron gates, such that only two or three dealers might service these interests nationwide.

There is nothing novel, however, about viewing an industry as a compilation of related market niches or segments, where each segment is recognisable by its separate characteristics and unique sets of attributes (Lancaster, 1966a, 1966b). Indeed, this perception contributes to an understanding of consumer behaviour for antiques and oldwares purchases, because it is not so much a demand for the goods *per se* but for the characteristics possessed by those goods (Lancaster, 1966b, p. 14). In economic terms, it could be said that the utility the consumer derives from the purchase of these goods comes from the bundle of attributes exhibited by them. Hence, for the broader industry it is the unique *bundling* of desirable attributes that provides the basis for segmenting different markets. To illustrate the point, French *Bergerac* chairs have been made since the eighteenth century, but in slightly varying styles and with different materials, so a consumer who wants such a chair to complement furnishings from the *directoire* period will perceive a late nineteenth century product as belonging to a different era and so to a different market segment.

It is perhaps easier to view any attempt to categorize the market segments in the antiques industry as a spectrum, ranging from rare and exotic antiquities to outright junk, with specialist markets and specialised dealers all along the continuum, as Table 6.1 demonstrates.

The industry predominantly comprises a trade in goods of a second-hand nature, but this is not exclusively the case as many firms also deal with current products and with goods that have been so extensively restored or remanufactured that they need to be classified as new productive output. It is also distinguished by the intrinsic value of the type of products that are traded, and by their non-essential and decorative nature. This pattern of segmentation, of specialisation within segments and of overlap between them, continues through all aspects of the industry.

An Industry Profile

There are a number of unusual features that characterise the operation of the antiques industry — *unusual* in the sense that they are not commonly found in other retailing industries, and bear the hallmarks that are typically associated with *service* industries. This appears to be the case even though it is the physical product that ostensibly forms the basis for trade. These features can be reviewed by looking more closely at the market structure and at the environment in which the industry operates.

One characteristic of the antiques industry in most western countries is the clustering of firms and businesses in close proximity to each other. While there certainly are many individual and isolated retailers, the common pattern is to find clusters of traders in close location, often forming distinct precincts in urban shopping areas or in rural towns. Another variant of the same pattern occurs where several traders operate jointly in the same premises, sometimes by renting stall space or occasionally in co-operative ventures. These specialist retail services provide *horizontal* synergies that serve to pool the customer base, to expand the range of products and the potential level of sales (see Chapter 3). Similar patterns have been described in the development of *Book Towns* in northwestern Europe to create "... a critical mass of single commodity retailing ..." (Seaton, 1999, p. 390). However, in the antiques industry it seems to be taken to another level where

Table 6.1: Broad market segments in the antiques industry.

Antiques
Physical goods and artworks of intrinsic worth that are at least one hundred years old: dealers often specialize in goods belonging to particular localities, time periods, types of manufacture, etc.

Collectables
Physical goods of a similar nature that are presumed to belong together, what makes something a collectable is not its intrinsic worth but the desire of consumers to collect examples of the product: dealers are usually highly specialized in product type (*stamp and coin* dealers, *maps* and *books* form distinct sub-categories)

Memorabilia
Goods that are related to or commemorate a particular past event or activity: dealers are usually highly specialized (Note: sporting memorabilia is the industry's fastest growing segment)

Bric-a-brac (curios)
Goods of curiosity value, oddments or decorative items, which are not regularly sought by collectors: dealers are diversified and usually sell items of lesser commercial value (*Oldwares*, comprising second-hand goods of the same nature, are often treated this way to avoid confusion with antiques.)

Junk (second-hand)
Goods of questionable commercial value but for which some market exists: dealers are highly varied in stocks and activities, includes voluntary shops for some welfare agencies

Note: These descriptors are provided to help differentiate market segments but are not exclusive in their own right.
Source: Adapted from Michael (2002).

dealers gain more by co-operative action than by competition. For them, there are not only gains in marketing from close proximity to each other, but there are also gains to be had from information sharing, stock sharing and supplier access. In short, they are able to tap into the synergies available from *vertical* clustering.

This visible pattern of co-location is not confined to the antiques and oldwares industry alone (*horizontal* clustering), but seems to demonstrate a close alignment with other types of tourism and hospitality businesses. A random site study (Michael, 2002, p. 122) around the rural fringe of metropolitan Melbourne, reported that without exception wherever an operating antiques industry retailer was identified, there existed a hospitality venue or service located within close proximity (*c.* 100 metres). In some examples, a café or tea room had been established as an integral part of the business itself. Visitor information, specific purpose parking and other such services were also common. In other words, the location sites for antique dealerships matched closely to the same infrastructure location patterns that are commonly found with any other tourism destination.

The industry also relies heavily on trade fairs and special events of all kinds. Major exhibitions, involving as many as 100 independent dealers, are regular features of the antique calendar in most Australian states, as they are elsewhere throughout the western world, but smaller fairs and a plethora of events for particular specializations are a routine part of the industry's functions. Of course, the quality of these exhibitions is highly variable, reflecting the wide spectrum of the market's segmentation. The industry's associations in Australia, New Zealand and the United Kingdom (and, perhaps, in other countries) are also known for the range of workshops and information courses they offer to the public. Simple economics would suggest that for such *extra-curricula* activities to be an endemic feature of the industry, they must be an effective aid to sales, but anecdotally the dealers often claim they are involved more to promote their specialisations, or to meet client needs, than for financial reward. The observation remains, however, that to stage them in such a quantum there must necessarily be a culture of co-operation and participation among the dealers.

The antiques industry, however, is not confined to retailing as might be supposed. Despite the small scale involved, much of the industry's cost structure is incurred in the retrieval, storage, restoration, renovation, wholesaling and preparation of oldwares to fit them for a commercial market. The industry, therefore, adds productive value as a manufacturing process, not just as a distribution item, and so generates employment across a diverse range of skilled occupations — restorers, upholsterers, cabinet makers, French polishers, etc. In this sense, it preserves skills that are often not required in contemporary manufacturing industries, but which perhaps are important for sustaining employment in rural areas. As a generalisation, this *production* process is labour intensive and highly skilled, but remains a high yield activity based on single items or small batch lots. The Australian case study suggests the industry is capable of sustaining small businesses, and requires only small work sites for restoration or repairs that can often be located in environmentally or socially sensitive areas without causing intrusion. Given the high value attributed to many products, and the small volumes, they can usually absorb high transport and storage costs, implying that the location of *production* facilities need not be dependent on the location of retailing outlets.

In short, there is no significant economic reason to inhibit the geographic spread of industry participants, so it becomes something of a conundrum to find that the supporting trade operators choose to co-locate with the dispersed nature of clusters of retailers. Arguably, of course, there are gains for them to be made from co-locating with other specialist producers or in close proximity to their customers, who in this situation are the retailers.

Customers or Tourists?

From the consumers' point of view, the antiques industry also exhibits many of the characteristics of a *service* industry. The most obvious of these is visible from the basic segmentation of the market. It is not just that the dealers are specialists in microcosms of the market, for their trade is based on differentiating the physical products, rather, it is that the products themselves engender a range of socio-psychological responses from consumers associated with images of past cultural and social practice. The consumption decision, then, is about access to *heritage*. The motivations to purchase stemming from the consumer's own predilections, based on family, kinship, artistic expression or human creativity. Even where antiques are purchased nominally as investment items, the attribution of a value to the asset stems from the rarity of this access. Antiques and other oldwares, as commodities, evoke a sense of association with both the consumer's history and sense of place, a merging of the real and the imagined (Herbert, 1999, p. 77). In other words, the same package of motivations that drive antiques sales are those that analysts have identified in other forms of heritage-based activity, including tourism (Stewart, 1990; Zeppel & Hall, 1991; Palmer, 1996).

The purchase of antiques or oldwares remains a highly *discretionary* activity in economic terms, and one that is pursued only after more basic needs have been met. The purchase decision is based on the individual consumer's perceptions of intrinsic worth, curiosity or perhaps the assumed contributory value to a collection, but it remains a decision which reflects the consumer's own appreciation of the relevance of heritage and culture in their life. Nevertheless, in this context as a consumption decision, it is similar to many other tourism purchase decisions (Bull, 1995).

Antique collecting, by its very nature, requires the buyers to operate in a *seek-and-find* mode, because stocks are normally held in very small quantities. Given that dealers are small-scale specialists and widely dispersed, and the market's stockpile is disaggregated and varies over time, the consumer has little choice but to search for the sources of the items they want. While there are agency and Internet services that can consolidate the search task for specific items, most consumers still find it necessary to visit the dealers to identify what they want, and must in any case physically check and verify the authenticity and relative condition of the product they intend to purchase. Buyers in this kind of market, then, must become travellers willing to visit different locations. In a normal retail market, the imposition of such a process would have led to a change in distribution systems long ago, but again there are substantial differences here. Indeed, part of the explanation might lie in a *Lancastrian* interpretation (Lancaster, 1966a, 1966b), which perhaps suggests that some element of the utility the consumer enjoys is the search activity itself — the requirement *to visit* the various locations to look for what is desired as this forms part of the bundle of attributes that makes up the collector's activity.

In Michael's (1999, 2002) study of the connection between tourism and the antiques trade in Australia, he observed that from the dealers' perspective there were three distinct types of consumer of antiques and oldwares products. Customer profiles, while of limited value, can provide useful indicators to distinguish differences in market behaviours or to help in identifying genuine synergies between markets. Possibly, then, the industry's customers can be categorised into these groups, where the first appears to be the serious *collectors* in search of specific items to add to their collections or to meet their specific interests. Second, there are consumers who might be described as *occasional collectors*, maintaining enthusiasm in the field over many years, but who purchase only when they have time and resources available — such activities, for this group, are more overtly discretionary and so are incorporated into their leisure functions as recreational pursuits on weekends and holidays. Both these groups of consumers are likely to repeat visits to dealers over protracted time periods as the dealer's stockholdings change. The final consumer category, perhaps, are the *browsers*, who visit dealers to view the stock out of interest rather than with a specific purchase decision in mind. For most firms, nonetheless, these impulse buyers are an important part of the customer base. Depending on the location, this group can form the largest proportion of visitors, but rarely do they match the value of sales to the previous consumer categories. While the different categories of consumers exhibit varying degrees of commitment to their pursuit of particular items or to the nature of the products themselves, the study suggested that most consumers held a general appreciation of the structure of the market and comprehended the variance and segmentation within it.

It might be noted at this point, of course, that if this is a fair reflection of the consumers of antiques and oldwares, it goes some way to explaining the locational choices of the antique dealers. If the core of the consumer market is willing to travel, but the balance are effectively browsers who will visit as part of some other holiday or leisure activity, then the rational location decision is to be positioned at the destination where the visitors intend to go, or on the routes to those destinations. In short, the customer profile suggests a rather obvious symbiosis between travel, tourism and the consumption of these goods.

This consumer profile is distinctive in other ways, too. For regional economic development planners and for tourism analysts, the consumers who purchase antiques and other oldwares may well be considered to form a premium market. They have by implication an intrinsic appreciation of heritage and culture and (as an implied prerequisite) the economic resources to obtain the products. Consumers are likely to be more mature, better educated and higher income earners than average. Many will be retired or semi-retired or have substantial amounts of leisure time and, of course, own homes or buildings suited to the storage (use) of their collections. In short, the customer base is a high socio-economic group with high levels of disposable income and available leisure time. Concentrations of consumers with these sorts of high-value characteristics are not common in any industry and, quite obviously, are highly prized in rural locations where development is an issue. Similar observations have been made by Seaton (1996, 1999), where the visitors to specialist *Book Towns* appear to exhibit like socio-economic characteristics, and who demonstrate travel patterns and consumption decisions that seem to be based on similar requirements and motivations.

Clusters as Trip Generators

Another of the factors to clearly distinguish the antiques and oldwares industry from other retail markets is that its normal distribution process functions as a trip generator. The Australian evidence, supported by anecdotal experience in New Zealand, North America, Sweden and the United Kingdom, suggests that the industry is generally made up of small-scale businesses that are highly specialised and widely dispersed, but with a location pattern that often sees these firms co-locating in small groups. While there are clusters of firms in metropolitan areas, the majority of firms appear to be located in rural communities. This does not mean that the value of sales or economic activity is similarly dispersed, for there are often significant differences in scale between city-based firms and rural ones. To illustrate the point as an example, around two-thirds of firms in Victoria are located

outside the metropolitan area (Michael, 2002). However, the nature of each firm's specialized trade makes it unlikely that any one business in a rural location would be commercially viable solely from servicing the needs of its local market; rather these firms must be
drawing a substantial volume of their customers from more distant locations. For most
forms of retailing this would constitute an impossible impediment to sustainable commerce, but the reality is that the need to travel, to visit and to inspect the merchandise,
makes up part of the activities associated with antiques and oldwares — from the customer's perspective, half the fun is finding it!

In this context, the key to the explanation lies in *visitation*. The antiques trade serves as
a *trip generator*, attracting people to locations where dealers operate. It can be seen as a
generator at two levels:

- As a *primary generator*, where it draws people to a location because the predominant
  purpose of their visit is the search for appropriate merchandise, thus serving as a destination like any other tourism product.
- As a *secondary generator* in that it provides an ancillary activity at a location that
  induces the traveller to extend their length of stay and, hence, increases the level of
  expenditure within the local economy.

Even for travellers with only a peripheral interest in antiques and oldwares, the very
existence of dealers at the location they have chosen to visit can add value to that destination, by contributing another activity to enhance the total basket of features that makes a
visit worthwhile.

As a trip generator there will be flow-on effects for the location that is visited, particularly in the range of visitor services that reflects the antiques industry's customer base,
including travel, accommodation and hospitality. Again, for comparison, the history of the
development of *Book Towns* manifests its success not so much in the emergence of clusters
of booksellers but in the symbiotic growth of accommodation, catering and other visitor
services (Seaton, 1999). If there is any accuracy in the antiques consumer profile, the need
will be for a concomitant development of services targeted at the independent traveller —
motor vehicle services, quality accommodation and middle to upper range hospitality services, and for appropriate visitor information facilities. Such services presumably will be
pitched at a more mature market, and their existence (or development) will encourage
these visitors to use their more extensive leisure time at that destination, adding further to
the growth of regional economies.

The multiplier impacts or flow-on effects of the antiques trade on local economic communities would also appear to be highly significant. As noted in Chapter 4, tourism multipliers for the macro-economy are well understood (Bull, 1995, p. 148), but less is known
about their effects on very small or niche markets in local or regional economies. Local
multipliers are difficult to measure and are highly variable between regions, depending on
the degree to which the local economy is contained. Guidance on this issue is made more
difficult in the absence of appropriate micro-economic research into the antiques trade,
either in the Australian or international context, to establish a framework for such an analysis. Logic, however, suggests that the antiques trade will generate substantial local impacts
both because it draws new spending to a region where it generates visitor travel and
because its mode of production is highly specialised. When the retailing function is

supported by a range of restoration services, it becomes a labour-intensive and value-adding industry. In this context, for a local community, it ought to exhibit multiplier effects that would be larger than might normally be anticipated for a small-scale industry.

One indicative industry study undertaken in Pennsylvania, USA, reports a regional multiplier impact greater than three (Grado et al., 1997), meaning that for every dollar of expenditure created by the local antiques trade more than three dollars are generated as income for that regional economy. While this outcome seems remarkably high, if applied to the somewhat similar environments in rural Victoria, a typical cluster of three or four antique dealers in a smaller country town, who might currently be creating around A$1 million in spending on average (adjusted from Australian Bureau of Statistics, 1994), would be generating a regional output of A$3 million. Production earnings of this magnitude are trivial at the macro level, but they translate to the equivalent of 20–25 full-time continuing employment positions that would be crucial to a small community's economy. Although the available evidence is fragmentary, and the Pennsylvania results cannot be assumed to be transferable to other environments, the existing indicators point to the probability that the industry is of much greater economic significance in some local circumstances than has previously been assumed, but only in those circumstances where the cluster acts successfully as a trip generator to enhance visitation.

At a broader level, the Antiques industry clearly offers opportunities in some appropriate localities for the expansion of tourism, and, in some circumstances might even kick-start a tourism function where none currently exists by drawing in a new stream of visitors. For regional planners, it is the very nature of the antiques trade that should place it at a premium for tourism development. The industry attracts consumers with an appreciation of heritage that manifests itself in a customer profile characterised by higher educational attainment, middle to higher income levels and more mature age groupings. Moreover it is a sedentary activity that imposes little dislocation to local communities and appears to have commercial and cultural synergies with local hospitality operators and with heritage-based activities.

Successful Clusters and the Existence of Networks

Using the results from an earlier study (Michael, 2004), it is also possible to use examples from the antiques and oldwares trade to illustrate differences in the success of firms and their locational choices and the factors that have enhanced the gains to be had from sharing in a clustering process. While there are myriad locations that might have been chosen for comparative purposes, this review considered the circumstances in two small towns outlying the rural fringe of metropolitan Melbourne (Australia). These two towns, *Flinders* and *Kyneton*, were selected in part because their physical differences illustrate two distinct forms of co-location, but also because they shared two commonalities for analysis — each relies on passing visitors as integral contributors to their local economies, and each has small groups of co-located firms in antiques' retailing that suggests *prima facie* they play a similar role as a secondary attribute in the delivery of each locality's tourism services.

Flinders is a coastal township at the southeastern tip of the Mornington Peninsula, around 75 km from Melbourne, with a permanent population close to 2000 people. It has a heritage based on pastoral farming and small-scale maritime and naval activities. Over the past 20 years it has evolved as a secluded recreation centre, which has grown more rapidly in the last decade as a consequence of the coastal property boom. In that time, the township's retail centre has also expanded to include half-a-dozen hospitality venues and six antique or oldwares retailers, positioned within 300 m of each other to form a distinct visitor's precinct. Its tourist traffic derives mainly from suburban Melbourne day-trippers and weekend visitors and from holidaymakers staying on the western side of the Peninsula.

Kyneton, on the other hand, is a slightly larger town that lies 80 km to Melbourne's north, with a regional population in excess of 3000. It originated as a transit point during the gold rushes (1850s), and developed as a transport junction in the latter nineteenth century. It remained an important rail depot until the end of the steam era in the late 1950s. Until 2000, the Melbourne-to-Bendigo highway passed through the town's main retail precinct, generating a substantial trade from passing visitors. As a consequence, a range of hospitality providers had located there to service traveller's needs. Despite the passage of time, Kyneton's commercial centre had retained its nineteenth century character, and so there had also evolved by the mid-1990s a concentration in the 'Piper Street precinct' of more than a dozen antiques, crafts, arts and oldwares dealers that both complemented and reinforced the heritage character of the local region. By 2002, however, when the study commenced, only six dealers remained in active trade.

The opening of a freeway bypass pushed the local economy into recession, 2001–2003. The immediate reduction in *passing trade* forced a number of the niche market retailers to close, despite the efforts of the roads authority and other government agencies to maintain local business activity. The 'Piper Street precinct' of antiques and oldwares dealers, and the associated craft and heritage businesses and their complementary hospitality providers, were particularly affected. By January 2004, only four dealers remained, and two of these, along with some other businesses, including hospitality operators, had converted to weekend trade only. Nonetheless, and despite the commercial ramifications of the freeway bypass, the town's residential population continues to grow at a sustained 2.5% per annum as it lies within an easy commuting distance of Melbourne's western suburbs and the CBD. This process is likely to accelerate in due course, as the town's future is almost certainly as a residential satellite to the neighbouring metropolis. Kyneton's relatively high population growth has encouraged some new retailing services to locate there, but it has not yet offset the economic consequences from the reduction in visitor numbers. With the support of the local municipal authority (Macedon Ranges Shire), the town has sought to re-establish its tourism base, but the focus has largely been on its built heritage and its access to nearby attractions. The role that the 'Piper Street' antique shops once played now seems to have been cast into history.

The core of the tourism product differed for each location: in Flinders it derived from its coastal recreation attractions, while Kyneton's stemmed from its nineteenth century built landscape and heritage and from its rural surroundings. Each locality was supported by hospitality and accommodation enterprises, which are natural complements for tourism. When the research project commenced in 2002, each also had a concentration of half-a-dozen co-located antiques and oldwares dealers, forming distinct (but compatible) additions to the local tourism products and adding to the mix of attractions for visitors to these towns. Rather surprisingly, this comparative study found that the structure of the co-located groups of antique retailers, and their approaches to business development, were markedly different. Initially, this difference seemed puzzling and counter-intuitive: for it might have been anticipated that a co-located group of firms under stress, such as those at Kyneton, would seek greater co-operation for their common benefit, while a co-located group in a rapid growth area, as was the case in Flinders, would be more inclined to compete for market share and profits, and be less concerned with long-term development.

The antiques' firms in Flinders are relatively new arrivals, with 4 out of 6 having opened premises for public trading since 1997, along with a number of new hospitality and bed and breakfast providers. Indeed, the level of new investment is itself an indicator of growing regional demand and the success of the local business development strategies. Interviews with these antique dealers demonstrated that without exception they perceived themselves as component parts of the local region's tourism industry, who necessarily had to work with the operators of other types of firms to expand the total number of visitors to *their* region. More importantly, they exhibit a real level of co-operative activity within their own group, building a network based on sharing resources, suppliers, stocks and information in effective ways, with the aim and deliberate intention to enhance both customer satisfaction and the reduction of overheads and costs. In effect, these firms were working as a co-operative cluster to expand their collective market and share the benefits from the synergies that exist between them. While the individual dealers clearly recognized that some "do better" in commercial terms than others, each seemed to recognize that there was some sense of gain to them from contributing to the collective process.

The circumstances in Kyneton, however, proved to be quite different. The antique dealers, or at least those that remained, had been established for some time, but the loss of passing trade from the freeway bypass had significantly impacted on them, forcing two to close or shift elsewhere, or to seek their commercial future in alternative markets (such as stalls at antique fairs or wholesaling for dealers located elsewhere). Two of the remaining firms (including one under new ownership) reconfigured the nature of their businesses to include hospitality services or coffee shops within their operating premises. The Kyneton dealers recognize themselves as part of the regional tourism product, and seek to gain from the benefits of a pooled market; but, as a collective group, they did not demonstrate a level of active integration with other elements of the local tourism industry. Indeed, their concern appeared to be with the declining position of their immediate locale, the 'Piper Street precinct', rather than with the broader region. In comparison with the dealers at Flinders, the Kyneton operators seemed less connected to each other and their co-operative actions more constrained, in some cases limited only to stocks and information. In effect, there was little evidence of effective networking here, but rather a sense of competition and the need by dealers to pursue their individual markets.

Two observations can be made at this point; the first concerns the differences that are being exposed in the mechanics of a micro-cluster's formation, while the second concerns the processes that occur within it. Flinders and Kyneton illustrate a similar pattern of geographic co-location by firms, with a similar *precinct effect* that offers a collection of like and compatible products and services, attracting more potential customers to the location than any one firm could do alone. This factor becomes more relevant for tourism destinations like these, as it simplifies the *search process* for visitors by providing them with a range of options within a concentrated area. In principle, this is the obvious advantage of a *micro-cluster* as it amalgamates the available pool of customers and leads potentially to a larger total market size.

Geographic co-location, however, may well be a necessary condition for effective clustering to occur, but as these two examples demonstrate, it is not sufficient by itself. The reason is that mere co-location may increase a firm's market potential, but only in terms of enhancing the potential customer base. The fact that complementary firms are in co-location does not by itself generate synergies between those firms, nor does it necessarily lead to cost efficiencies. Rather, it creates an *opportunity* for those firms to put in place the mechanisms and strategies to capture these benefits; and, as each micro-cluster is a unique formation, the business development processes needed to identify those synergies and shared cost benefits differ in every case. The rationale for clustering stems from the process of optimizing the gains from both economies-of-scale and of-scope but these gains come in the form of a continuum which progresses as firms enhance their ability to co-operate (see Figure 6.1). Co-location offers common marketing advantages, but the benefits from clustering require common business strategies to evolve, and in truly successful formations that process moves still further as the participants learn to adopt or share common business practices (labelled here as *tactics*).

The evidence from Flinders suggests that the existing firms operated as an effective micro-cluster, with co-operative strategies for marketing both within their own industry (antiques retailing) and with the broader region's tourism industry. More significantly, they appear to have moved further along this spectrum by developing an effective network process that permits them to share a range of common business practices to obtain resources and manage their communications with customers and suppliers — including, just for illustration, common computing software for stock control and accounting purposes. Kyneton's Piper Street precinct of antique dealers, on the other hand, present themselves only as a group of firms in co-location, extracting common benefits from the pool of customers but exhibiting few gains from other co-operative business strategies.

This comparison of the behaviour of firms in Flinders and Kyneton demonstrates that understanding the economic dynamics of clustering and the mechanics of a cluster's

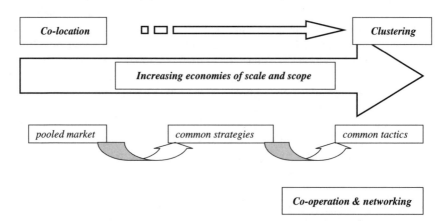

Figure 6.1: Co-location to clustering – a continuum.

formation are essential elements for analysing how a successful cluster operates; but, by itself, this will not explain why some groups of co-located firms are able to optimize the benefits from clustering when others are not. What needs to be considered is why some groups of firms are able to co-operate and share a common set of outcomes, even if the rewards are asymmetric. What persuades them to make and sustain such a choice?

Economics provides part of the answer in terms of motivation, for firms and their host communities have the potential to gain more through co-operation in a specific location as a means to compete in a broader market, but such a proposition is only viable if all firms contribute. (The motivation for this behaviour is explored further in Chapter 9.) The circumstances in Flinders might be said to support the validity of this explanation, while the contra argument is perhaps visible in the Kyneton case, for it is obvious that a co-operative process will not emerge or will collapse if any firm or substantive element of the host community seeks only to extract the immediate benefits from the group's synergies and externality gains in pursuit of their own self-interest.

A more effective answer is required to explain why firms in real world situations will co-operate and *trust* each other in these circumstances. One route to such an explanation appears to lie in contemporary networking theory, or at least in those variants that have been applied to tourism destinations and to the social nexus between business and the community. As Dredge (2004, p. 197) points out, network theory has generally been used as a retrospective tool for analyses of policy issues and destination planning cases, but it can also serve to explain how and why different interests in small communities interrelate within a network — which is the issue of interest here. In a small cluster formation, the network of business and community interests needs to handle common problems for its membership, but there is inevitably diversity and difference in aspirations, implying that a successful network provides a means for resolving conflicts as much as it provides a mechanism for building consensus. Networking theory offers another contribution to cluster analysis, for at its core it seeks to identify the range of reasons for different individuals and groups to associate; which, as was pointed out in the previous chapter, includes a raft of issues about 'learning and exchange', 'community' and 'business activity' that traverse well beyond short-term economic gains. These *human* factors suggest that the network's members are motivated by longer-term interests that might include a sustainable relationship between the needs of businesses and their community hosts.

This comparative evaluation of two micro-cluster formations, in Flinders and Kyneton, serves as only an incremental step in the exploration of the concept, but it does provide some empirical backing to confirm the principles that have been developed earlier. In a practical context, it has explored the benefits that favour and reward micro-clustering as both a business and a strategic planning tool. As an empirical review of only two locations, of course, its value is limited, but the purpose is only to demonstrate how the synergies between complementary firms can be captured to enhance growth and opportunity in real-world circumstances. The results appear to accord with expectations, in that groups of firms that are simply co-located do not generate benefits beyond *pooling* the customer base (Kyneton), while those that adopt co-operative strategies to share their synergies with complementary firms are actually able to extract cost benefits and to enhance the collective group's market performance (Flinders). The implication is that co-location by itself does not lead to integration with other aspects of tourism, nor to synergies with other parts of the market; rather, that effective clustering is a deliberate business development strategy based on co-operative practices, not just between firms within a market segment but across a broader industry.

References

Australian Antique Dealers Association. (1999). *List of members and approved service providers 1998*. Malvern (pamphlet).

Australian Bureau of Statistics. (1994). *Retail industry Australia 1991–92*. Cat. no. 8622.0, Canberra.

Bull, A. (1995). *The economics of travel and tourism* (2nd ed.). Melbourne: Longmans.

Dredge, D. (2004). Networks, conflict and collaborative tourism planning. *CAUTHE 2004: Creating tourism knowledge*. School of Tourism & Leisure Management, University of Queensland, Brisbane, 10–13 February 2004 (pp. 195–207).

Garmony-Burton, S., & Russell, L. (Eds). (1999). *The antiques and collectables trail* (2nd ed.). Victoria, Horsham: Brantome.

Grado, S. C., Strauss, C. H., & Lord, B. E. (1997). Antiquing as a tourism recreational activity in southwestern Pennsylvania. *Journal of Travel Research*, 35(3), 52–56.

Herbert, D. T. (1996). Artistic and literary places in France as tourist attractions. *Tourism Management*, 17(2) 77–85.

Lancaster, K. J. (1966a). A new approach to consumer theory. *The Journal of Political Economy*, *LXXIV*(Feb–Dec), 132–157.

Lancaster, K. J. (1966b). Change and innovation in the technology of consumption. *American Economic Review*, *LVI*(2), 14–23.

McHone, W. W., & Rungeling, B. (1999). Special cultural events: Do they attract leisure tourists? *Hospitality Management*, 18, 215–219.

Michael, E. J. (1999). The antiques trade — A tourism generator. *Tourism: Policy and Planning Conference, Proceedings of Research Papers*, Oamaru, N.Z., August–September, (pp. 84–95).

Michael, E. J. (2002). Antiques and tourism in Australia. *Tourism Management*, 23(2), 117–125.

Michael, E. J. (2004). Tourism micro-clusters: From principles to practice. *Proceedings of 'Tourism: State of the Art II'*, Glasgow, June 2004 [CD, refereed paper no. 099].

Palmer, C. A. (1996). The making of a nation: Heritage tourism and the British national identity. In: G. Prosser (Ed.), (1996) *Australian tourism and hospitality research conference* [pp. 481–488]. Canberra: Bureau of Tourism Research.

Seaton, A. V. (1996). Hay on Wye, the mouse that roared, book towns and rural tourism. *Tourism Management*, 17(5), 379–382.

Seaton, A. V. (1999). Book towns as tourism developments in peripheral areas. *International Journal of Tourism Research*, 1, 389–399.

Stewart, J. K. (1990). Heritage attractions and tourism: Myths and issues. *Tourism research; meeting the needs of industry – conference proceedings* [pp. 91–98] Canada: T.T.R.A.

Zeppel, H., & Hall, C. M. (1991). Selling art and history: Cultural heritage and tourism. *The Journal of Tourism Studies*, 2(1), 29–45.

Chapter 7

Wine Tourism Networks and Clusters: Operation and Barriers in New Zealand

Richard Mitchell and Chrissy Schreiber

Objectives

- This chapter explores the relationship between the wine and food industries in New Zealand and, more particularly, in the Central Otago region.
- It introduces into the discussion issues concerning the institutional framework for networking and cluster development in New Zealand, including funding for tourism and wine projects.
- A number of examples of national, regional and sub-regional wine tourism networks are identified and their differences are discussed.
- Central Otago is examined as an example of a region where the vertical integration between elements of the tourism and wine industries continues to offer further opportunities for development.
- As an illustration of the issues confronting further development, the results from a number of key informant interviews are used to identify the barriers which exist to formal cooperation between the wine and tourism industries within this region.

Micro-Clusters and Networks: The Growth of Tourism
Copyright © 2007 by Elsevier Ltd.
All rights of reproduction in any form reserved.
ISBN: 0-08-045096-2

The very concept of wine tourism suggests that opportunities for network and cluster development abound, as wine tourism is the symbiotic relationship between two very different industries: one is based on agriculture and manufacturing, while the other is service related (Mitchell, 2004). In fact, relationships between wine and tourism have existed since Greek and Roman times (Getz, 2000), but it is only recently that governments and analysts have begun to recognise the value of supporting and encouraging formal network and cluster behaviour between the two (Hall, Johnson, & Mitchell, 2000). Governments in a number of countries now support wine tourism clusters and their associated networks, which have grown out of a recognition of the benefits for regional development from less formal cooperative projects, such as wine trails in Australia and New Zealand, *La Strada del Vino* in Italy, *Die Weinstrasse* in Germany and the *Route des Vin* in France (Hall et al., 2000; Mitchell, 2004; Mitchell & Hall, forthcoming).

Wine Tourism and Wine Networks

There have been a number of studies that have explored the role of cooperative behaviour between the wine and tourism industries, including several studies focusing on Australasia (e.g., Hall, 1996, 2002, 2003, 2004; Hall Cambourne, Macionis, & Johnson, 1998; McRae-Williams, 2002, 2004; Schreiber, 2004; Simpson & Bretherton, 2004), South Africa (Bruwer, 2003; Meyer, 2004), parts of North America (Dodd, 1995; Telfer, 2001a, 2001b; Wilkins & Hall, 2001; Barham, 2003; Taylor, Woodall, Wandschneider, & Foltz, 2004) and various regions in Europe (Hall & Mitchell, 2000; Arfini, Bertoli, & Donati, 2002; Correia, Passos Ascenção, & Charters, 2004; Karafolas, 2005). According to Hall, Johnson, and Mitchell (2000, p. 208), "…in the context of wine tourism such networks are critical as there is a need to create linkages between businesses which have previously identified themselves as being in separate industries with separate business foci." As such, true wine tourism network development will see integration both horizontally (within the wine industry *or* the tourism industry) and vertically (between the two industries) (Mitchell, 2004). A useful example of such behaviour is that of the Niagara wine tourism cluster, which was presented as a network case-study in Chapter 5. Here, Telfer (2001a) not only identified interactions between wine and tourism organisations, but with other clusters (including agricultural clusters and food clusters), organisations (such as wine councils and marketing committees and the visitor bureau) and governmental and research bodies. Porter (1998) has also examined inter-cluster cooperation in the Californian wine cluster.

However, Hall (2003) has noted there are a number of barriers to the formation of effective links between wine producers and the tourism industry. These include:

- poor perceptions among wineries of the benefits of tourism for the wine industry;
- a dominant product focus on the part of wine producers;
- a general lack of experience in and understanding of tourism within the wine industry;
- a lack of entrepreneurial skills and abilities with respect to marketing and tourism product development;
- spatial separation — distance between vineyards and physical and perceived barriers to access;

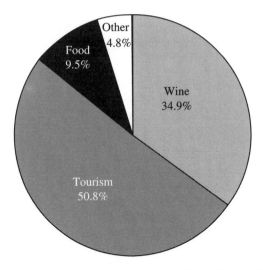

Figure 7.1: New Zealand Food and Wine Tourism Network membership categories.

- administrative separation — in particular multiple public administrative agencies within a region; and
- the lack of 'champions' to promote formal cooperative behaviours.

In New Zealand, until recently, the relationship between the wine and tourism industries could at best be described as ad hoc and largely informal. Perhaps the most important network to have been established recently, and then only in October 2004, is the *New Zealand Food and Wine Tourism Network* (NZFWTN). This has 63 members from a wide range of businesses including: regional and national tourism organisations; regional wine and food bodies; tour operators; accommodation providers; small and large wineries; a range of food producers; Air New Zealand, and the Department of Tourism at the University of Otago (see Figure 7.1 for a breakdown of membership). This network undertakes such activities as the development and dissemination of generic marketing collateral, preparation and presentation of best practice case studies, cooperative presence at trade and consumer events, and the development and delivery of education and training. It was provided with seed funding by *Tourism New Zealand* and has undertaken contract work for *New Zealand Trade and Enterprise*.

Telfer and Wall (1996) identify a range of *vertical* (between wine and tourism industries) and *horizontal* (within the wine industry or tourism industry) linkages between Canadian wine and food tourism businesses. However, in New Zealand, despite some recent examples of cooperative behaviour, few regional or local initiatives could be considered as being vertically and horizontally integrated, for most are dominated by either the tourism or the wine industry members: that is, they are *horizontal* linkages. Table 7.1 demonstrates that there are a range of commitments to networking/clustering behaviour, with three of New Zealand's wine regions exhibiting the most advanced level of such cooperation: Wairarapa, Marlborough and Hawke's Bay. In each of these regions winery visitation is a core element of the tourism product (Mitchell & Hall, 2000; Hall & Mitchell, 2002). As such, the wine industry is a key part of the tourism industry and wineries are therefore active in tourism product delivery and in regional tourism organisations. Wairarapa, Marlborough and Hawke's Bay are also actively

Table 7.1: Formal wine tourism relationships in New Zealand wine regions.

Region	Inter-industry cooperation	Inter-regional cooperation	National cooperation
Very low formal cooperative behaviour			
Gisborne	• Little evidence of formal cooperation beyond *dyadic* relationships and *action sets*	• No evidence	• No members of NZFWTN
Little formal cooperative behaviour			
Auckland	• Little evidence of formal cooperation beyond *dyadic* relationships and *action sets*	• No evidence	• 3 tourism & 3 food members of NZFWTN • A small amount of active par ticipation from tourism
Canterbury	• Little evidence of formal cooperation beyond *dyadic* relationships and *action sets*	• No evidence	• 3 tourism members & 1 food member of NZFWTN • Little evidence of active participation
Nelson	• Little evidence of formal cooperation beyond *dyadic* relationships and *action sets*	• No evidence	• 1 tourism member & 2 wine members of NZFWTN • Little evidence of active participation
Waikato/Bay of Plenty	• Little evidence of formal cooperation beyond *dyadic* relationships and *action sets*	• No evidence	• 2 tourism members & 1 wine member of NZFWTN • Little evidence of active participation
Some formal cooperative behaviour			
Central Otago	• Little evidence of formal cooperation beyond *dyadic* relationships and *action sets*	• No evidence	• 8 tourism, 2 wine & 2 food members of NZFWTN • Active participation from tourism • Role on management committee of NZFWTN • Degree of suspicion from some in the wine industry

Northland	• Some evidence of formal networks in sub-regions • Cooperation relatively immature	• No evidence	• 1 tourism member & 2 wine members of NZFWTN • Little evidence of active participation
Considerable formal cooperative behaviour Wairarapa	• Largely *action sets* and *organisation sets*, but some relatively mature relationships via 'Toast' Martinborough event	• Strong formal cooperation through membership of 'Classic New Zealand Wine Trail'	• 3 tourism & 2 wine members of NZFWTN • Involved in NZ food & wine tourism strategic plan • Active participation from tourism
Marlborough	• Strong mature formal network via the 'Love Marlborough' regional brand & 'Destination Marlborough'	• Strong formal cooperation through membership of 'Classic New Zealand Wine Trail'	• 2 tourism & 7 wine members of NZFWTN • Involved in NZ food & wine tourism strategic plan • Founding member of NZFWTN • Active participation from wine and tourism • Role on management committee of NZFWTN
Hawke's Bay	• Strong mature formal network via the 'Hawke's Bay Wine Country' regional brand & 'Hawke's Bay Inc.'	• Strong formal cooperation through membership of 'Classic New Zealand Wine Trail'	• 1 tourism member & 4 wine members of NZFWTN • Involved in NZ food & wine tourism strategic plan • Founding member of NZFWTN • Active participation from wine and tourism • Role on management committee of NZFWTN

Note: NZFWTN = New Zealand Food and Wine Tourism Network.

participating in formal inter-regional (*Classic New Zealand Wine Trail*) and national (NZFWTN) networks. Some of the wine regions, such as Gisborne, Auckland, Canterbury, Nelson and Waikato/Bay of Plenty, on the other hand, exhibit only a limited level of formal interaction between the tourism and wine industries.

Hall (2003) suggests that the Hawke's Bay region is the most advanced in the context of food and wine tourism networks. In 2000, the *Hawke's Bay Food and Wine Group*, a membership-based organisation, was established following a private sector initiative to establish a strong regional brand identity that would benefit the individual members. After its foundation, the group developed promotional brochures, expanded signage, and created a regional tourism brand, *Hawke's Bay Wine Country* (Hall, 2003) and an export-led network, known as *Food Hawke's Bay*. The *Hawke's Bay Wine Country Tourism Association Inc.*, (HBWCTA), as the network's formal entity is now known, also receives public sector funding and works closely with the local regional tourism organisation (HBWCTA, 2004).

Despite Hall's (2003) suggestion that there is little evidence of cooperation between the wine and tourism industries in the Marlborough region, and some reports of disagreements between the two industries on matters relating to tourism (McIntyre, 2005), recent activities suggest that this is set to change. Indeed, some of the more recent innovations highlight the emerging degree of cooperation between the two industries, including:

• the development of the 'Love Marlborough' brand identity: designed to encompass tourism, wine, seafood and other food products from the Marlborough region (Cluster Navigators Ltd, 2001);
• the *Marlborough International Marketing Group*, a tourism marketing initiative, now includes two winery operators as members (Destination Marlborough, 2005a);
• one of the more prominent Marlborough winery owners has joined the six member board of *Destination Marlborough*, the local regional tourism organisation (Destination Marlborough, 2005b);
• *Destination Marlborough* is a founding member of the *Classic New Zealand Wine Trail*, which is a commercial venture that cooperatively markets wine tourism activities in five regions; and
• Marlborough members of the New Zealand Food and Wine Tourism Network are increasingly active participants in that network's cooperative activities.

Simpson and Bretherton (2004) provide still further evidence of sub-regional wine tourism networking behaviour in the Matakana region, which lies north of Auckland. They suggest that:

> "The Matakana coast cluster is much more [sic] broadly based than the wineries-only Wine trail group, and currently has between 60 and 70 members drawn from a wide range of participants in the local tourism industry. From this perspective, it has clearly been recognized by respondents as a very necessary element in the overall promotion of the local area, and an initiative that offers significant avenues for synergistic cooperation between individual members. Several wineries have combined with a local motelier to produce a wine tour weekend package; one small winery has partnered with a Warkworth gift shop to create an exclusive retail distribution channel; and another is keen to develop a calendar of annual wine-based events that would involve an inclusive cross-section of local business. These types of partnership

have on occasion developed into a form of cooperative merchandising, where local produce (such as cheeses, pickles, and other condiments) are made available at the cellar door as a complement to the core winery product." (Simpson & Bretherton, 2004, p. 117)

The Matakana cluster is listed as an 'active cluster development initiative', one of just 7 of the 95 clusters that have been identified nationwide that have a tourism focus (NZTE, 2005). This list of active clusters is prepared by New Zealand Trade and Enterprise, a government agency which serves in an active role to develop and support the networks and clusters in New Zealand. New Zealand Trade and Enterprise provides the implementation component of enabling policy that promotes cluster development, capability and capacity building.

New Zealand—Government, Networks and Clusters

The New Zealand government follows the *New Regionalism* model for development which "…tends to favour bottom-up and region-specific policy actions, based on regional governance" (Nischalke & Schöllmann, 2005, p. 560), and this has been used to develop a planning concept known as *Regional Innovation Systems*. According to Nischalke and Schöllmann (2005) Regional Innovation Systems result in collaborative efforts which, when combined with geographic proximity, encourage the development of innovative ideas and knowledge generation. While a key component of this approach arises from the spatial concentration of firms, it also includes aspects of regional research and development infrastructure, and seeks to incorporate the brokers between supply and demand (e.g., technology brokers and venture capitalists) within the development scheme. However, they also point out that there are significant barriers to the implementation of this approach in New Zealand, including low population density, isolation and the distance to the main markets (e.g., Japan, USA and UK), and the significant limitations imposed by its physical geography — a long narrow country with high mountain ranges. In fact, until recently, the barriers have not been limited only to physical ones; with Oram (2003), for example, suggesting that past government policies and business attitudes have severely stifled the development of clusters in New Zealand. Even Michael Porter's assistance could not help, with Oram (2003, n.p.) noting that:

"More than a decade ago, Michael Porter, the Harvard Business School guru of economic development, identified the power unleashed by clusters. The message was so inspiring for small New Zealand companies that the government of the day paid Porter to tell us how to do it. But the so-called Porter Project, in the early 1990s, flopped. Lacking buy-in from a laissez-faire government and "kill-not-cooperate" industries, clustering was shuffled off into the too-hard basket."

However, successive Labour governments, first in 1999, again in 2002 and most recently in 2005, have developed and implemented a pro-cluster/network 'whole of government' approach to regional development (Nischalke & Schöllmann, 2005). Following the 1999 election, the Ministry of Economic Development was established by the Labour-led government. It set about preparing a 'blueprint for economic growth' in its *Growing an Innovative*

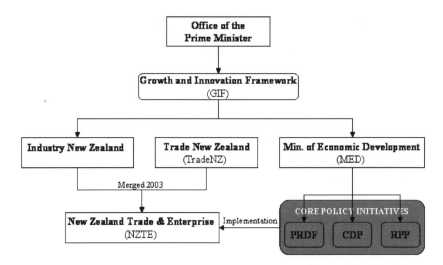

PRDF = Polytechnic Regional Development Fund. CDP = Cluster Development Programme.

RPP = Regional Partnerships Programme.

Figure 7.2: New Zealand regional development framework.

New Zealand policy (or Growth Innovation Framework). The Ministry of Economic Development is responsible for policy relating to economic, regional and industry development and works closely with New Zealand Trade and Enterprise to design and implement programmes that deliver these policies. New Zealand Trade and Enterprise was formed in 2003, as a merger between 'Trade New Zealand', which had been established in 1991 by the National Party Government of the time, and 'Industry New Zealand', which had been established in 2000 (NZTE, 2004a). The new entity is charged with implementing the Ministry of Economic Development's core initiatives: including the Cluster Development Programme, the Regional Partnerships Programme and the Polytechnic Regional Development Fund (Nischalke & Schöllmann, 2005). Figure 7.2 shows the different threads of economic development policy and programme implementation and the agencies responsible.

The Cluster Development Programme, the Regional Partnerships Programme and the Polytechnic Regional Development Fund each have different sets of objectives and each has funded a range of projects since 2000 (detailed in Table 7.2). The Regional Partnerships Programme is the principle fund for regional development and provides up to $NZ2 million for major regional initiatives. The Cluster Development Programme is focussed entirely on supporting the development of industry-based clusters, and has provided seed funding for dozens of projects for formal cluster start-ups. It is administered jointly by New Zealand Trade and Enterprise and the Ministry and attempts to allow clusters to move along 'the cluster development process and life cycle'. According to Gray, Harvey, and Brimblecombe (2003), this is a four-stage process:

• Initiation — analysis and organisation (lasting around three to four months);
• Incubation — cluster engagement (lasting around 18 months);
• Implementation — collaborative support (lasting around 18 months), and;
• Improvement/renewal — building market innovation and market leadership (ongoing).

Table 7.2: Outline of New Zealand's core regional development initiatives.

	RPP	CDP	PRDF
Key objectives	• Facilitate & promote sustainable regional development • Facilitate learning & cooperation • Improve under standing of the value of local strategic development processes	• Build skills, knowledge and expertise of cluster facilitators • Address barriers to collaboration • Build capacity & capability for collaboration • Assist stakeholders to identify & exploit opportunities for growth	• Enable & encourage institutes of technology and polytechnics (ITP)/regional industry collaboration • Build capability of ITPs to be responsive to regional training needs • Improve regional economic development
Funding basis	• Regional Economic Development Strategies= $100,000 per 3 year cycle • Capability Building= $100,000 in any 1 year • Major Regional Initiatives (MRI)=up to $2 million per 3 year cycle	• A national co-ordinator (unspecified amount) • Cluster identification & implementation • Iinformation, tools & workshops ($157,000 in 2002/2003) • A maximum of $50,000 per cluster and to 50% of running costs in Year 1 & 33% in Year 2) • Up to $5,000 for other costs beyond operational funding (e.g., web site, brochure) • Research & evaluation into clusters (unspecified)	• Up to $300,000 (GST inclusive) per year • Maximum of 70% of overall project cost
Funds allocated	• $14.24 million (Dec 2000–Mar 2003) • Average per region of $508,500 • Average per project $219,000	• $3.35 million (Feb 2002–June 2005) • Average per allocation of $24,000	• $3.86 million (Dec 2002–June 2004) • Average per ITP funded of $241,000
Projects	• 28 regional partnerships established by June 2003 • Includes 4 Major Regional Initiatives (MRIs) @ $2 million	• 140 separate funding allocations to Feb 2005 • Includes some clusters that received multiple funds	• 16 ITPs funded 32 different projects

PRDF, Polytechnic Regional Development Fund; CDP, Cluster Development Programme; RPP, Regional Partnerships Programme.
Sources: Nischalke and Schöllmann, 2005; Ministry of Economic Development, 2003; Chen, 2004.

The Cluster Development Programme also provides funding for a facilitator to assist clusters to move through this process. The Polytechnic Regional Development programme has a role to play in cluster development in New Zealand, albeit indirectly, as it assists capability building in regions, which are often focussed around cluster activity, by regional partnerships between industry training and education providers (primarily polytechnics).

Table 7.2 shows that New Zealand Trade and Enterprise administered projects totalling NZ$3.35 million under the Cluster Development Programme between February 2002 and June 2005. During this same period, four wine-related projects received funding that accounted for around 5.1 percent of all Cluster Development Programme funds, while four tourism-related projects accounted for a further 4.7 percent of these funds (see Table 7.3). Together, these wine and tourism projects have accounted for almost 10 percent of the total funds available through the Cluster Development Programme in the first three and half years of operation.

Table 7.3: Cluster development funding for wine and tourism projects: February 2002–June 2005.

Recipient	Region	Project description	Amount
Wine cluster funding			
Marlborough Winegrowers Assoc. Inc.	Marlborough	Marlborough Winegrowers cluster development	$28,000
Central Otago Pinot Noir Limited	Otago	Central Otago Pinot Noir cluster funding	$61,625
Hawke's Bay Winemakers	Hawke's Bay	Hawke's Bay wine cluster funding	$50,000
Waipara Valley Winegrowers Inc.	Canterbury	Wine cluster funding	$30,000
All wine cluster funding			***$169,625***
Tourism cluster funding			
Poutama Trust	Wellington	Development of NZ Maori Tourism Assoc.	$14,063
Fernmade Limited	Auckland	Golf tourism cluster	$46,875
Destination Rotorua Limited	Bay of Plenty	Rotorua tourism cluster funding	$25,000
Auckland Tourism & Visitors Trust	Auckland	Tourism operators cluster/ strategy development	$72,000
All tourism cluster funding			***$157,938***
All wine & tourism cluster funding			**$327,563**

Source: New Zealand Trade and Enterprise, 2005.

Two of the 15 'major regional initiatives' funded by New Zealand Trade and Enterprise are also dedicated to tourism (one in Northland and one in Wanganui), (NZTE, 2004b) while both the Auckland region (Auckland Regional Economic Development Strategy (AREDS), 2004) and the West Coast region (West Coast Development Trust, 2005) are developing similar tourism-related proposals. A further three 'major regional initiatives' are dedicated to the development of the food and beverage industry, in Hawke's Bay, Marlborough and Tairawhiti, in the Gisborne/East Cape area (NZTE, 2004b). In short, a further NZ$10 million has been invested in these two highly synergistic industries, yet there is little or no evidence of formal acknowledgement and funding of cross-sectoral cooperation. This has occurred despite the fact that: "NZTE's [New Zealand Trade and Enterprise] sector engagement strategies in the food and beverage ... cover businesses that sell to the international tourism trade. New Zealand Trade and Enterprise recognises that international visitors offer significant opportunities and value to businesses' growth prospects in these sectors" (NZTE, 2004c, n.p.). Hawke's Bay and Marlborough are perhaps the two regions with the highest degree of cooperative behaviour between the wine and tourism industries (as per Table 7.1) and both have food and beverage 'major regional initiatives' funding, but still there appears to be little direct support from the national economic development agencies for wine and food tourism cluster development.

Winery Attitudes to Tourism in New Zealand

Hall, Johnson, and Mitchell (2000, p. 217) suggest that in New Zealand, "while positive attitudes towards wine tourism are often strong in the tourism industry there appears to be a much lower level of support in the wine industry." Johnson (1998, p. 97) also found that "... wine producers perceive an imbalance in the partnership between the wine and tourism industries, with the wine industry having more to offer the tourism industry than vice versa." As a result, network development between the industries is uneven, and barriers often exist that reduce the capacity to establish inter-firm cooperation (Hall, 2003). One such barrier appears to be that many wineries do not recognise that they too are part of the tourism industry, for they perceive the region's visitors as *customers* at the winery. As one Martinborough winery put it: "As I don't consider being a tourist operator, I am in the business of selling my wine, all the rest is carried out by us to welcome people to us" (Hall, Johnson, & Mitchell, 2000, p. 216). Despite this, there are still many wineries that do see the benefit of cooperation between the wine and tourism industries. According to Hall, Johnson, and Mitchell (2000, p. 217), this was even prevalent among those that had a generally negative view of tourism, including one Central Otago winery that "... noted that New Zealand wineries were 'Just babies at wine tourism ... [We] need local and central government financial assistance to get further down track'."

The Case Study Region: Central Otago

It is within this context that a study of the Central Otago wine region was carried out to further illuminate the nature of relationships within and between the wine and tourism industries in Central Otago (see Schreiber, 2004). The study used key informant interviews with eight stakeholders in the wine and tourism industries, as well as one other from an independent business development agency, to assist in identifying the potential for — and

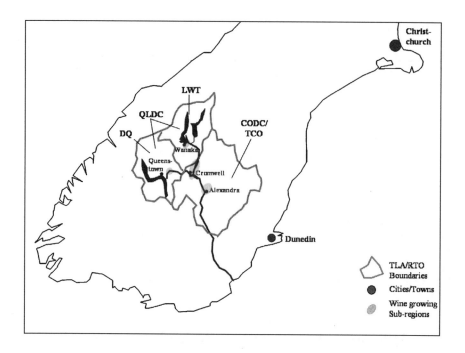

Key:
Territorial Local Authorities:
> QLDC = Queenstown Lakes District Council;
> CODC = Central Otago District Council;
Regional Tourism Organisations:
> DQ = Destination Queenstown;
> LWT = Lake Wanaka Tourism;
> TCO = Tourism Central Otago

Figure 7.3: Central Otago regional map.

the barriers against — formal (horizontal and vertical) wine tourism network development. A summary of the findings of this Central Otago case study begins with a brief insight into the region, its wine and tourism industries and the extent of wine tourism in the region. Figure 7.3 identifies its location.

The Central Otago region is located in the South Island of New Zealand. The region is administered by two territorial local authorities: the Central Otago District Council and the Queenstown Lakes District Council. There are three regional tourism organisations that service the needs of local operators: *Destination Queenstown, Tourism Central Otago* and *Lake Wanaka Tourism* (see also Figure 7. 3). The region is dominated by its alpine geography and a number of natural and man-made lakes. Rather surprisingly, for those who have never visited the region, it has a semi-arid continental climate.

Pastoral agriculture and horticulture have long dominated the Central Otago economy. While a lone Frenchman had planted grapes in the region in the 1860s, production did not last beyond the end of the 19th century; however, viticulture was reintroduced into Central Otago in the late 1970s and 1980s. Growth was slow in the first 15 years or so, but the last decade has seen the industry expand at around 9 percent annually (see Table 7.4) (Cull, 2001; Oram, 2004). Central Otago now has 5 percent of the national vineyard area, with more than 75 percent of the grapes planted being the Pinot Noir variety. Central Otago can be divided into four main sub-regions: Wanaka, Gibbston Valley (near Queenstown), Alexandra and the Cromwell Basin, which includes Bannockburn, Lowburn, Wanaka and Bendigo (Cooper, 2002).

Tourism has been an important component of the Central Otago economy since at least the 1920s (Kearsley, 1998). Table 7.5 shows that Central Otago's three Regional Tourism Organizations have distinctly different visitation patterns: Queenstown, a highly developed mature resort, dominated by international tourism; Wanaka, a secondary but rapidly developing resort; and, the Central Otago region, where tourism is less well-developed and international visitors are unlikely to stay. Both domestic and international visitors are attracted to the area's diverse and unique landscape of mountains, lakes and gorges, to its mixture of historical and cultural sites, and to its adventure and outdoor activities, as well

Table 7.4: Central Otago wine region growth indicators: 1996–2005.

	Vineyard area (Hectares)	Winegrowers (Members of NZW)	Vintage (tonnes crushed)
Year end 1996	92	11	376
	(9)	(8)	(9)
Year end 2005	942	82	1441
	(4)	(3)	(6)
Average annual increase	9.0%	8.7%	7.4%

Note: Bracketed figure is rank out of New Zealand's nine wine regions.

Table 7. 5: Central Otago tourism performance indicators (Year End 2004).

RTO	Visits (000's)	Nights (000's)	Spend ($millions)
Queenstown	1742.8	3448	472.6
	(51%)	(64%)	(73%)
Lake Wanaka	677.2	1422	147.5
	(42%)	(40%)	(53%)
Central Otago	651.8	976.2	100.9
	(8%)	(12%)	(14%)
All RTOs	3071.8	5846.2	721
	(40%)	(50%)	(61%)

Note: Bracketed figure is the percentage attributable to international tourists.

as to its wine tourism services (Central Otago Economic Development, 2004; Queenstown Lakes District Council, 2004).

After the first phase of vine planting, with wine successfully produced, vineyard owners in the Gibbston Valley decided to take advantage of their proximity to Queenstown, one of New Zealand's main tourist destinations, and began to build facilities to encourage wine tourism (Austin, 1993). Alan Brady, the owner of Gibbston Valley Wines, was the first to construct a purpose-built tasting room and restaurant to cater for tourists (Cull, 2001). Today Gibbston Valley Wines, with its restaurant, boutique cheese factory and regular tours through its wine cellars, is New Zealand's most visited winery (Cooper, 2002). Other wineries in the region followed Gibbston Valley's example and constructed purpose-built facilities for tourists, such as cellar door sales rooms and restaurants.

A study of New Zealand winery visitors in 1999 (Mitchell, 2004) found that the visitor profile for Central Otago wineries is generally similar to that of the national sample — with a higher proportion of females, mainly Baby Boomers and Gen-Xers (i.e., those aged 35–60), well-paid, well-educated professionals. More than 90 percent of visitors came from outside the region, including almost 20 percent from overseas, and almost two-thirds stayed in the region for three to seven days. While staying in the region, the survey suggested they visited an average of three wineries, but less than 15 percent were motivated to visit the region primarily for its wine and wineries (compared with more 39 percent in Marlborough and 57 percent in Wairarapa). As noted in Chapter 6, this suggests that wine tourism in this region is an important *secondary generator* of visits. The main reason for visiting was general holidaying or touring and as such it is likely most visitors were attracted by a combination of the region's outstanding natural beauty and its many adventure and outdoor pursuits. The most enjoyable aspects of visits to wineries were reported as the wine, the level of service and the setting in which the grapes are grown, reflecting the region's growing reputation for quality wine, high levels of service and the natural scenery of the region.

Network Behaviour by the Central Otago Wineries

A number of *formal* and *informal* networks (see Chapter 5) were identified in this study. The data suggest that, while there is strong support for inter-organisational relationships, the form that these relationships take, and their intensity, varies substantially between both the wine and tourism industries and the particular location of the business within the region.

In the Central Otago wine industry, there is clear evidence of horizontal integration between firms, which is clearly demonstrated by the strong formal regional network relationships among the 'Central Otago Winegrowers Association' and in 'Central Otago Pinot Noir Limited'. Membership of the Central Otago Winegrowers Association network can be considered to be mandatory, as every winemaker or grape grower is required by law to pay an annual levy to the New Zealand Wine Institute or the New Zealand Grape Growers Council. By paying the annual levy, the winemaker/grape grower automatically becomes a member of the particular region's wine tourism body. The Central Otago Winegrowers Association's primary role is to support and educate its members: for example, with seminars, addresses by guest speakers and the provision of printed information on the industry or compliance issues. One of its initiatives has resulted in the publication of the *Central Otago Wine Map*, which provides a location guide to the member's wineries and vineyards.

However, perhaps more importantly in relation to networking behaviour, the Central Otago Winegrowers Association is active in promoting social relationships between its members. One key informant commented that "… it is important that we meet with each other, share our concerns, failures, what we tried, what did work." This is supported by another respondent, who stated that "… I also work informally with other wineries in tasting each others wines. We provide a peer review, where we critically examine each other's wine and give advice or views."

Central Otago Pinot Noir Limited is responsible for the domestic and international promotion of the wineries in the region; with a primary focus to market and brand the area's wines for international markets. The company was founded by the winegrowers association in 2002 as the marketing arm of the regional body. One of the reasons that this occurred is that, under New Zealand Trade and Enterprise criteria the Central Otago Winegrowers Association was not able to receive government funding for cluster/network development. As a result it formed its own company — Central Otago Pinot Noir Ltd — in effect, as a commercial cluster. To join this *commercial* cluster a prospective member must first become a member of the Central Otago Winegrowers Association, but, to date, not all its members have sought to become members of Central Otago Pinot Noir Limited. According to one survey respondent, it is only those actively producing wine (around 70 of the 200 winegrowers) that have chosen to participate in Central Otago Pinot Noir Ltd. Each member is required to pay an annual generic fee, which, combined with Cluster Development Funding from New Zealand Trade and Enterprise (refer Table 7.3), pays for the basic administration of the cluster. Additional fees are charged to supplement the cost of specific promotions, but participation in these is optional, and the amount charged depends on the type of function and the potential of the event to help raise the profile of the region or the individual winery. The sorts of activities Central Otago Pinot Noir Limited sponsored in 2003/2004 included: media and trade promotions in partnership with New Zealand Trade and Enterprise's '*marketnewzealand.com*', USA Wine Fairs, a promotional event in London, promotional events in Wellington, such as 'the Beehive Tasting' and 'Pinot Noir 2004', and the cost of bringing wine writers, buyers and chefs to Central Otago (COPNL, 2004).

It is worth noting at this juncture, that it appears that New Zealand Trade and Enterprise, by funding Central Otago Pinot Noir Limited under its 'Cluster Development Program', may not necessarily be adhering to the traditional definition of the cluster concept. New Zealand Trade and Enterprise supports the industry with government funding of so-called 'commercial clusters' and Central Otago Pinot Noir Limited is defined as such. According to New Zealand Trade and Enterprise (2002, n.p.) a commercial cluster exists when: "a group of companies decide to work together on specific projects". The primary focus of a commercial cluster is to support the networking of small to medium sized enterprises so that they can achieve aims they cannot realise alone and enable them to compete more effectively with other regions (NZTE, 2002). The areas in which companies can collaborate vary depending on the industry.

The theoretical concept of the cluster is the agglomeration of one core industry surrounded by supporting industries that are together involved in the creation of a complete value chain (refer Chapter 3). However, all members of Central Otago Pinot Noir Limited are wineries and, as its membership is limited to Central Otago Winegrowers Association members — no other industry can become directly involved in this network. Central Otago Pinot Noir Limited also appears to have little in the way of informal or formal linkages with other businesses in the value chain outside the network, perhaps with the exception of wine distributors and wholesalers. This is the result of the narrow focus of the network on marketing and promotion, which as a consequence seems to limit the range of benefits that can be gained from a commercial cluster arrangement. In fact the co-location of the wineries appears to be more to do with the presence of optimum grape growing conditions (e.g., soil and climate) than it is to do with the benefits of working cooperatively. There is little doubt that the subsequent cooperative behaviour is of benefit to the region as a whole, but this is clearly post-hoc and, as such, Central Otago Pinot Noir Limited might perhaps be better described as a *network* rather than as a *cluster*. Porter's (1998) discussion of the Californian wine cluster demonstrates that, while the wine industry is at the core of the cluster, the cluster itself includes supporting and complementary industries throughout the value chain and interacts with other complementary clusters.

Nevertheless, Central Otago Pinot Noir Limited aims to benefit every member. This is important because the markets for wine at the relatively high price level sought by the wineries in Central Otago are very small, and by using the organisation's marketing network, marketing costs are reduced. This allows the members of Central Otago Pinot Noir Limited to actually achieve economies-of-scale and greater market penetration, especially in export markets. As a result small companies and not just the larger, more established ones are able to gain access to international and domestic markets. However, participation in such marketing initiatives is optional and it is up to the individual members to decide whether or not take advantage of the full range of services that can be provided.

In this sense, Central Otago Pinot Noir Limited is a strong commercial cluster that is achieving good success internationally, but their activities are focussed entirely on product marketing and, as such, there appears to be little scope for cooperative behaviour outside the wine industry. The fact that its members must also be members of Central Otago Winegrowers Association also means that Central Otago Pinot Noir Limited is perhaps an inappropriate structure for vertical integration with other industries in the region. There are less formal networks between the wineries located in the wine producing sub-regions of Central Otago, and these may in fact be more conducive to the development of cross-sectoral cooperation with the tourism industry. As an illustration, according to one key survey informant, five Bannockburn wineries joined forces "… Just on simple things — developing signs and working together to extend the experience of visitors to Bannockburn. So, that they [wine tourists] don't just attend one winery, they attend more than one." Other examples of similar relationships are also to be found, for example the wineries in Gibbston Valley work together on similar projects, and the wineries around Alexandra have cooperated to organise an Easter Harvest Festival in Clyde.

There is also some evidence of informal cooperation relating specifically to wine tourism. In particular, one winery in the region has organised for cellar door managers to meet regularly to discuss issues relating to visitors. This has included a seminar by University of Otago staff and informal and infrequent 'get-togethers' to taste each other's wines and chat about things that have arisen during the 'season'. Participation in this group is by invitation only and is largely (but not exclusively) limited to the 'new kids on the block' in terms of wine production or cellar door development.

Like the wine industry, the Central Otago tourism industry also exhibits the elements of strong horizontal networks. The three Central Otago Regional Tourism Organisations ('Destination Queenstown', 'Lake Wanaka Tourism' and 'Tourism Central Otago') are themselves formal networks (see Figure 7.3 to identify the boundaries for each regional tourism area). Although the Regional Tourism Organisations cooperate in a broader regional marketing network, each is responsible for the support, promotion and tourism development of its own region. As a consequence, the tourism activities in the different wine producing sub-regions are administered by different Regional Tourism Organisations. This means that 'Tourism Central Otago' is responsible for the promotion of wine tourism in the Alexandra and Cromwell Basin, 'Destination Queenstown' for Gibbston Valley and 'Lake Wanaka Tourism' for the Wanaka sub-region. As such there is a lack of region-wide cooperation and coordination, which creates significant barriers to inter-organisational networking across the entire region. This is further exacerbated by the fact that the broader wine region is also administered by two Territorial Local Authorities (municipalities) with differing approaches to economic development, different rating (local tax) bases and differing political agendas.

Vertical Integration between the Wine, Tourism and Other Industries

There is some evidence from the Schreiber (2004) study of the value to be gained from these relationships between wineries and tourism operators in the Central Otago region and of the benefits of working together. For example, one of the respondents associated with the tourism industry argued that the small size of New Zealand compared to other tourist destinations, and the distance from its main markets, makes it essential that industries work together and undertake joint promotion. Another, associated with the wine industry, said: "... I think as a country we should do more together. We are not good at promoting ourselves together." Further, it seems that the wine industry is aware that Queenstown, as a major international resort, offers the potential for wine tourism development, with one wine industry key informant suggesting: "... There is probably no other wine region in New Zealand that would have such a great concentration of international visitors on its doorstep. So the potential for wine tourism is massive and I think there are a lot of untapped opportunities there."

However, relationships between the wine industry and the tourism industry are less formal, or at least not as strong, as the linkages that exist within each industry. For example, a wine industry respondent explained the relationship between the Central Otago Regional Tourism Organisations and both the Central Otago Winegrowers Association and Central Otago Pinot Noir Limited as follows: "... We have relationships with the regional tourism groups in just presenting promotional material to them and just advising them of what's happening in the industry." While the relationships are somewhat limited, key informants from both industries acknowledged that they have worked together for some time, with a tourism operator suggesting that "… we have *always* worked closely with the wineries here." According to one wine industry respondent, it is also apparent that "… the Gibbston/Queenstown wineries are much more aligned to Queenstown tourism activities and promotions", reflecting larger visitor numbers and a greater influence by tourism on the economy of this particular locality.

Despite the lack of formal relationships at a regional and industry-wide level, some wineries at least acknowledge the role of tourism in their business, and some are members of their local Regional Tourism Organisations or promotional groups. It could be suggested that this is evidence of *vertical integration*, but membership of a tourism organisation by an individual winery does not result in truly cooperative behaviour as these wineries are not necessarily active players in their tourism networks. In fact, in many instances they become members simply to have their winery included in destination promotional material or to display their brochures at the local visitor information centre — perhaps, this could be better described as a client–service provider relationship.

However, there is evidence of *informal* relationships that have developed between individual wineries and winery tour operators. For instance, one respondent associated with the wine industry commented: "… We certainly have a relationship — far less formal — with wine tour operators, who either visit the winery to taste wine or to bring in clients to eat [sic]." Meanwhile, other respondents have explained that in addition to five 'official' wine tourism operators, there are also other tourism operators who offer exclusive, tailor-made trips to wineries. Once again there is evidence to suggest that these relationships are particularly important in the Gibbston Valley, but there are also wine tours that regularly visit wineries in Bannockburn and around Wanaka. Gibbston Valley Wines is perhaps the winery with the greatest relationship with the tourism industry as it operates a wine cave, regular winery tours, a restaurant and function centre, a cheese factory and a gift shop. These activities and facilities are part of Gibbston Valley Wines' long-standing strategy to engage the tourism market and to optimize the advantages from their location on the main route into and out of Queenstown. They receive visitors from all over the world, including large numbers of coach tours which are popular in New Zealand. Consequently, they work closely with other tourism providers, wine tours and inbound tour operators. On the other hand, smaller wineries unable to cater for large groups are happy to arrange wine tours by appointment for smaller groups. One respondent suggests that "… A few people can come to us, but we do not encourage large tours, because we do not have the facilities like Gibbston Valley [Wines]. It's just another dimension of the industry."

Finally, there are informal linkages that see wineries and tourism businesses provide referrals for each other. For example some wineries refer their visitors to some accommodation providers, cafés and other attractions and vice versa. These are largely based on personal relationships between the winery owner and the tourism operator. At another level, there exists a less obvious connection between the wine and tourism industries in relation to the Otago Polytechnic, which trains staff for both industries through their tourism, hospitality, winemaking and viticulture training programs. Importantly, the Polytechnic trains staff to work at the cellar door with sets of skills from both industries (i.e., hospitality skills and knowledge of winemaking and viticulture).

Categorizing the Inter-Organizational Relationships in Central Otago

While the distinction between *informal* and *formal* networks was clearly established in Chapter 5, it is worth noting Birley's (1985, p. 109) comments in this context:

- an 'informal network' consists of relations to friends, family and business contacts resulting from previous employment and work experience;
- a 'formal network' consists of relations to regional and national government agencies, consultants and advisors, such as lawyers, accountants and banks and other formal sources of help.

Hall et al. (1998) takes this distinction one step further, describing inter-organisational linkages as:

- *Dyadic linkages* — two organisations find they can gain mutual benefit in a common goal;
- Organisation sets — a cluster of dyadic relationships around a focal organisation;
- Action sets — interacting organisations working together to achieve a specific purpose; or,
- Networks — a (formal) group of organisations with common organisational ties with an identifiable bounded inter-organisational system.

These classifications of networks have been combined with Telfer and Wall's (1996) distinction between horizontal and vertical relationships (see above) to classify the relationships that exist in Central Otago (See Table 7.6).

The relationships identified in this study suggest that the vertical integration between the wine and tourism industries of Central Otago is somewhat limited (as dyadic relationships between individual organisations and simple action sets based around Regional

Table 7.6: Existing network categorisations and intensity in Central Otago.

Inter-organisational relationships			Existing relationships in Central Otago
Informal	Vertical	Dyadic relationships	• Winery & tour operator • Winery & other tourism operator • Winery & Otago Polytechnic
	Horizontal	Organisation sets	• Cooperation of wineries in sub-regions: e.g., Bannockburn, Alexandra & Gibbston Valley
Formal	Horizontal	Action sets	• COWA
	Vertical	Action sets	• Visitor centre, RTO or promotion group with individual winery • Visitor centre, RTO or promotion group with COWA or COPNL
	Horizontal	Networks	• Southern Lakes marketing collective • COPNL

Adapted from Schreiber (2004).

Tourism Organisations and visitor information centres). Some positive attitudes towards inter-sectoral cooperation are evident: there is a high recognition of the value of the two industries working together (especially around Queenstown) and there are strong networking relationships within each of the wine and tourism sectors (especially wine) evident from this study. However, there appear to be several barriers to vertical integration between the Central Otago wine and tourism industries.

Barriers to Inter-Organisational Relationships

The first identifiable barrier to vertical integration and cluster formation is the perception that wineries are not part of the tourism industry. This view is relatively widespread in Central Otago, reflecting Hall, Johnson and Mitchell's (2000) findings across New Zealand. In the 2004 survey, one respondent stated that, "… we see ourselves primarily as winemakers", while another explains that "a lot of people in the wine industry don't understand that they are in the wine *tourism* industry. They don't see that they are in the *tourism* industry." However, this perception is not uniform across the region and depends partly on the stage of development of tourism facilities in the wine growing sub-region. According to a tourism respondent, one way this is manifest is the different, number, scale and style of cellar door developments across the region that largely reflect a higher concentration of international visitors the closer you get to Queenstown. The respondent highlighted that this was no different to tourism infrastructure more broadly (e.g., accommodation, cafés, restaurants, etc). As such, those with a high level of cellar door sales to visitors have a more obvious appreciation of their role in tourism.

It was suggested that the Gibbston Valley and Bannockburn sub-regions were more 'sophisticated', as both regions have purpose-built facilities to better cater for tourism needs. "… Alan Brady is the innovator, who started Gibbston [Valley] off and his winery [Gibbston Valley Wines] has moved into expansion now … [with a]… cheese factory, cave tours, restaurants and a big range of merchandise." Others have followed suit, with six significant cellar door developments in Gibbston Valley, some with cafés and restaurants incorporated, and five similar developments in Bannockburn, three in Alexandra, but only one in Wanaka. Furthermore, only one of the Alexandra wineries offers year-round cellar door facilities; the rest are open during the summer season or by appointment. The differences between the sub-regions reflect, at least in part, the history of the Central Otago wine industry. Wineries around Alexandra, established in the 1980s, were "pioneers" and lacked the resources to invest in sophisticated tourist facilities. Wineries around Bannockburn had a more entrepreneurial, strategic focus from the beginning, as they were established in the 1990s, a time when more money was available to invest in the construction of propose-built cellar door facilities. The Gibbston Valley also developed in the 1980s, but their location meant that even the pioneers developed cellar door facilities from the outset. As one operator put it: "… Chard Farm and Gibbston Valley [Wines] were the leaders [of wine tourism]… Their positioning is fantastic. They couldn't get a better position at the main road." While another suggested: "… Queenstown wineries [are] taking advantage of the tourists on their doorsteps." Despite this view, it remains moot as to whether or not Alexandra wineries would have a greater level of tourism development if they had been developed in the 1990s and not the 1980s. Certainly, an Alexandra wine producer that established in the 1990s has had a cellar door with café from its inception, and another of the original 'pioneering' companies has recently built a café and tasting facility at a more strategic location away from their original site. Interestingly, however, both businesses rely heavily on local patronage at their cafés, and it could be suggested that these developments meet a gap in the local market rather than a tourism one.

One of the main barriers that was commonly referred to by the survey respondents was a perceived lack of cohesion within the tourism sector. In particular, the fact that the broader wine region is controlled by three Regional Tourism Organisations appears to be a cause for concern, particularly among the wine industry respondents. Several appear to believe that the structure of the tourism industry, with its various promotions groups, is ineffective; as one said: "... The wine industry position is that all of the tourism groups should be amalgamated into a single body", or in the words of another: "... I believe the structure of the promotion groups involved in tourism generates a lack of cohesion in that sector." Indeed, the attempt to form a broader regional — Southern Lakes — marketing collective in the 1990s did appear to be the best way forward for improved networking potential, but the withdrawal of 'Tourism Central Otago' from these initiatives seems to have caused somewhat of a rift with the other regional partners.

This is in stark contrast to the wineries in the region which cooperate across the wine region despite local authority political boundaries. However, the tourism respondents considered that joint promotion of the region is not possible, precisely because of these political boundaries and the different ways Regional Tourism Organisations are funded. For instance, 'Destination Queenstown' is funded by membership fees from participating tourism businesses as well from a levy on tourism businesses, whereas 'Tourism Central Otago' is funded by ratepayers as a whole. According to a tourism industry respondent in Queenstown, those funding 'Destination Queenstown' "... don't like spending [their] money in Australia promoting Central Otago product." It was also suggested by another tourism stakeholder that the differences in the stages of tourism development meant that 'Destination Queenstown' and 'Tourism Central Otago' necessarily had different objectives. 'Destination Queenstown's' focus is to promote and market the Queenstown region, while the Central Otago is still not yet fully developed and, hence, part of the role of 'Tourism Central Otago' lies in the development of products, the education of operators and the introduction of different distribution channels.

It was also suggested that there were some issues within Central Otago that act as significant barriers to wider cooperation. In particular, the different stages of development between Alexandra and Cromwell have created a long-standing sense of animosity between the towns. As one respondent stated: "... There has always been issues [sic] with Alexandra and Cromwell. Alexandra was seen as the service town yet Cromwell is positioned in the middle of the region and feels it should be the main town." Alexandra is also the administrative location of the Central Otago District Council, as well as 'Tourism Central Otago', and among some Cromwell residents it seems there is a perception that this is retarding growth in Cromwell, which may have a greater potential for development in tourism, wine and other economic activities. For example Cromwell has a well-developed social infrastructure and housing capacity, which was built to support hydro-electric dam construction, which in turn has created an attractive lake surrounding the town; it has land available for more grape planting and a significant investment in winery development; it is located on the main route into Queenstown for international visitors and lies at a major cross-roads for domestic tourists; and it is proving to be an attractive location for the movie industry and vehicle testing by major car manufacturers. In this instance, there are perhaps good grounds for local rivalry.

It should also be noted that there are also significant topographical constraints, which on their own are not likely to stop effective networking, but serve to reinforce the other psychological and administrative barriers. Each wine-growing sub-region is separated from the other by a mountain range. The road between the Gibbston Valley (near Queenstown) and Bannockburn (near Cromwell) is normally around a 35–45 minute drive, but in winter it can be difficult to negotiate. There are two roads between Gibbston Valley and the Wanaka sub-region, one of which is New Zealand's highest sealed road and can be closed in winter and the other includes the stretch between Bannockburn and Gibbston Valley. The travelling times between the wineries that are furthest apart could be as little as an hour in summer, but as much as two in winter. Needless to say, while the actual distances are not long, the presence of mountain ranges between the sub-regions, the treacherous nature of winter driving and the time taken to drive between the sub-regions mean that, without a strong desire and otherwise conducive conditions for networking behaviour, a formal wine tourism network is necessarily difficult to maintain across the broader region.

Prospects for Clustering in the Central Otago Region

Despite the presence of the barriers identified by the respondents to Schreiber's (2004) survey, there was some optimism that there could be greater vertical integration in the future. Two respondents associated with the tourism industry were very positive about the future: both pointed out that the launch of the 'New Zealand Food and Wine Tourism Network' in October 2004 offered the potential for industry stakeholders to work more closely together and could be the catalyst for a more formal regional wine tourism network. However, while 'Destination Queenstown' has already joined that network, 'Tourism Central Otago' was still considering the concept in mid-2006. Despite the tourism industry's positive attitude towards the New Zealand Food and Wine Tourism Network, the wine industry stakeholders expressed concern about the operational effectiveness of the network in Central Otago, one suggesting: "… We would have reservations about it. It wasn't really trying to fit into the overall activities of wineries in the region. I think there is still quite a lot of work to do to develop that strategy into something which is operationally effective." These concerns seem to stem from the lack of consultation with wineries in the region, as well as from a perception that Hawke's Bay and Marlborough regional wineries had developed that network for their own benefit. Another wine industry respondent took this further, suggesting that "… it seems to me that we are better just starting a small group doing things like the farmers market. I don't think it necessarily has to be driven from the top." Another respondent involved in both industries believed that if the region wanted to develop a formal wine network, it would be essential for the wine and tourism industry to first work together to develop a strategy for wine tourism in the region.

In general, respondents were positive about the concept of a wine tourism strategy as they knew of other regions in New Zealand and Australia that have successfully implemented similar strategies. As one respondent in the wine industry states: "… Most things have been done before somewhere else. It doesn't take much for people to travel in the Barossa Valley [Australia] or in Hawke's Bay or in the Rheingau [Germany] to look and see what sort of wine tourism ideas work and what doesn't work." It is not surprising, then, that all respondents believed that more communication between the two industries is essential.

One significant unanswered question is who should take the lead in the development of this communication process? As the respondent associated with the economic development agency asks:

> "Is it another form of parochial behaviour? Possibly. Is it a lack of vision and dialogue between protagonists, or the fact that Regional Tourism Organisations are too scattered? I am not too sure, but this shows that a round-table with representatives of both industries and representatives of local councils should be initiated. The question is who is prepared to take a lead on this?"

Opinions about who should take the initiative varied from respondent to respondent. One tourism stakeholder suggested that the wine industry could work under the umbrella of Central Otago Pinot Noir Ltd. or the Central Otago Winegrowers Association, but the counter view from a wine industry respondent was that perhaps it was the individual wineries that should be taking the lead: "... I think it's up to the group of wineries [with a cellar door] to say we need to promote ourselves better in Queenstown and Wanaka ... It all comes down to a user pays ... for the wineries who have a cellar door." Meanwhile, the economic development agency's representative said: "I think the initiative should be for the local councils or someone else, because it's a regional benefit." So, while there is agreement about the need for more dialogue, there is no agreement on who should lead the process. This would suggest that unless, as has been the case in regions like Hawke's Bay, there is an individual willing to *champion* a vertically integrated wine tourism network, there is unlikely to be any significant progress.

Conclusion

In New Zealand, there is substantial evidence of networking between the wine and tourism industries at both a regional (e.g., Hawke's Bay) and a sub-regional (e.g., Matakana) level. There is also evidence of recent developments at a national level to support the process (e.g., the New Zealand Food and Wine Tourism Network). The national government also provides strong policy support for the development of clusters and networks at a regional level; but, while there is both financial and administrative support for wine regions and for wine and tourism 'clusters' independently, there is as yet little encouragement for vertical integration between the two industries.

Central Otago is one wine region that has received funding for the establishment of a formal commercial cluster — Central Otago Pinot Noir Limited. The study reported in this chapter has identified a high degree of networking behaviour within this cluster and varying degrees of inter-organisational cooperative behaviour within the industry. However, unlike regions like Hawke's Bay, horizontal integration is largely limited to informal *dyadic* relationships between individual wineries and tourism businesses, with some *action sets* based around visitor centres also present. Despite this apparent lack of inter-sectoral cooperation, there appears to be widespread support for cooperation at the regional and sub-regional level. Nevertheless, the evidence suggests there are several barriers to constrain the extension of this cooperation. Key informants to the survey cited administrative and physical barriers as significant impediments to cooperation, as well as the perception by many wineries that they are not engaged in tourism and therefore they are not part of the tourism industry. It would seem, then, that without the presence of a champion willing to drive the development of common industry relationships, as has happened elsewhere in New Zealand, there is likely to be little or no progress in this area. While the material presented here relates to just one case study, and it would be dangerous to generalise, it does serve to highlight the need for a greater understanding of the barriers, both real and perceived, to vertical integration between tourism businesses and those in other industries. It might also reflect what Leiper (1990) once called *partial industrialisation*, where 'nontourism' businesses have still to learn how to engage with the mainstream of tourism.

References

Arfini, F., Bertoli, E., & Donati, M. (2002). The wine routes: Analysis of a rural development tool, *Les systèmes agroalimentaires localisés: Produits, entreprises et dynamiques locales, Proceedings*, Montpellier, France, 16–18 October 2002. Montpellier: Groupement d'Intérêt Scientifique Systèmes Agro-alimentaires Localisés (GIS SYAL). http://www.gis-syal.agropolis.fr/Syal2002/FR/Atelier/ 204/DONATi/ 0ARFINI.pdf [Accessed: 23 November 2005].

Auckland Regional Economic Development Strategy (AREDS) (2004): *Tourism MRI progress update and plan for progression*. http://www.areds.co.nz/Doc_Library/ AREDS_Tourism_MRI_ Stakeholder_Update.pdf [Accessed: 27 December 2005].

Austin, P. (1993). The *Central Otago Vineyard Industry: A supply side view of one of Otago's newest tourist attractions*. Department of Tourism, University of Otago, Dunedin. [Unpublished Diploma in Tourism Dissertation].

Barham, E. (2003). *Missouri Wineries: Present status and future scenarios*. Department of Rural Sociology, University of Missouri-Columbia. http://www.ssu.missouri.edu/Faculty/EBarham/ MO/Wineries/Report/2003.pdf [Accessed: 1 December 2005].

Birley, S. (1985). The role of networks in the entrepreneurial process. *Journal of Business Venturing, 1* 107–117.

Bruwer, J. (2003). South African wine routes: Some perspectives on the wine tourism industry's structural dimensions and wine tourism Product. *Tourism Management, 24*,(4), 423–435.

Central Otago Economic Development. (2004). Growth prospects and economic development. http://www.centralotagonz.com/index.cfm/growth_prospects [Accessed: 30 October 2004].

Central Otago Pinot Noir Limited (COPNL). (2004). *Annual report 2003/2004*. Central Otago Pinot Noir Limited.

Chen, E. M. (2004): *Review of the polytechnic regional development fund: Evaluation report*. Ministry of economic development: Industry and regional development research, evaluation and monitoring, Wellington, New Zealand.

Cluster Navigators Ltd. (2001). *Cluster building: A toolkit (A manual for starting and developing local clusters in New Zealand)*. [Unpublished].

Cooper, M. (2002). *Wine atlas of New Zealand*. Auckland: Hodder Moa Beckett.

Correia, L., Passos Ascenção, M. J., & Charters, S. (2004). Wine routes in Portugal: A case study of the Bairrada wine route. *Journal of Wine Research, 15*(1), 15–25.

Cull, D. (2001). *Vineyards on the edge — the story of central Otago Wine.* Dunedin: Longacre Press.

Destination Marlborough. (2005a). *International marketing group.* http://www.destinationmarlborough.com/international-marketing-group/ [Accessed: 3 January 2006].

Destination Marlborough. (2005b). *Destination Marlborough Strategic Plan 2005 — 2010.* [Unpublished].

Dodd, T. (1995). Opportunities and pitfalls of tourism in a developing wine industry. *International Journal of Wine Marketing*, 7(1), 5–16.

Getz, D. (2000). *Explore wine tourism: Management, development and destinations.* New York: Cognizant Communication.

Gray, C., Harvey, O., & Brimblecombe, T. (2003). *Cluster classification and costing research, Report for New Zealand Trade and Enterprise.* Wellington: Innovation & Systems Ltd.

Hall, C. M. (1996). Wine tourism in New Zealand. In: J. Higham (Ed.) *Proceedings of tourism down under II: A research conference*, University of Otago, Dunedin (pp. 109–119).

Hall, C. M. (2002). Local initiatives for local regional development: The role of food, wine and tourism. In: E. Arola, J. Kärkkäinen, & M. Siitari (Eds), *The 2nd tourism industry & education symposium, tourism and well-being* (pp.47–63). Finland: Jyväskylä Polytechnic..

Hall, C. M. (2003). Wine and food tourism networks: A comparative study. In: K. Pavlovich, & M. Akorrie (Eds), *Strategic alliances and collaborative partnerships – A case book* (pp. 258–268). Palmerston North: Dunmore Press.

Hall, C. M. (2004). Small firms and wine and food tourism in New Zealand: issues of collaboration, clusters and lifestyles. In: R. Thomas (Ed.), *Small firms in tourism: International perspectives* (pp. 167–181). Oxford: Elsevier.

Hall, C. M., Cambourne, B., Macionis, N., & Johnson, G. (1998). Wine tourism and network development in Australia and New Zealand: Review, establishment and prospects. *International Journal of Wine Marketing (special Australasian edition)*, 9(2/3), 5–31.

Hall, C. M., & Johnson, G. (1998), Wine and food tourism in New Zealand: difficulties in the creation of sustainable tourism business networks. In: D. Hall & L. O'Hanlon (Eds), *Rural tourism management: Sustainable options, conference proceedings*, Edinburgh: Scottish Agricultural College.

Hall, C. M., Johnson, G. R., & Mitchell, R. D. (2000). Wine tourism and regional development. In: C.M. Hall, E. Sharples, B. Cambourne, & N. Macionis (Eds), *Wine tourism around the world* (pp. 196–225). Oxford: Butterworth Heinemann.

Hall, C. M., & Mitchell, R.D. (2000). Wine tourism and rural restructuring and reimaging. *Mediterranean Thunderbird International Business Review Special Issue: Mediterranean Tourism in the Global Economy: Transition and Restructuring*. 42(4), 443–463.

Hall, C. M., & Mitchell, R. D. (2002). The tourist terroir of New Zealand wine: The importance of region in the wine tourism experience. In: A. Montanari, (Ed.), *Food and environment: Geographies of taste* (pp. 69–91). Rome: Societá Geografica Italiana.

Hawke's Bay Wine Country Tourism Association Inc. (2004). *About Hawke's Bay Wine Country Tourism Association Inc* (HBWTCA), http://www.hawkesbaynz.com/trade_media/about_hbt/hbw-cta/ [Accessed: 30 October 2004].

Johnson, G. (1998). *Wine tourism in New Zealand — A national survey of wineries 1997.* Department of Tourism, University of Otago, Dunedin. [Unpublished Diploma of Tourism dissertation].

Karafolas, S. (2005). Creating a non profit network of producers for the development of the local culture and local tourism: The case of wine roads of Northern Greece. In *ICA international research conference, the contribution of co-operatives to community culture.* ICA and Centre for Co-operative Studies, University College Cork, Cork.

Kearsley, G. (1998). Rural tourism in Otago and Southland, New Zealand. In: R. Butler, C. M. Hall, & J. Jenkins (Eds), *Tourism and recreation in rural areas* (pp. 81–95). Chichester: Wiley.

Leiper, N. (1990). Partial industrialization of tourism systems. *Annals of Tourism Research, 17*(4), 600–605.

McIntyre, A. (2005). Wine industry tapped for tourism drive. *The Marlborough Express,* 6 December 2005. http://www.stuff.co.nz/stuff/0,2106,3504093a7775,00.html [Accessed: 6 January 2006].

McRae-Williams, P. (2002). *Wine and regional tourism: Strengthening complementarity to facilitate regional development.* School of Business, University of Ballarat. [Unpublished].

McRae-Williams, P. (2004). Wine and tourism: Cluster complementarity and regional development. In: K. A. Smith, & C. Schott(Eds), *Proceedings of the New Zealand Tourism and Hospitality Research conference 2004,* 8–10 December 2004. Victoria University, Wellington, (pp. 237–245).

Meyer, D. (2004). *Tourism routes and gateways: Key issues for the development of tourism routes and gateways and their potential for Pro-Poor tourism,* overseas Development Institute, Durban. http://www.pptpilot.org.za/Routes/52Oreport.pdf [Accessed: 3 December 2005].

Ministry of Economic Development. (2003). *Regional partnerships programme review — background report.* Wellington: New Zealand Ministry of Economic Development.

Mitchell, R.D. (2004). *Scenery and chardonnay: An exploration of the New Zealand winery visitor experience,* University of Otago, Dunedin. [Unpublished doctorate].

Mitchell R. D., & Hall, C. M. (2000). Touristic terroir: The importance of region in the wine tourism experience. In *Proceedings of the 1st World Forum on Agritourism and Rural Tourism,* 17–27 September 2000, International Association of Experts in Agritourism and Rural Tourism, Perugia, Italy, (pp. 362–378).

Mitchell, R. D., & Hall, C. M. (2006). Wine tourism research: The state of play. *Tourism Review International, 9*(4), 307–332.

New Zealand Trade and Enterprise (NZTE). (2002). *Cluster building: A toolkit — a manual starting and developing local cluster in New Zealand,* New Zealand Trade and Enterprise, Wellington. http://www.nzte.govt.nz/common/files/cluster-builders-toolkit.pdf [Accessed: 30 October 2004].

New Zealand Trade and Enterprise (NZTE). (2004a). *History of New Zealand trade and enterprise.* http://www.nzte.govt.nz/section/11919.aspx [Accessed: 20 December 2005].

New Zealand Trade and Enterprise (NZTE). (2004b). *Major regional initiatives: Funding assistance.* http://www.nzte.govt.nz/section/11962.aspx [Accessed: 1 December 2005].

New Zealand Trade and Enterprise (NZTE). (2004c). *Tourism: A key sector for the New Zealand economy.* http://www.nzte.govt.nz/section/14196.aspx [Accessed: 1 December 2005].

New Zealand Trade and Enterprise (NZTE). (2005): *New Zealand Trade and Enterprise (NZTE) under the cluster development programme since February 2002 parliamentary question response.* Wellington: New Zealand Trade and Enterprise.

Nischalke, T., & Schöllmann, A. (2005). Regional development and regional innovation policy in New Zealand: Issues and tensions in a small remote country. *European Planning Studies, 13*(4), 559–578.

Oram, R. (2003). Clustering to compete, *unlimited,* vol. 53. http://idg.co.nz/unlimited.nsf/ [Accessed: 4 November 2005].

Oram, R. (2004). *Pinot pioneers — tales of determination and perseverance from Central Otago.* Auckland: New Holland Publishers.

Porter, M. E. (1990). *The competitive advantage of nations.* London: Macmillan.

Porter, M. E. (1998). *On competition.* Massachusetts: Harvard Business School Press.

Queenstown Lakes District Council. (2004). *Tourism in our council.* http://www.qldc.govt.nz/portal.asp?nextscreenid=201.102.101.101&categoryid=508&sessionx=41CEEF2B-0916-489B-86C0-A2C1DC9D0B80 [Accessed: 30 October 2004].

Schreiber, C. (2004). *The development of wine tourism networks: An exploratory case study into established networks and issues in Central Otago.* Department of Tourism, University of Otago, Dunedin. [Unpublished Diploma in Tourism dissertation].

Simpson, K., & Bretherton, P. (2004). Co-operative business practices in the competitive leisure destination: Lessons from the wine tourism industry in New Zealand. *Managing Leisure, 9,* 111–123.

Taylor, R. G., Woodall, S., Wandschneider, P., & Foltz, J. (2004). The demand for wine tourism in Canyon county, Idaho. *International Food and Agribusiness Management Review, 7*(4), 58–75.

Telfer, D. J. (2001a). From a wine tourism village to a regional wine route: An investigation of the competitive advantage of embedded clusters in Niagara, Canada. *Tourism Recreation Research, 26*(2), 23–33.

Telfer, D. J. (2001b). Strategic alliances along the Niagara wine route. *Tourism Management, 22*(1), 21–30.

Telfer, D. J., & Wall, G. (1996). Linkages between tourism and food production. *Annals of Tourism Research, 23*(3), 635–653.

West Coast Development Trust. (2005). *Tourism-based major regional initiative funding,* Press release. http://www.scoop.co.nz/stories/AK0512/S00093.htm [Accessed: 15 December 2005].

Wilkins, M., & Hall, C. M. (2001). An industry stakeholder SWOT analysis of wine tourism in the Okanagan Valley, British Columbia. *International Journal of Wine Marketing, 13*(3), 77–81.

Chapter 8

Networks: Comparing Community Experiences

Laila Gibson and Paul Lynch

Objectives

- This chapter explores the role of networks within a tourism cluster from the perspective of community involvement and participation.
- It suggests that there are a set of clearly identifiable benefits that are achieved through the networking process, which deliver gains to both the network's membership and its host community — these benefits are categorised as accruing from 'learning and exchange', enhanced 'business activity' and from the pursuit of 'community' values.
- It would be entirely inappropriate to simply claim that networking delivers a range of social and economic benefits, hence this chapter uses three case studies (from Guldriket and Jukkasjärvi, in Sweden, and from Leith in Scotland) to demonstrate the gains made by three distinctly different kinds of network formation.
- The chapter sets out the community background for each case study, and argues that this level of social understanding is imperative for any kind of network analysis.
- The comparison of the three case studies demonstrates that each circumstance is very different, and while not all have been successful, they have delivered substantial benefits for the development of local tourism destinations.
- One of the lessons apparent in this comparative analysis is the difficulty networks face in building linkages with local public sector development agencies, largely because their value sets are contradictory; nevertheless this examination of networks in practice demonstrates how local communities can find ways to interact and become engaged in the process of local development.

Micro-Clusters and Networks: The Growth of Tourism
Copyright © 2007 by Elsevier Ltd.
All rights of reproduction in any form reserved.
ISBN: 0-08-045096-2

Being part of a network often involves going through turbulent stages of formation, frustration, sacrifices and compromises. For its members, however, network participation can also mean making valued social contributions and creating an exciting tool that facilitates local tourism development. The question is then: How do you do it? Why do some networks succeed in contributing to local tourism development, while others stay frustrated and stagnant — or in a state of constant turbulent change?

This chapter, then, seeks to build on the principles and the experience noted in the earlier chapters, and seeks to provide more insight into some of the critical factors that determine the success of networks. This is done by drawing on case studies from Scotland and Sweden with comparisons of community experiences in rural and urban settings.[1]

Tourism Networks

While there has been interest in *business* networks for some time in the generic management literature, it is only more recently that the topic has received concerted attention in the specific context of tourism development (see reference list). Lynch, Halcro, Johns, and Buick (2000) undertook an analysis of tourism-related network literature and identified a range of benefits that networks contribute to building profitable tourism destinations. They categorised these according to *learning and exchange, business activity* and *community*. These outcomes and their associated dimensions are presented in Table 8.1.

Through learning and exchange between network participants benefits are leveraged that have the potential to be translated into positive business activity and community outcomes. In each of these categories it can be observed that there is a strong bias towards those benefits of a largely qualitative nature. This highlights a key issue in relation to the value of networks; there exists a lack of measured benefits from networks, in part, because many of the issues associated with network behaviour are qualitative and not easily quantified (Nilsson, Petersen, & Wanhill, 2005). Significant factors that have been attributed to the success of tourism networks have been identified by Morrison, Lynch, and Johns (2004), drawing on the work of Augustyn and Knowles (2000), Littlejohn, Foley, and Lennon (1996) and Morrison (1994, 1996). These are set out in Table 8.2 in the form of a checklist. Again, this indicates the dominant qualitative content, with network success dependent on social structures, relationships embeddedness and the competence of participants in the process of effective networking.

There are two reasons for the emphasis on *community* networks. The first is that tourism is connected to geographical places or communities with a social and cultural history that needs to be accounted for in any discussion of a tourism destination's development. This makes it very difficult to study tourism development at a local and regional level without being aware of, and taking into consideration, the relationship with the wider development of a society. In short, tourism has important political, economic and social dimensions, especially in rural areas, which stem not just from the fact that a destination draws visitors who spend money and so contribute to the local economy — a point that is well recognised by many analysts (see, e.g., Elbe, 2002; Karlsson, 1994; Müller, 1999; Hall, 2000).

---

[1] The cases are based on studies conducted during 1999–2001 within the research project 'Local and Regional Destination Development' at the European Tourism Research Institute (ETOUR), Östersund. See also Frisk (1999, 2000, 2003) and Gibson, Lynch, and Morrison (2005).

Table 8.1: Benefits of networks for building profitable tourism destinations.

Benefit category	Identified network benefits
Learning and exchange	Knowledge transfer Tourism education process Communication Development of new cultural values Accelerating speed of implementation of support agency initiatives Facilitation of development stage of small enterprises
Business activity	Co-operative activities, for example, marketing, purchasing, production Enhanced cross-referral Encouraging needs-based approaches, for example, staff development, policies Increased visitor numbers Best use of small enterprise and support agency resources Extension to visitor season Increased entrepreneurial activity Inter-trading within network Enhanced product quality and visitor experience Opportunities for business development interventions More repeat business
Community	Fostering common purpose and focus Community support for destination development Increases or reinvents a sense of community Engagement of small enterprises in destination development More income staying locally

Source: Adapted from Lynch et al. (2000).

The second reason is the complexity and multiplicity of tourism, which makes it difficult to distinguish separately from other kinds of phenomena and from other industries in modern societies (Urry, 1990). The complex nature of tourism includes all parts of society; private enterprises, public organisations and voluntary associations. Tourism community networks are therefore seen as broadly common *interest groups* with actors involved in tourism to varying degrees at a local or regional levels. Interest groups, in the context of social organisation can be defined as:

> An identifiable group of people who share common goals and values, who come together in a formal or informal organisation to influence the outcome of particular economic or social processes to deliver decisions in their favour (Michael, 2006, p. 109).

Table 8.2: Network success factor checklist.

Success factor	Description
Benefits	Learning and exchange translates into perceived and tangible commercial outcomes that provide social and economic gains within communities
Communication	Effective systems are in place that makes efficient use of business environments, social space and virtual cyber-space
Engagement	Comprehensive understanding, manipulation and management of a diverse set of member economic, social and psychological motivations
Inclusivity	Membership represents a healthy balance and interplay of public agencies, academic institutions, and the private sector as appropriate
Inter-organisational learning	Connects with a hub organisation, core participants and is stimulated by a supportive infrastructure of formal and informal mechanisms, ultimately translating into commercial benefits
Leadership	A combination of hub organisation and network champion play catalytic roles that are stimulated and supported as appropriate to the life cycle of the network
Objectives	Clearly identified, articulated and communicated
Purpose	Aims are linked to local, regional, national and international priorities that are able to transcend issues that may deflect the driving purpose, achieving commercial outcomes as appropriate
Resourcing	Continuity of sufficient financial, human and physical resources as the network starts-up and evolves
Structure	Fit for purpose, recognises the benefits of the creation of communities of learning involving inter-connecting of a multi-tiered pyramid of networks as appropriate, and is supported by key public sector organisations

Source: Morrison et al. (2002).

Successful tourism community networks are conceived to be those groups that have fulfilled the role of producing the kinds of benefits described previously in Table 8.1; thus making a *vital contribution* to the development of tourism in their particular community. It might be during a specific point in time or for a longer period, as this depends on the type and purpose of the network.

Another element in the study of community networks is the vital role that entrepreneurs in the private, public or voluntary sector play in starting up and working with those networks. The patterns that appear to be evolving from a range of research analyses in these fields seem to suggest that a core of 'entrepreneurial' key persons are crucial for tourism and community development to take place (see for example, Brulin & Nilson, 1997; Frisk, 2000, 2003; Gibson et al., 2005; Johannisson, 1988, 1997; Karlsson & Lönnbring, 2003; Philips, 1988).

A Comparison — Three Destinations as Communities

Three cases are considered here to illustrate three distinct types of networks that have achieved varying degrees of success. Each of these networks is presented and analysed below, but, in accord with the caveats noted earlier, each seeks to build some understanding of the nature of the local community as part of how they can be regarded as a tourism destination.

'Guldriket', Västerbotten County, Sweden

Västerbotten is a county situated in the North of Sweden, with an area of 59,300 km^2, nearly the same size as Scotland and Wales together. There are around 256,700 inhabitants, with approximately 72,000 living in the coastal municipality of Skellefteå. This local area, along with its three neighbouring municipalities of Lycksele, Malå and Norsjö, together form the tourism destination known as 'Guldriket' — which translated from Swedish loosely means the *Golden* Kingdom — reflecting the region's heritage in gold mining. The Lycksele municipality has around 12,800 residents and is situated inland in the centre of the region; between the mountains and the coast (www.lycksele.se). Malå is the smallest of these communities, with about 3,500 inhabitants, and is situated north of Lycksele (www.mala.se). Norsjö is located east of Malå, next to Skellefteå, and has a population of only 4,500 residents (www.norsjo.se).

The town of Skellefteå and the tourism area called 'Guldriket' are located in the so-called 'Skellefteå field', one of Europe's richest ore fields (www.guldriket.net). Apart from mining, people in the region have mainly earned their livelihoods out of forestry, farming, fishing and reindeer herding. Forestry still employs a large number of people and there is also an engineering industry in the region. Västerbotten county does not have a long tradition of tourism; although the tourism sector as an employer has become increasingly important in recent years (www.mala.se; www.skelleftea.se; www.norsjo.se; www.vasterbotten.se). The exception is the town of Lycksele which, due to its central location, has been a meeting place for centuries for Norwegian, Swedish and Finnish people and, in particular, the people from the southern part of the Samic region. Over the last decade, investments in business tourism in terms of conferences, congresses and other events have also been made in Skellefteå. Some nature-based tourism, including fishing, canoeing and skiing, exists as well. However, it is the investments and focus on tourism clearly connected to mining and other geological activities that make this area a bit different from many others in northern Sweden.

Leith, Edinburgh, Midlothian County, Scotland

This locality is part of the waterfront area that marks the northern boundaries of Edinburgh. Edinburgh is the administrative capital of Scotland with a population of approximately 450,000 people, of whom nearly 30,000 live in Leith. Edinburgh is situated in the county of Lothian, where 15% of Scotland's population live although the area is no more than 2% of Scotland's land area (www.scottish-enterprise.com). Edinburgh has an area of approximately 160 km^2, but Leith is only about 10 km^2.

Leith was once an important port and gateway to Scotland, from the late 13th century until the beginning of the 18th century when The Clyde, Glasgow, became more significant due to its deeper waters and the increasing trade with North America. Apart from trade, shipbuilding was also a major industry for Leith, but the last shipyard was closed in 1983. Nevertheless, it remains the fifth biggest port in the UK, with increasing numbers of cargo vessels and cruise ships arriving. Besides the port, there are also other industries and businesses that have replaced the old ones, such as graphic design computer software, retailing, restaurants and galleries. For example, a new large shopping centre has recently opened where one of the old docks used to be. This and the permanently moored former Royal Yacht 'Britannia' are now the main visitor attractions for Leith.

Leith has undergone periods of social dislocation, and it is only in the last 10 years that the major changes, both tangible and social, have begun to have an impact, with new businesses and professionals moving there and new houses and offices being built. This development involves issues regarding restoration of buildings, cleaning up of the 'Water of Leith', improvements to its streets and streetscapes and efforts to resolve its transport problems. Leith is now part of a waterfront regeneration scheme and is gaining a reputation as an interesting tourist destination. Even though people have met at this sometimes thriving port for centuries, Leith cannot be said to have been a tourism destination for very long. It was only a few years ago since the area was included on Edinburgh tourist maps for example. One explanation, apart from the lack of 'tourism infrastructure' is the reputation of Leith as being a rather *rough* or socially undesirable area. Despite this past, Leith has however a tradition of welcoming people into its community and that is what they are trying to build on with today's tourism developments.

Jukkasjärvi, Kiruna, Norrbotten County, Sweden

Kiruna is the northernmost and largest municipality in Sweden. It has an area that is half the size of Switzerland, about 20,000 km^2. Kiruna is situated in the county of Norrbotten, which borders both Norway and Finland, and includes the highest mountain in Sweden, called Kebnekaise, 2117 m. There are around 23,300 inhabitants in the municipality, with about 80% living within the town of Kiruna itself (www.kommun.kiruna.se).

The region has developed largely around the mining of iron ore. The first mine opened in 1647 and, as the industry subsequently developed, it has left its mark on the daily life of Kiruna ever since. The town, Kiruna, is however much younger and celebrated its 100-year jubilee during 2000. The first church was also built in the 17th century, in the village of Jukkasjärvi, situated 17 km outside Kiruna by the Torne river. Jukkasjärvi is called 'Cohkiras' in Samic language, which means 'meeting place'. This village of around 800 people and about 600 dogs (for dog sledding!) has been a royal market place since the 14th century, but has an even longer history as an important place on the trade route between Russia and the Norwegian coast. The area today comprises a social mixture of Samic people, Swedish people and people with a Finnish-influenced culture (www.kommun.kiruna.se). Just as the cultural mix of Kiruna is based on three parts, so is its business life. While the mines laid the foundation for its industrial business sector, over the last 20 years the dependence on mining has been complemented by the emergence of two other industries: environmental and space sciences and a services industry, with tourism as an important component.

Tourism is an important industry for Kiruna in general and for Jukkasjärvi in particular and the area is a crucial destination within the region. The northern location attracts tourists, with the somewhat extreme climate, with darkness, snow and northern lights during the winter and midnight sun during the summer. Tourism really started at the end of the 19th century, when the Swedish Touring Club, a voluntary association founded in 1885, among other things built the first tourist mountain stations. Nowadays, the main attraction in this area is the famous 'ICEHOTEL' — located in Jukkasjärvi, and built of ice and snow (www.icehotel.com). This facility, which was constructed for the first time more than 20 years ago, has since gained an international reputation and become an attraction in itself.

Comparing Destinations

These communities have several characteristics in common. For example, they have long histories as meeting and trading places; *Leith* as a harbour has seen people from many countries coming and going, and *Lycksele* in Västerbotten and *Jukkasjärvi* in Norrbotten have served as Nordic trading places for centuries. They are all also destinations on the periphery of Europe, yet not too difficult to access for the mass markets. However, for the same reason, they are unlikely to be 'transient' destinations that people travel through in order to get to somewhere else, and, consequently, are less likely to be chosen as stopovers by potential visitors. Moreover, these places are located on the periphery of *northern* Europe, which suggests that they are likely to be perceived by the majority of the world's potential tourists as having a cold and wet (in the case of Leith) and dark (in the case of Västerbotten and Norrbotten) environment. This is not very far from the reality; hence, the challenge for these destinations is how to turn these conditions into some perception of a unique opportunity, and perhaps, an even more difficult challenge, of how to turn these weather conditions into a business opportunity.

In recent times, there has been a shift from traditional ways of making a living in these communities to an increased focus on the tourism industry. The shipping and shipbuilding industry in Leith has steadily declined over the last century, but the retail, hospitality and tourism sectors have grown rapidly over the last two decades. The foresting industry in the county of Västerbotten has declined substantially since the 1950s, while the demand for and the supply of nature-based tourism and outdoor recreation has increased. People living in Jukkasjärvi and its surrounding communities in the county of Norrbotten have been dependent on the mining industry, in combination with reindeer herding, fishing and hunting; but, again, the more difficult conditions and competition within these fields has led to a booming tourism industry, based on collaborating with the environmental and space science institutes located in the area and on the utilisation of traditional skills in fishing, hunting, etc. to attract visitors.

Tourism Community Networks in Scotland and Sweden

Guldriket

The *Guldriket* — or Golden Kingdom — is a *formal* network (see Chapter 5) at a geographical destination within the county of Västerbotten, as well as being a 'brand' label to market the attractions within the area. It is a network that aims to create a brand that represents good quality and establish the basis for a long-term, sustainable local and regional tourism industry.

In the late 1980s, the local community considered how it might go about protecting the cultural and historical heritage of Västerbotten, given the extent of its mining and geological history. The brand identity of Guldriket was chosen and launched in June 1993. It is now based on seven main attractions, supplemented with other additional features and services. The main attractions are

- Adak — a renovated mining community cinema from the 1940s, which conducts an annual film festival.
- Boliden — one of the world's largest gold mines, with a museum and visitor centre.
- Kristineberg — a mine offering tours, including a unique underground church.
- Malå Geomuseum — a newly built geological museum.
- Rönnskär — a folk museum of the daily life of gold miners.
- Varuträsk — a mineral park of international status.
- Örträsk — the world's longest cable car journey.

The *Guldriket's* complementing products and tourism services include, for example, fishing, hunting and other nature-based tourism activities, spa and health facilities; arts and crafts; film festivals and a range of Samic cultural experiences. The facilities operated by the network's members are also used for conferences, concerts, parties and other events.

Initially, Guldriket operated as an *informal* network of loosely connected volunteers. During 2000, however, the collaboration became well established and the association now known as *Guldriket* was formalised: it then had 19 members, of which about half were private businesses and the rest public organisations or voluntary associations. Up until 2003, around €3.8 million had been invested in the different attractions to make them suitable as tourist facilities; e.g., converting old mines to visitor centres and the provision of exhibition space. Apart from private investment, money has been provided through the European Union's structural funds, the County council, other regional agencies and the four local councils involved.

Today, it is supported as a European Union project, but the aim is for each of the attractions to be independent or profit making, but this requires further investments in attractions, the development of clear growth strategies and an increased knowledge within the organisation of Guldriket. The network has therefore been focusing on marketing, sales, booking and the future form of Guldriket. In recent years, it has also extended its co-operation with other networks and destinations in the vicinity to cement its market position.

This network has developed rapidly over the past five years. At the end of the 1990s, they were still a semi-formal group of attractions with a rather basic website giving general information about the various attractions, which were fewer then than they are today. The network has since become more formalised, a legal association has been created, it has achieved European Union project status, and has attracted financial and other support from a variety of public organisations. *Guldriket* now provides a more sophisticated internet service, offering accommodation bookings, package trips, virtual tours and a brochure ordering service (www.guldriket.com), and has increased its marketing efforts, through for example local and regional radio. The number of attractions and other businesses involved has doubled in five years and there are activities all year round, although summer is still the peak season. There is also an intranet for the existing members, with an open invitation for potential members to join.

One of the strengths of this network is that its participants have a common theme to gather around. This has led to the creation of a somewhat different and in some ways unique product, compared to many of the competing destinations in the northern regions of Scandinavia — particularly for those visitors who seek to combine tourism with research and education about mining, minerals, geology, etc. Together, with other networks in the area, e.g., Ostriket ('Cheese Kingdom'), they can provide excellent excursions for schools as well as for business visitors and for the more curious tourists. The network has also received other forms of non-pecuniary support from public organisations, sometimes in the form of time from leading individuals to be members of the board or in other forms of organisational effort, which gives further legitimacy to the network's activities. Once again, in line with the findings from studies in many similar circumstances, it is the enthusiasm and interest of the key people running some of the attractions, e.g., Adak and Varuträsk, which has made it possible to turn these facilities into tourism success stories.

Nevertheless, the *Guldriket* network still faces some difficulties — the *barriers* referred to in Chapter 7. First, the public administrative system, or, more accurately its consequential political influence, appears to strongly impact on the network. Given that there are four municipal administrations involved, this seemingly causes the focus to steer towards structural issues and imperatives rather than to an action-oriented approach. Second, some of the key attractions are run by voluntary associations, but these are dependent on the enthusiasm and energy of their current contributors, but from the network's position there needs to be contingency plans in place when these key individuals are no longer able to contribute, or contribute to the same extent. Third, the network's mixture of public, private and voluntary organisations continues to expose difficulties in collaboration as they have different reasons and motivations for their participation. Finally, the future growth of *Guldriket* is inevitably confronted by its rather specialised market position, which makes its future expansion more difficult to achieve in an efficient way: in short, the unique nature of the *Guldriket* product makes it harder to attract the 'traditional' tourism market, in terms of families, general holiday makers and day trippers.

Leith Initiatives for Tourism

In studies conducted by Lynch and Gibson in 2001 and 2004, the 'Leith Initiatives for Tourism' (LIFT) was identified as a *semi-formal* network. The network was created in 1999. Like many such initiatives, its origins are curiously accidental: its two female initiators, having trained staff for the former Royal Yacht 'Britannia', invited interested people to a discussion session regarding the future development of tourism in Leith and the regeneration of north Edinburgh. From this beginning, a group emerged who started to hold regular monthly meetings. These were open to everyone interested in tourism development and, while in the beginning the initiators used their own networks and contacts to engage people to attend the meetings, the network quickly became an entity in its own right.

The mission statement for LIFT presents it as a voluntary partnership with the aim to develop Leith, both in social and tourism-related terms (minutes from LIFT meeting, 2001). The founders were initially focussed on a core ethos of networking, co-operation and the pursuit of social goals, and not just on tourism development; but from a bottom-up perspective that sought to include the local community. Initially, the network did not have a formal membership; interested persons could in theory come and go as they pleased. In reality, there were approximately 110 people on LIFT's mailing list, representing about 70 private, public and voluntary organisations. Around 30 of these were identifiable as tourism-related businesses, such as restaurants, hotels and guiding services. Among the people on the mailing list, there was a committed core group of about 30–40 persons who were involved from the beginning of the network. Of these, there were 10 or so members who formed the Board of LIFT, who necessarily exercised a somewhat higher degree of responsibility and involvement in its activities.

In the beginning, LIFT focussed on networking or social activities as well as marketing actions, such as: 'familiarisation trips', a 'waterfront festival' and various 'social drinks and networking events'. The marketing activities have included exercises for example to put Leith on the tourist maps of Edinburgh, public presentations, articles in the local press and the like. A website was also established that served for some years as a gateway for Leith, providing information about accommodation, restaurants, events, attractions and its local history.

Three years after its inception, the network sought to make some crucial changes to the way it operated. They wanted to reflect on their network, enhance its focus and refine its structure (chairman, board, action plan, etc.), and they saw a need to seek out some level of core funding in order to continue their work. They also started working in groups around projects more so than they had in the beginning when the group was smaller and they were doing most things together. After reconstructing themselves and as part of their new, more formalised way of working, they secured funding, created an action plan for 2002 and appointed a new board of management. The following year, however, debates recurred regarding the network's future direction and it was again restructured, but this time as a private company, LIFT Ltd, with a more commercially focused chairperson and initial funding from local public agencies. Its primary aim now became unambiguously the development of small tourism businesses in Leith, and one of its first goals was to develop a Tourism Action Plan.

As an action-oriented network, as was noted earlier, the LIFT network delivered a number of positive outcomes during the early years of its existence; and, perhaps the most important of these was its success in bringing together a range of actors from the public sector, voluntary organisations, business interests and other individuals concerned with the community's development. These actions were possible through the many strengths of LIFT, which the researchers suggested included:

- The existence of a few very communicative initiators.
- The close geographical proximity of its membership.
- The diverse social mix of people from Leith and from outside the area.
- The availability of initial financing, providing some people with the ability to dedicate some time to the network.
- The mixture of types of organisations, giving vitality and understanding for each other.
- A relatively open culture and atmosphere.
- The low degree of structure and a clear focus on actions.
- The original initiatives and ideas were derived from the bottom-up — a 'grass-roots' level of involvement driven by the needs of community participants.

One of the problems for the longevity of LIFT lay in its structure, where the network was dependent on the initiators for its formation but there was no planning for transferring the knowledge and contacts the key individuals had gained over the years. This created a dilemma, as contacts are the crucial element for building a network but they are often personal and hard to sustain without the individuals who first establish them (see, e.g., Elbe, 2002). Furthermore, the mixture of private, public and voluntary organisations involved, and their confusing focus on both tourism business and community development, became too complex over time. With hindsight, this appears to have been the cause of disagreements about the aims of the network and its lack of focus, which affected the goals and actions taken to reach them.

As has been noted in other studies, in order to change the image and identity of a local area, visible results are critical (Pettersson, 1999). This is difficult for organisations to accomplish in the beginning when there often is a lack of resources. It must be stressed, however, that achieving these early outcomes is very important in order to get the majority of a local community to recognise the network and what it does. Given the short time that the network existed in its initial form, LIFT made vital contributions at a crucial time in Leith's development.

Jukkasjärvi

The story concerning the Jukkasjärvi network was uncovered in a research exercise by Laila Gibson in 2000 and 2005. Jukkasjärvi and its surrounding area form a tourism destination that is very much centred on a leading enterprise and an *informal* network based on a few key entrepreneurs. Following the decline of the mining and forestry industry in the 1970s, a few enterprising people started to offer a range of nature-based tourism packages and outdoor recreation activities, such as rafting, fishing, hunting, guiding, etc. This business developed through the 1980s with a focus on the summer months. In 1983, the local heritage trust, where these entrepreneurs were active members, founded the company *Jukkas AB* to further develop the region's tourism potential. The company was restructured in the early 1990s as a private enterprise with nine partners who are still active within the business.

The year 1989 was important for tourism in the area. First, an exhibition of ice art and sculptures was held by a visiting group of Japanese ice artists, and this was followed by another exhibition by a French artist, for which an igloo — the *Artic Hall* — was built. From that moment, the focus started to shift from summer activities in favour of winter as the potential peak tourism season. Given that Jukkasjärvi is situated away from the mountain ski sites, the local community was initially quite sceptical. Fifteen years on, the company is now called ICEHOTEL AB and has developed from a small igloo to offering the world's largest ice hotel of 5000 m², built with 30,000 tonnes of snow and 4,000 tonnes of ice. The development includes a shop, restaurant, ice art exhibitions, ice bar and ice church and now ranks as one of the leading attractions in Scandinavia. Its success has made the development of several other tourism businesses possible within the surrounding area. The businesses within this destination mostly work in informal networks with the ICEHOTEL AB as the hub, while the independent businesses provide a range of complementary activities, such as dogsledding, rafting and snowmobile excursions as subcontractors.

Other groups also form part of the network surrounding the ICEHOTEL. There are for example Samic people with tourism businesses based on their own culture; the local church, which performs weddings in the ICEHOTEL, and the science centres and universities which act as excursion places for guests at the hotel and vice versa. The ICEHOTEL needs to be rebuilt every year (ice melts!) and these works involve local artists, engineers and construction workers, while local artists are also engaged in an exhibition programme throughout the season. The other complementary tourism businesses mainly use the locality's existing resources, such as its mines, research stations or nature itself. Destination development in this area has to a large extent been based on the development of innovative ideas that have been turned into saleable products, targeting new and niche markets. In short, they have used the existing physical resources and turned some of the region's characteristics features (such as cold, darkness, snow, etc.) into something that is more positive and attractive for consumers.

The present structure of the destination allows it to have a high degree of flexibility: temporal, functional and to some extent spatial (Hjalager, 1999). In other words, the businesses are able and willing to arrange their product according to the visitors' wishes. They also work independently with smaller groups of guests and then work jointly when a large group of visitors comes. This flexibility is possible because the business operators know each other and can optimise their capacity by working through co-ordinating centre at the ICEHOTEL. This way of working may also be seen as an example of *co-operative competition*, which was referred to in Chapter 4 and, as a conceptual explanation, seems to particularly suit the circumstances of the small businesses situated in this area.

Once again, the main strength identified in this network appears to rest in the enthusiasm of the people who make up its membership. The majority of the people involved in tourism in the area have had a long history together and been through a 'collective learning process'. They have thus built up *trust* and forms of working together. The entrepreneurs in Jukkasjärvi are also seen as pioneers and role models for other destinations in the northern hemisphere that want to develop their tourism products for a winter season. Another strength, of course, is that the ICEHOTEL, and the group of 'partners' who established it, are in a strong position: the venture is financially secure and has an extensive worldwide public relations function, which gives them still further means to realise their visions and ideas to continue developing the product. Ironically, in this particular case, the climate is a natural strength for the destination, making it possible to build the hotel and offer a distinct and different set of activities.

Nevertheless, the network is not without its risks. The company who initially introduced the concept of the ICEHOTEL was effectively founded by only one of the 'partners', who has been very influential and is still very active in the business. This makes the enterprise, and thus the network, vulnerable as it is based on personal contacts and an established way of working. At some point, when the founder is no longer able to participate as actively, this is likely to create substantial changes to the concept. The informal network is very flexible and allows a degree of independence for its members, but it remains dependent on the same people staying in the group. Its test will come as time progresses and change occurs.

Benefits and Implications

Arguably, there are three main types of benefits inherent in the formation of tourism networks (described previously in Table 8.1). These are explored here in the context of the three case studies that have been presented above.

Learning and Exchange

There are several prominent elements of the *learning and exchange* process in *Guldriket*. First, there has been increased communication between the operators of attractions across local municipality borders, helped by the website and an Intranet. The network has also contributed to the development of new cultural values, including an enhanced appreciation of the region's industrial heritage. The provision of some financial support from public agencies has also facilitated the development of attractions and provided the infrastructure to support the establishment of small enterprises.

In *Leith*, there is further evidence of *knowledge transfer* through visits to LIFT members' businesses and through participation in a tourism education process through e-commerce seminars and the like. Considerable efforts have been made at developing new, or at least much stronger, cultural values of 'co-opetition' (see Chapter 4). Collectively, these benefits can be seen to have contributed to facilitating the development of small enterprise members. While a number of local support agencies have sought to include LIFT in particular roles, there is little evidence that they have acted upon them, but this would seem to be due to the organisation's desire to initiate and own the ideas for action themselves. From the point of view of the network's members, however, LIFT's own initiatives might be said to have pre-empted those of the public support agencies; for example, LIFT initiated and developed a tourism map and set up a website, and so raised the profile of Leith more quickly than the agencies had planned or could have done themselves.

The flexibility of the *Jukkasjärvi* network suggests that learning played a large part in its development. The destination and the businesses involved have gone through difficult periods where they have learnt by sharing their experiences with each other. Much of the learning has been through experiences from the past — trial and error — combined with a continuous dialogue between the groups membership. This, perhaps, is a practical example of the theoretical concept of 'dialogue learning' (Beeby & Booth, 2000) or 'collective innovation and learning' (Mitra, 2000; Nilsson, 2000). For example, the tacit knowledge held by the ice sculptors, or the Samic people, has been combined successfully with the explicit strategic knowledge about issues and processes like marketing, business and packaging held by the managers of the ICEHOTEL.

Business Activity

Although the *Guldriket* study did not specifically measure any quantitative benefits from business activities, a range of qualitative benefits is evident. To illustrate, there has occurred a range of co-operative activities, including the development of packaging of trips, marketing and booking via the website, that have provided the catalyst for further increased entrepreneurial activity. The outcomes are visible in terms of an extension of the visitor season and an increased number of visitors through a stronger focus on the corporate market and a capacity to offer a wider range of activities.

Direct measures of business activity benefits were not employed in the study of LIFT either. Although some restaurants reported increasing economic returns during the period of LIFT's activities, most businesses found it difficult to give immediate examples of commercial gains that were attributable to their participation in the network. Rather, they suggested that the benefits were more in terms of the insights they gained into the connections between tourism and community development, and how to leverage those advantages.

In *Jukkasjärvi*, the key benefits to business activity stem from establishing the routines for joint packaging, booking and marketing with the ICEHOTEL as its hub. The network's membership demonstrates a needs-based approach, where an *ad hoc*, flexible form of co-operation allows them to collaborate to deliver services for larger groups of visitors, but to act individually at other times. The focus on winter products has extended the tourism season and significantly increased the number of visitors over the years, given that there still is some activity in the summer season. Various groups in the network (artists, constructors, hospitality and activity businesses, science, etc.) are also continuously enhancing the quality of the region's product and the visitor's experience in terms of developing new, complementary elements to the core activities.

Community

Members involved in the *Guldriket* network have contributed to a reinvented sense of community, in terms of an increased awareness, knowledge and pride in the industrial heritage of the area. This has been made possible largely through the engagement of small enterprises, voluntary associations and the key representatives of public agencies taking an interest in the revival of the traditional mining community, and, as a community group, finding ways to turn this heritage into a range of sustainable business opportunities.

Fostering a stronger sense of common purpose around the concept of the local community was integral to the original purpose for the formation of LIFT. Engagement of the community in destination development was its primary goal. One could therefore say that a sense of community has been increased, or perhaps recreated. Even if no other criteria are applied, one of LIFT's successes has been the engagement of small enterprises in the development of Leith as a destination.

Gathering around a *common purpose* has also been a central part of the network's achievements in developing the destination of Jukkasjärvi. It has taken many years of positive outcomes to build an understanding within the local community of the benefits to be gained from shifting the tourism focus from a summer season to a winter one. The informal network of enterprises and other actors in the area has also contributed to an increased sense of community identity, by for example encouraging collaboration between the diverse cultural and ethnically different Samic and other populations. For Jukkasjärvi, there is an added advantage for the community, as the income earned from tourism stays largely within the local economy because the majority of enterprises and the services they use are owned by local residents.

Implications for Community Management

One of the observations for community planning and development, which can be drawn from these three illustrations of networks in practice, is that they might well follow an identifiable *life cycle*. In this sense, a network can be seen as a social arrangement that goes through a series of processes or transitions from its formation (or start-up), through a period of growth and, if it is to succeed, of reinvention. Morrison, Lynch, and Johns (2002) have proposed such a model (detailed in Table 8.3) but, its categorisations should be seen as organic rather than as implicit or fixed. The model seems to fit remarkably well with the developmental stages of the Guldriket, LIFT and Jukkasjärvi and provides insights into the analysis of their growth phases. The need for reinvention is still not apparent in the

Table 8.3: Business network life cycle model.

	Start-up	**Growth**	**Reinvention**
Benefits	Conceptual benefits of membership	Demonstrable achievements of network and valued benefits of membership	Ongoing achievements of network and valued benefits through membership
Core	Hub organisation/network entrepreneur	Broader membership	Reinvigorated membership
Membership	Enthusiast and enlisted members	Broader membership	Enlarged membership
Objectives	Fuzzy — idealistic	Concrete	Revised
Resourcing	Goodwill or core funding	Attracting resources	Sustainable resourcing

Source: Morrison et al. (2002).

Swedish examples, but, in the case of LIFT, the model does not convey the substantive tensions that underlay the reality of that network's evolution — the compromises, especially to community values, that had to be reached, or the arguably less inclusive nature of the network that has since arisen.

Despite the tentative focus of these kinds of networks, and difficulties in their working, they may well contribute to the development of a locality and to the businesses within the given area. Differences and multiplicity in many cases spur development (Kuhn, 1996; Törnqvist, 1990). They create arenas for meetings and discussions among a variety of organisations and persons, as well as a range of other learning and exchange, business and community benefits.

Arguably, however, the evidence from the three case studies might suggest that the level of initial funding is critical to a network's formation and survival. The realisation of the Guldriket network was not possible without funding from private and public organisations, and the case history for LIFT suggests that the funding received tended to be too little, too late, in that it missed the most creative start-up phase, when membership was at its highest, most inclusive and most enthusiastic. On the other hand, the relatively strong financial position of entrepreneurs who established the Jukkasjärvi network allowed them to develop more independently.

One might wonder how successful an organic network such as LIFT might have been if it had received some resourcing at an earlier stage, along with some guidance on how to manage such a network to a level of economic independence. The timing of financial support emerges from these comparative studies as an important lesson: early stage support to the community networkers appears to be desirable, or even a precondition, if the full benefits are to be realised. The difficulty of arguing a case for financial support from the public sector, in terms that might be acceptable to local development agencies, suggests a need for measurable network performance indicators. A clearly relevant set of such indicators would permit the appropriate local development authorities to co-operate with emerging networks, and take other supporting actions to facilitate their growth in a more transparent and timely manner than is now the case.

One proposal along these lines has been made by Morrison et al. (2002), and is described further in Table 8.4: it covers issues including membership, performance benchmarks and the community. The existence of *success measures* for a network could provide public administrators with an objective basis for the provision of funding, but as the objective remains local economic development, it would be appropriate to include indicators that relate to increased job opportunities and to development of the physical environment — to focus on outcomes that appeal to both community and commercial audiences. In Scotland, the national enterprise responsible for economic development has now introduced an 'innovation toolkit' for businesses working together and which includes the possibility of securing early stage funding to support the formation of projects involving business networks (Scottish Enterprise Innovation Toolkit, 2004). One of the problems, of course, as is apparent from the three case studies examined here, is that the requirements placed on public development agencies stem from the needs of governance and administration, which can be quite separate from the needs of private companies, which in turn can be quite separate from the social needs that some community-based voluntary associations seek to pursue. In practice, these 'separate worlds' (Frisk, 1999, 2003) can make it very

Table 8.4: Success Indicators for Business Networks.

	Indicator
Learning and exchange	• Regular sampling of members' views on network benefits and efficiency • Collaboration between private, public and voluntary groups • Product development based on social and cultural capital and heritage • Regular informal and/or formal communication between actors • Support of key enterprising people, in particular in initial stages
Business activity	• Additional income generated and retained within communities • Evidence of extended visitor season • Evidence of market development, innovation and new product development • Evidence of a resource plan • Increased numbers of business start-ups • Increased repeat business • Increased visitor numbers • Leverage of resources that could not have been achieved without the network • Regular monitoring of business activity • Regular sampling of members' views on network benefits
Community	• Membership numbers • Organisational and sectoral analysis of membership • Regular sampling of members' views on network membership • Network conformity and contribution to social and ethical business policies

Source: Morrison et al. (2002).

difficult for public support agencies to comprehend the operations of a network that is a composite of such mixed values, and perhaps more so when community values are strongly weighted. The consequence, then, is that any suggested set of performance indicators needs to reflect community development goals and not just those that lead to commercial development goals (Swarbrooke, 1999). There are some cases where public development agencies have moved in this direction, as for example with '*Highlands and Islands Enterprise*', Scotland, but in general there are few illustrations to demonstrate that these agencies understand how best to work with such mixed organisations.

In summary, it might be noted that the three network case studies have demonstrated that each was quite effective in delivering the kinds of benefits that the theory suggests ought to arise from these forms of association: learning and exchange, business activity and community. The *learning* benefits for the network members and their host communities were apparent in each case, although the evidence of accelerating support agency initiatives is somewhat absent. However, the networks presented here were found to have raised the profile of each local destination, and to have done so in relatively short periods of time. The evidence from the case studies in Sweden, and perhaps somewhat indirectly for Leith, also indicates that the networking processes contributed to a level of increased economic activity for businesses arising from an increased level of tourism activity. The main business benefits, however, are perceived to be long term and of a non-tangible nature. Importantly, the case studies clearly indicate that the networks have been relatively successful in delivering community benefits, at least in the short term, but equally they have each identified some deficiencies in the networks' capacity to communicate effectively with key public sector stakeholders.

References

Augustyn, M., & Knowles, T. (2000). Performance of tourism partnerships: A focus on York. *Tourism Management, 21*(4), 341–351.

Beeby, M., & Booth, C. (2000). Networks and inter-organisational learning: A critical review. *The Learning Organisation, 7*(2), 75–88.

Brulin, G., & Nilson, M. (Eds.) (1997). *Identiprenörskap — Företagande med Regionalt Ursprung*. Rapport från NUTEK 1997:22, Stockholm.

Elbe, J. (2002). *Utveckling av Turistdestinationer Genom Samarbete*. Doctoral thesis no. 96, Företagsekonomiska Institutionen, Uppsala University.

Frisk, L. (1999). Skilda världar — om samarbete inom lokal och regional destinationsutveckling. *Forskarforum 1999*, Lokal och regional utveckling, 16–17 November, Östersund.

Frisk, L. (2000). Mission impossible? — Industrial development centres for tourism. 9th Nordic Tourism Research Conference, 12–14 October, Research Centre of Bornholm, Nexø, Denmark.

Frisk, L (2003). Samarbete inom lokal destinationsutveckling. In: Larson, M. (Ed.), *Svensk Turismforskning — En Tvärvetenskaplig Antologi om Turister, Turistdestinationer och Turismorganisationer*. ETOUR V 2003:13, Östersund.

Gibson, L., Lynch, P. A., & Morrison, A. (2005). The local destination tourism network: Development issues. *Tourism and Hospitality Planning & Development, 2*(2) 87–99.

Hall, C. M. (2000). *Tourism planning: Policies, processes and relationships*. Singapore: Prentice-Hall.

Hjalager, A-M. (1999): Tourism destinations and the concept of industrial districts. ERSA Conference, August 1999, Dublin.

Johannisson, B. (1988). Images of the entrepreneurial spirit — Swedish experiences. *Rapport Ser.1 Ekonomi och politik 19*, Högskolan i Växjö.

Johannisson, B. (1997). Organizational networks and innovation. In: M. Zineldin (Ed.), *Strategic relationship management: A multi-dimensional perspective*. Stockholm: Almqvist & Wiksell.

Karlsson, S-E. (1994). *Natur och Kultur som Turistiska Produkter: En Början till en Sociologisk Analys*. Research report 94:11, University of Karlstad [Doctoral Thesis].

Karlsson, S-E., & Lönnbring, G. (2003). Turismföretagarens livsstil och livsform. In: Larson, M. (Ed.), *Svensk Turismforskning — En Tvärvetenskaplig Antologi om Turister, Turistdestinationer och Turismorganisationer*, ETOUR V 2003:13, Östersund.

Kuhn, T. S. (1996). *The structure of scientific revolutions.* Chicago: University of Chicago Press.

Littlejohn, D., Foley, M., & Lennon, J. (1996). The potential of accommodation consortia in the Highlands and Islands of Scotland. *Proceedings of IAHMS Spring Symposium,* Leeds Metropolitan University, Leeds (pp. 55–66).

Lynch, P. (2000). Networking in the homestay sector. *The Services Industries Journal, 20*(3) 95–116.

Lynch, P. A., Halcro, K., Johns, N., & Buick, I. (2000). Developing small business networks to build profitable tourist destinations. *Destination Development Conference,* 13–14 September, Östersund.

Michael, E. J. (2006). *Public policy — the competitive framework.* Melbourne: Oxford University Press.

Mitra, J. (2000). Making connections: Innovations and collective learning in small businesses. *Education and Training, 42*(4/5) 228–236.

Morrison, A. (1994). Small tourism business: Product distribution system. *Proceedings of 3rd CHME Annual Hospitality Research Conference,* Napier University, Edinburgh.

Morrison, A. (1996). Marketing strategic alliances: The small hotel firm. *Proceedings of IAHMS Spring Symposium,* Leeds Metropolitan University, Leeds.

Morrison, A., Lynch, P. A., & Johns, N. (2002). *International networks — scoping study.* Report for Scottish Enterprise, Scottish Hotel School, University of Strathclyde, Glasgow.

Morrison, A., Lynch, P. A., & Johns, N. (2004). International tourism networks. *International Journal of Contemporary Hospitality Management, 16*(3) 197–202.

Müller, D. K. (1999). *German second home owners in Sweden: On the internationalization of the countryside.* Umeå: The Department for Human Geography & ETOUR.

Nilsson, P-Å. (2000). Forms for transmission of different types of knowledge within small scale business in peripheral areas. The Arjeplog case. *9th Nordic Tourism Research Conference,* 12–14 October 2000, Research Centre of Bornholm, Nexø.

Nilsson, P. A., Petersen, T., & Wanhill, S. (2005). Public support for tourism SMEs in peripheral areas: The Arjeplog Project, Northern Sweden. *The Services Industries Journal, 25*(4) 579–599.

Pettersson, M. (1999). *Förtroende i samverkan: en studie av småföretagare i ett regionalt utvecklingsprojekt.* Thesis no. FiF-a26, University of Linköping.

Philips, Å. (1988). *En studie av aktörsskap i arbetsorganisatoriskt utvecklingsarbete.* Doktorsavhandling, Stockholm: Handelshögskolan.

Scottish Enterprise Innovation Toolkit. (2004). www.scotexchange.net/business development/innovation_2004-2/innovation_toolkit/, accessed 27 October 2005.

Scottish Executive. (2001). A smart successful scotland: Ambitions for the enterprise networks (pp. 1–24). http://www.scotland.gov.uk/library3/enterprise/smart-successful-scotland.pdf, accessed 31 January 2006.

Swarbrooke, J. (1999). *Sustainable tourism management.* Wallingford: CABI.

Törnqvist, G. (1990). Det upplösta rummet: begrepp och teoretiska ansatser inom geografin. In: A. Karlqvist (Ed.), *Nätverk: teorier och begrepp inom samhällsvetenskapen.* Värnamo, Fälths Tryckeri.

Urry, J. (1990). *The tourist gaze: Leisure and travel in contemporary societies.* London: Sage.

Websites

www.edinburgh.gov.uk, accessed 31 October 2005.

www.guldriket.com, accessed 8 September 2005.

www.icehotel.com, accessed 8 September 2005.

www.kommun.kiruna.se, accessed 31 October 2005.

www.lycksele.se, accessed 8 September 2005.
www.mala.se, accessed 31 October 2005.
www.norsjo.se, accessed 31 October 2005.
www.scottish-enterprise.com, accessed 31 October 2005.
www.skelleftea.se, accessed 31 October 2005.
www.vasterbotten.se, accessed 31 October 2005.

Chapter 9

A Path for Policy

Ewen J. Michael and C. Michael Hall

Objectives

- This chapter explores the approaches to micro-cluster formation and the role of networks as mechanisms for inclusion in tourism growth policies for rural communities.
- It emphasises the need for policy mechanisms that sit consistently within the practices and frameworks of existing approaches to public administration.
- The discussion is set within the context of a changing role for government in regional development, where the demands for a competitive allocation of public resources impose new requirements on public administrators for transparency and accountability in the nature of the decisions that they can make.
- The rationale for public intervention in tourism development is reconsidered, particularly in the way it can contribute to the growth of opportunity within some rural areas over the short and longer term.
- Within this new paradigm, the chapter explores the roles that public sector authorities are best positioned to fulfil in support of those local communities that seek to pursue their own preferences in tourism development. Here, consideration is given to concepts that involve government acting as mutual assurance agents in the locational decisions of firms, as communicators between diverse market segments, as information providers in the search for complementarities, and as sources for infrastructure support in the development and maintenance of networks.

Micro-Clusters and Networks: The Growth of Tourism
Copyright © 2007 by Elsevier Ltd.
All rights of reproduction in any form reserved.
ISBN: 0-08-045096-2

While the focus of micro-cluster analysis is to provide industry participants and regional communities with a strategic response to promote positive forms of development in their local environments, its significance rests on its application as part of a framework for revitalizing growth and developing new opportunities that are consistent with the needs of those who live in these regions. In short, its real value will be revealed if it can form part of the basket of tools to implement regional development policy.

The micro-clusters and networks approach, if applied to tourism development, does not supplant the need for more traditional analyses of market competition. Business and destination planning still requires a full assessment of the customer base (demand behaviour) and the factors affecting production (supply). Whatever form the local product takes, how will it be produced? What complementarities are there with the existing infrastructure and the other related industries in the region? What sort of response might come from existing firms — will they see new entrants as rivals or as allies? As already observed, these commercial assessments all form part of the information requirements for existing firms to determine whether geographic concentration can be converted into more strategically sophisticated clustering relationships (Porter, 1991; Saxenian, 1994; Doeringer & Terkla, 1995; Henton & Walesh, 1997; Rosenfeld, 1997; Waits, 2000; Enright & Roberts, 2001).

For policy purposes, however, the intent of the micro-cluster and networks model is to service more than the private interest associated with the commercial viability of any particular firm. As a mechanism for delivering economic growth, its purpose is to establish the existence of any symbiosis between compatible firms and the potential alignment for complementarity that will affect the growth of other firms that choose to co-locate, or which already exist. Cluster formation, as a strategic tool, appears possible in limited circumstances; but, where those circumstances apply, the externality benefits to be derived may be substantial and fall well within the domain of the public interest. Politically, it offers another advantage that may be important in regional areas, for the pattern of cluster growth can be shaped to accord with the host community's needs (Hall, 2000). The hypothesis, which may now emerge, is that successful clustering in tourism-based micro-markets might deliver superior community benefits in comparison with more traditional growth pole strategies. For example, in the case of tourism this has often constituted the development of infrastructure such as convention and exhibition centres, stadiums and art galleries and museums. However, many of these more traditional development strategies have not brought the desired long-term economic and social returns (Hall, 2000, 2004a). The issue that remains, however, is whether or not there is a need for public sector intervention to enhance this process (Hall, 2005; Michael, 2006).

Role of Government

The concept of *micro-clusters* provides a framework for explaining how businesses can optimise their prospects for growth through co-location in some circumstances, while the *networks* model demonstrates how the operators of those businesses can extract the benefits, both collectively and individually. This approach also implies the potential to create a pro-active path for policy that deliberately fosters the formation of *micro-clusters* and enhances the range of opportunities for residents in small regional communities (Hall, 2004b). The micro-clusters model, then, has applications beyond the broader *clusters* approach proposed by Porter (1991), which has proved useful in the analysis of the benefits from co-location in large-scale regions, but which has less relevance to the circumstances that apply in micro or local environments. Indeed, one of the inherent weaknesses of the Porterian model is that it provides no direction for public sector intervention — in fact, Porter warns specifically of the dangers of market failure where government actions might lead to alliances between firms, which reduce competition or lead to monopolistic practices, arguing instead that governments should: "... sharply limit direct co-operation among industry rivals ..." (Porter, 1998, p. 187). In practice, Porter's model provides little in the way of a prescription for establishing a cluster formation, for it is more an analytic tool than a prescriptive one; but, even so, it still offers some guidance for identifying the business success factors amenable to the policy development processes used by local authorities to encourage the location decisions of local industries (Rosenfeld, 1997).

If the micro-cluster approach is to have a policy application in the processes for local development, its practice will still need to be compatible with, and supportive of, the contemporary economic and social roles of government, and accord with the differences in those roles at the national, regional and municipal levels. Over the past two decades, the OECD (Hugonnier, 1999) claims to have observed a substantial change in the direction of public sector intervention in local development, particularly among the governments of the European Union and those of Canada and the United States (see Chapter 2). While these more mature economies engage in the rhetoric of using public resources only to further allocative efficiency, they have simultaneously moved to deliberately rebuild the infrastructure and development base of regional communities to reverse the trend of declining employment and economic opportunity (Ward, Lowe, & Bridges, 2003), albeit using new models for economic growth which are often articulated within the frameworks of neoliberalism and competitiveness (Tickell & Peck, 2003; Malecki, 2004). In summary, the OECD is arguing that the *old* concepts for policy, based on **regional equalisation** schemes and sporadic *icon* developments, have given way to new approaches based on enhancing the competitiveness of localities and the decentralisation of resource allocation decisions to the affected communities (Hugonnier, 1999).

Not all states of course, are following the same path. Some of the peripheral states in the European Union, such as Ireland, have found it effective to return to taxation and subsidy practices that seek to encourage emerging industries to decentralize, in an effort to spread the benefits of economic growth across a wider community base, using the argument that the costs of support are temporary and will be offset as these industries become more sustainable in the future. In much of continental Europe, the welfare of regional communities remains a priority for public decision makers, particularly at the core in France, Germany and the Benelux countries, but the same commitments are not so apparent in many other states (Sarris, Doucha, & Mathjis, 1999; Fernández, 2002).

In Australia and New Zealand, for example, the intervention practices of governments over the past 20 years have often been more issue-based than sectoral; with the consequence that some matters are attended to as policy priorities, such as improving telecommunication services, while others, like health and social services, are not. In rural Australia, as a particular illustration, policy implementation has been even more problematic for there are greater opportunities between the State and Commonwealth governments to differentiate between geographically separated interests in the application of development policies, with the perhaps unintended outcome of promoting one region or economic interest ahead of another. Indeed, it could be argued that these discrepancies have contributed to the high level of electoral dissatisfaction among rural voters, where many now perceive the differences in the distribution of benefits between regions as inequitable (Regional Australia

Summit, 1999, in passim). The Australian examples demonstrate a broader pattern of incon-sistency in the frameworks used by many other countries for enhancing rural economic development and, more particularly, for expanding social *opportunities* in ways that deliver positive outcomes to match expectations with existing community needs and values.

From the perspective of government, however, the need to adhere to the strictures of *competition policy* does not imply the existence of simultaneous requirements that might preclude intervention in any local development programme, but rather sets conditions on such actions so that they are taken only to support the common needs of the market sys-tems' participants. In short, governments are expected to pursue efficiency gains, even at a local level, but through mechanisms that ensure resource costs are transparently identified and that any benefits are accessible to all users. In this way, the sponsorship of competi-tive practice remains equitable for all and subject to public oversight.

The issue, of course, is that there is a fine line to be drawn between supporting co-operative arrangements between firms in a competitive environment and the potential for those arrangements to become collusive. The danger that exists for government is that policies, which seek to encourage co-operation between firms within any given region, rely for their success on the ability of firms to extract the benefits from their co-location, but the existence of these benefits may encourage those same firms to collude to prevent others from gaining the same outcomes. In the same vein, of course, the cooperative arrangements and decision-making practices between public–private interests may also lead to the exclusion of policy alternatives (Hall, 1999). What constitutes the distinction between *co-operation* and *collusion* is therefore a critical element of the micro-cluster approach, for at the heart of the model lies the notion that the co-operative practices of the cluster's firms will occur only to extract the synergies between them, to lower production costs, enhance product quality and generate a competitive advantage for that locality's particular package of outputs. Clustering in itself does not contradict the principles of com-petition, though it may increase the risks of collusion if no vigilance is in place (Hall, 1999; Michael, 2003). In a fair market, however, the dynamics of competition remain unchanged; both for the cluster, where like firms continue to compete for sales, and between the cluster and those firms located outside it (see Chapters 3 and 4).

There are significant policy implications to be drawn from these observations by regional planners, more especially by those responsible for non-urban tourism develop-ment. There is real danger in the contemporary trend of many public sector policy-makers to focus solely on large-scale or macro regional projects. While such *icon* activities may be politically appealing, there is a tendency to forget basic economics principles in that there is often more to gain in aggregate from myriad smaller micro developments, which contribute collectively to community welfare, than from single large-scale projects. As Hall (2000) emphasised, the scale and pattern of ownership of land and property is extremely important for the way in which places change. Small lots allow for ongoing fine grain change as opposed to the sudden wholesale change that can occur with large parcels of land. Appropriate tourism development may well mean relatively gradual small-scale change with the inclusion of large numbers of stakeholders as opposed to large-scale developments with limited numbers of 'owners' of a project.

While the large-scale project may well be a grand gesture that politicians and lobbyists sup-port by virtue that 'they are seen to be doing something' in a time of increasing competition between places (Malecki, 2004), it is more likely that unspectacular gradual change will be more economically and socially sustainable (Hall, 2007). As Hughes (1993, p. 162) argued with respect to the Olympics, tourism:

> "can only be a component of an overall strategy for urban regeneration rather than a major force in its own right. Tourism associated with the Olympics, given its short-term nature, provides even less direct opportunity for urban regeneration. The hopes of regeneration lie largely in the belief that inward investment in other industries and increased long-term tourist flows will result. The prospect is based on improvements to the environment and infrastructure and a generally enhanced image or awareness of an area. The case for this has, however, not yet been demonstrated."

Indeed, Hughes (1993, p. 162) went on to note that the hosting of a mega-event, such as the Olympics, may even disturb "... the 'normal' development of tourism and other activity ...", with the possibility that they will be "... a distraction from the pursuit of a more fundamental development strategy that will ensure long-term sustainable growth."

In rural environments, problems arise when the growth of tourism impacts on local lifestyles or delivers benefits only to particular interests. The consequence is that development policies are sometimes viewed with scepticism, and the policy-making process itself may be perceived as dissociated from local needs and values (Hall, Jenkins, & Kearsley, 1997, p. 136; Braithwaite, Greiner, & Walker, 1998, p. 78). A spread of small-scale developments is more likely to be received favourably as they deliver broader economic benefits to a wider range of interests and with less dislocation to the existing communities. The irony is that for the same reasons small-scale tourism development policies engender less political support and action even though the economic outcomes may be substantial and the social impacts less intrusive.

Clarke alludes to these issues in his reconsideration of the economic rationale for public sector involvement in the management of Australia's tourism industries. He notes that there is little interest in policy development when an industry is obviously successful and growing well ... *"if it isn't broken don't fix it"* (Clarke, 1997, p. 361). The trouble is that such a position ignores the very purpose of policy:

> "Even if the tourism industry is performing well, one can (and should) ask how potential gains from tourism can be *optimized.*" (Clarke, 1997, p. 362)

In other words, the purpose of policy is to deliver the best possible outcome as the allocative impacts flow through to the rest of the economy, and, hence, to all members of the community. Indeed, successful industries that can be enhanced still further may be the ones likely to deliver the most significant positive economic and social impacts.

While this argument applies to the tourism industry in general, it applies equally to its constituent sub-industries. The antiques trade is an example of a successful small-scale private market that contributes to tourism but which has attracted no attention from the public sector's planners (Michael, 2002). It is perhaps not surprising to note that Australia's national tourism policies make no reference to it whatsoever. At the State level, Victoria's

'Tourism Industry Strategic Plan', for example, acknowledges the antiques trade's existence only as a passing reference among the state's shopping attractions (Tourism Victoria, 1997; Tourism Victoria, 2002), even though it is a focal point for the marketing campaigns in several regions. In Tasmania, at least, there is a flicker of recognition that the antiques industry, along with other micro markets, can generate trade for the accommodation industry and that this clustering effect should be recognised and marketed accordingly (Tourism Tasmania, 1998). At the municipal level, however, there is an emerging interest in many localities about the industry's potential as a force for local economic development. The point is not that the antiques trade is of any particular significance by itself, rather that there are many small niche or micro markets that generate tourism activity in regional areas, and these may well be amenable to further growth and development with the support of appropriate public intervention.

New approaches to regional development will continue to evolve, as public administration seeks to keep pace with social expectations. The form it takes, however, must accord with the other aspects of national and regional frameworks for economic management, and so will be cast from the same mould that is forged around the principles of competition, budget transparency and social equity. Tourism development raises critical issues for regional communities, particularly where inappropriate activities impact on community lifestyles and the choices made by existing residents. On a transnational scale, one option for governments and their attending agencies, which appears to match the tenor of democratic demands, is to devolve much of the decision-making process that controls development back to the affected communities. This does not absolve governments from their responsibilities for development, but instead imposes on them a need to support the unique choices of local communities with information and infrastructure that helps them determine their own social cost–benefit outcomes. In this context, the provision of such services enhances the competitive framework by improving the efficiency gains from local choices — provided, of course, that the same services are available to all communities on an equitable basis.

Arguments for Public Intervention

Given a global policy regime that seeks to minimise public intervention in the market's operations, there is a need for some caution when considering arguments that suggest governments ought to engage as the appropriate agents to foster particular types of economic development. Any assumption that governments might serve an effective role in sponsoring micro-cluster formations in rural communities might then seem to be even more uncertain, particularly as the core of these clusters would normally comprise a collection of private firms.

At a social level, however, it could be argued that within the rural regions of many countries there now exists a perception of an imbalance in the provision of public infrastructure and the physical conditions for economic growth to support regional communities compared to what is made available for those in the more densely populated urban areas. In effect, so this argument goes, the potential for development and the opportunities for future growth have *actually* diminished. If this perception were to be demonstrated in reality, then the case for public intervention would be substantiated, and there would be a need for redress. The argument would be strengthened still further if it identified a *public good* outcome from those collective actions that lead to a resurgence of regional activity to promote employment and new forms of production. Social equity has its price, but it may well be that approaches to policy that enhance regional potential can be deemed a reasonable expectation on government in these circumstances.

Arguing for public sector intervention on the basis of social equity, however, is unlikely to be sufficient on its own, but it may be that a stronger case to warrant active intervention in regional tourism development can be illustrated through the gains in economic efficiency. In any event, such an argument would need to be established to justify any approach that calls for public support in the formation of micro-clusters. Set out in its simplest terms, the case for government intervention in regional development relies almost entirely on proof that a policy action will deliver some substantive increase in social benefit, creating a *positive externality*, or some substantive reduction to existing social costs, reducing a *negative externality*, or some combination of the two (see for example, Sloman & Norris, 2002, p. 271). The net gains, of course, must offset their budgetary costs, although how this might be measured is often problematic. More often than not, the issues that concern tourism development are localised, as their impacts are largely confined to the immediate destination. In this context, the effects are small-scale, but nevertheless still focus on the accumulation of social gains to be derived from establishing new and efficient industrial processes to replace those that are in decline, and more particularly in those regions where new employment opportunities will serve to reduce the pressure on existing social costs.

An additional justification for public intervention in the development of micro-clusters is the part they play in the development of social capital, which has positive externalities beyond the role they play in assisting a cluster's formation and development. As already noted, geographical co-location does not necessarily lead to cluster development and activation. Instead, communicative relationships need to be established between partners. Without an appropriate cluster champion and associated relationship creating strategy (formal or otherwise), co-location may just as easily lead to rivalries that works against cluster development as much as behaviours that do. The creation of trust becomes a critical component in this exercise; and, outside independent knowledge brokers, who may be from or supported by the public sector, might well be important in providing an understanding of the economic and social context of a cluster's development for the potential cluster's participants (Hall, 2004b).

The further development of social capital through the creation of networks is extremely important in terms of the cluster's capacity to reduce the level of uncertainty for entrepreneurs in the creation of new businesses, as much as it is for enhancing the wider range of community benefits. Network-based relationships can provide entrepreneurs with critical information, knowledge and resources. Social and intellectual capital, which has often come into existence with the support of public intervention at various scales, can therefore be used to maximise the scarce economic resources available to some micro-firms and small- to medium-sized enterprises. In the case of wine and food tourism development in the Hawkes Bay region of New Zealand, for example, Hall (2004b) observed that social capital assisted in the development of relationships between network members that helped to overcome the issues of firm's 'smallness' and 'newness'. Such a strategy represents a classic model of resource acquisition by new small business ventures (Starr & MacMillan, 1990; McGee, Dowling, & Megginson, 1995), the significance of which has only recently been recognised in studies of tourism entrepreneurship (e.g., Hall et al., 1997a).

These principles, however, merely serve as generic guidelines for what is or is not effective intervention practice. Intervention in local tourism development, of course, can take myriad forms; hence each specific approach requires its own analysis and validation. There is no 'one size fits all' approach in the context of clusters, tourism and regional development, although as this book has demonstrated there are a number of factors that are recognised as significant (Hall, 2004b). The micro-clusters model is no exception, and so must fit within the context of broader approaches to development practice, public administration and the competitive framework.

Assurance — A Critical Role for Government

One theoretical response is to see the formation of a micro-cluster as a mutual *assurance game* (Dixit & Nalebuff, 1991, p. 126). The social benefit from clustering for the host community stems from its success in delivering multiplier and externality effects (employment, wealth creation, etc.), but the host community cannot determine the location decisions of potential entrants to the cluster, even if it can exert some influence on the process through inducements or the promise of lower costs. On the other hand, the rationale for clustering by one firm with a group of other firms rests on that firm's own perceptions of the superior cost and market benefits (and perhaps quality gains) that they can obtain from co-location. The incentive for an individual firm to join the cluster where these benefits will be created, however, exists only when they know with *certainty* that other firms will make the same location decision. Unless sufficient firms make the same locational choice to join the cluster and participate within its network, the benefits will not materialize and a firm could be left stranded with higher costs and isolated from its intended market — a recipe for commercial disaster! Firms confronted with this decision, then, will seek some assurance of the reality of the cluster's existence before making any decision to join it.

One way to demonstrate this is by using a simple example from *Game Theory* (which, admittedly, for most readers will sound more complicated than it really is). Suppose, just for the purposes of illustration, that there are two tourism firms (labelled as Tourism Firms A and B) that are in a position to choose where they will locate their business operations. Given the promise of the benefits from joining a new micro-cluster these two firms, A and B, could choose to join the new cluster or choose to make their location decision elsewhere on the basis of normal expected commercial returns. In this scenario, the normal return to a firm is nominated at $2 million but by joining the micro-cluster, it could increase to $4 million — but this would only be achieved if the other firm also joins. The problem that confronts each firm is that it knows that engaging in a co-operative exercise is not costless, and if it should join a micro-cluster that is dysfunctional then its returns would be reduced (say, just for illustration, to $1 million). In this situation, each Tourism operator would prefer to join the new micro-cluster because it delivers the maximum possible payoff; but, in

Table 9.1: A Micro-clustering assurance game.*

		Tourism firm B	
		Co-locate	Locate elsewhere
Tourism firm A	Co-locate	A = 4, B = 4	A = 1, B = 3
	Locate elsewhere	A = 3, B = 1	A = 2, B = 2

*Benefits in $millions.

reality, each will choose to locate elsewhere and accept the normal level of profits, rather than risk exposure to a lesser return if they suspect the other firm is not likely to co-locate.

This decision matrix is shown in Table 1, where each firm has two choices (to *co-locate* or *locate elsewhere*) giving rise to four possible outcomes. In effect, there are two optimal choices available for each tourism firm's location decision: where both firms A and B choose to *co-locate* within the micro-cluster, or where both firms choose to *locate elsewhere*. In effect there are two Nash equilibrium positions (co-locate/co-locate: locate elsewhere/locate elsewhere), where the sets of choices deliver the greatest certainty to the firms, given the decision of the other firm (Varian, 1990, p. 473). It needs to be remembered, of course, that with the initial formation of the cluster there is no *first mover advantage*, because the benefits from association with the micro-cluster are *only* attainable through shared synergies, so a firm might well be worse off if it chose to locate in the potential cluster only to find its competitors chose to pursue some other location for normal commercial reasons.

Some mechanism is needed here for each firm to *assure* the other that it will choose to locate in the cluster. At this point, it might be argued that the choices faced by the competing firms are simply part of the dynamics of the competitive market structure, but where the outcome can lead to demonstrable social benefits it takes on another dimension. If a micro-cluster can lead to enhanced social outcomes only some fraction of these gains will accrue to the private operators — for their concern is with costs and profits — then there is a need for some collective action to secure these gains for the community's benefit. Here, the need for some form of public sector intervention is established. One obvious role for local administrators is to secure the intermediary communication needed between firms to assure the grounds for co-operation to optimise both the payoffs to the firms and the benefits to the host community. Moreover, public intervention does more by servicing this function because it can simultaneously layout a transparent basis for future new entrants to the cluster. If the *assurance* task is left solely to the market, the initial firms might still choose to co-locate but perhaps with a collusive understanding to limit the potential for other entrants to join the cluster, or to limit the host community's involvement in the cluster's benefits.

In this sense, Government can play a substantive role in initialising the cluster's formation to increase the payoffs for firms that choose to co-locate, irrespective of the decisions of other firms. The provision of infrastructure, community support or marketing, as examples, may deliver benefits to a locating firm, which may not equal the sum of the gains anticipated from a cluster of firms, but which remain sufficient to shift the optimal decision to one choice only, 'to co-locate'. This now becomes a *dominant strategy* for either firm (Varian, 1990, p. 462), for each knows it is better off in the cluster and each is assured that the other will make the same decision.

Engaging Producers — the Issue for Tourism Planners

The growth and development of tourism in non-metropolitan regions has emerged as a public issue in many local communities, but for a variety of reasons it often remains low-key and unaddressed in the political process. Perhaps, this reflects the perception of tourism as a substantive growth industry that requires only a little leverage in order to be successful (Hall, 2005), or perhaps it simply reflects the limited participation by government in tourism generally. The problem is not unique to tourism, but may reflect the nature of its market structure, which, like many other competitive industries, is dominated at by a plethora of small to medium sized enterprises that cannot easily be engaged in an effective dialogue by government agencies. In any event, these small business operators lack both the resources and the willingness to participate in the protracted processes normally associated with public sector planning (see, e.g., Cioccio & Michael, 2006).

The particular problem that confronts the development of tourism in regional areas is that small-scale destinations and activities are often ignored as one of the factors that motivate the demand for travel, even by the operators of co-located complementary services. The significance of this issue has been exposed in an extensive study of 13 tourism product regions in Australia as a factor constraining tourism development (Braithwaite et al., 1998). In Australia, the administrative model that structures the industry's development focuses the evolution of policy through Regional and Local Tourism authorities, made up variously of industry, community and municipal representatives. Unless the myriad micro-market operators (like antique, wine and food, and ecotourism businesses and a host of other segmented complementary providers) actively seek involvement and participation, they tend to be presumed to be part of a locality's general commercial environment and, hence, are ignored in the decision-process.

The extensive surveys conducted for that project demonstrated that many of the stakeholders in given local regions do not interact across the range of tourism activities and, consequently, are unaware of the issues affecting some groups or are unaware of the role they also play in bundling the localities' attractions for potential visitors. Obviously, the niche market operators are the ones most easily isolated, for they see themselves as belonging to a separate industrial activity (see Chapter 6). The failure to recognise the role of these operators as integral parts of the broader tourism market was shown to be a source of mistrust or antagonism towards those supposedly responsible for local tourism development. The evidence from antique dealers (Michael, 2002) in regional Australia or wineries in New Zealand (Hall et al., 1997a; Christensen, Hall, & Mitchell, 2004) would appear to support these findings wholeheartedly.

The Braithwaite study highlights the critical role that local tourism organisations play in enhancing regional outcomes, and emphasises the difficulties in bringing regional collections of disparate operators together. In the search for common ground, many regard "... marketing and promotion as 'sine qua non' or the fix for every problem" (Braithwaite et al., 1998 p. 79), but, inevitably, such approaches favour the major attractions rather than the smaller complementary players, and serve only to further dislocate the communication process. Enhancing local tourism development requires an understanding of the range of factors that generate tourism and of the interrelationship and connectivity between those factors — and this sophistication seems to be consistently absent amongst both operators and planners. For the operators of small segments or complementary activities within the broad construction of a local tourism industry, as is the case for example with antiques and oldwares dealers, hospitality providers or motoring services, there is often more to be gained by devoting their limited resources to those means that directly interface with their core clientele, rather than engage in the development of the regional product (Michael, 2002). What is being observed here is not a *free-rider effect*, where non-members enjoy the benefits created by some other association, but rather a process of inadvertent exclusion that generates apathy or active disinterest.

Given that these micro segments act as generators of travel demand by drawing visitors to given locations, there is a need for the local and regional planners to develop a better understanding of the synergies and flow-on effects between them and the consequences for the growth and development of their local tourism products. Ideally, this needs to include not only the interplay between tourism micro segments and firms but also the enhancement of interrelationships between firms in different sectors which have strong economic ties. For example, in many regions the purchasing and investment of even very small tourism businesses will have implications for firms in other sectors, like construction and food. Consequently, the activities of tourism micro-clusters can have considerable economic multiplier effects at a local or regional scale that governments are often in the best position to enhance for the mutual benefit of these different industry sectors. In these situations the same issues of trust and network creation that apply in tourism micro-clusters clearly also apply to broader sets of inter-firm relations.

From the perspective of regional development policy, there are short-, medium- and long-term economic benefits from encouraging denser sets of inter-firm relations through micro-clustering and inter-sectoral linkages (Hall, 2007). In the short-term there may be immediate, identifiable economic multiplier effects that lead to increased local expenditure. In the medium term there are secondary and indirect multiplier effects as the economic activities of tourism micro-clusters flow through different industry supply chains to bring benefits to suppliers in other sectors and stimuli for further employment generation. Indeed, at this level much government activity at the local level is guided towards creating supply chains that enhance the link between tourism businesses and other local producers, for example with food producers. In the longer term, improving the density of network relations between firms can lead to enhancement of local brand values that not only expand perceptions of 'quality of product' but which also serve as a point of differentiation in the market.

Venkataraman and Van de Ven (1998) argue that it only makes sense to leverage social capital in the early stages of a new venture. According to their research, as ventures progress, businesses base their decisions on economic criteria, and social capital has less impact. Ironically, this means that the very network relationships that help to reduce risk and uncertainty in small business start-ups fade in importance as the perception of uncertainty diminishes. Such an interpretation may mean that the importance of social ties may therefore be a function of the level of uncertainty facing a small business entrepreneur (Hall, 2004b). However, in the case of food and wine tourism, and arguably more generally with the interrelationship of tourism firms with other firms that also leverage value from *place* promotion, Hall, Mitchell, and Sharples (2003) have argued that the significance of social ties and trust continues to be significant over time because of the importance of regional brands as mechanisms for both destination promotion and for *place* and *product* differentiation (see also Bengtsson & Kock, 2000). Once a geographical designation is established and accepted in the market, it then becomes extremely difficult for ventures to withdraw from networks that support the place brand — for it would potentially mean the loss of significant intangible capital and a direct economic resource.

Indeed, in some such situations in which geographical designation is transformed into regulatory structures such as *appellation* controls, Champagne, Burgundy, or Napa Valley, it may be a distinct business disadvantage to withdraw unless there are exceptional circumstances that have led to a decline in place brand values (e.g. publicity given to the adulteration of a product). This observation may have substantial implications for the longevity and success of place and brand-oriented clusters and networks. Once place-brands have established their presence in the market they not only contribute to the success of the cluster and individual businesses, but they also contribute to the development of further social capital because they become integral to the identity of place and the firms and individuals within it (Hall, 2004b). This iterative and recursive process does not mean that tourism micro-clusters and place-bound networks have an infinite lifespan, nor does it mean that regions automatically shift from building a basic co-location configuration to one that forms dense network sets of social, economic and intangible capital, which are deeply embedded in the region's social, cultural, economic, industrial and political formations. However, the particular congruence of intangible capital to be found within tourism and related industries, such as food and wine, does potentially lead to longer cluster lifecycles and the associated longer-term maintenance of social networks and capital, and to potentially significant flow-on effects for the maintenance of regional brand identity (Hall, 2007).

In terms of regional policy, there is a clear need for public-sector planning agencies to enhance their understanding of what draws visitors to a region and to lead a process that communicates the strengths of these interrelationships to all the industry's participants: for the actions that will increase the level of visitation will be those that build on the interconnected package or bundle of attributes that the region has to offer. While the benefits that this growth can deliver will indubitably benefit both the tourism ventures and their complementary providers in the same region, it also serves as the platform from which the community can extract its own welfare gains. However, as this chapter, and this book as a whole, has indicated there is also a need to better understand how tourism production is created and how this may best be encouraged so as to bring benefits to regional communities.

Ironically, tourism has long been subject to what Faulkner (2003, p. 300) once described as 'advertising fundamentalism', which sees "… the key to gaining the competitive edge in the quest for maximising market share [residing] in the manipulation of consumer awareness and choice through advertising programmes". Such an approach has often translated in the past to an emphasis in tourism policy that asks only how can we best advertise our products, rather than seeking to understand how the product that the tourist consumes is actually put together and how inter-firm relations can best be leveraged to bring about the desired economic and social benefits from tourism. Nevertheless, as this chapter has highlighted, there are clear policy roles for government — at different levels — to intervene at different scales within the tourism market in order to assist both firms and regional development. Indeed, in an increasingly competitive marketplace, it is actually likely that these forms of public intervention have the potential to become greater mechanisms for long-term sustained regional competitiveness, able to deliver substantial gains to community welfare, than any continuation of the policy approach that seeks yet another short-term advertising campaign — no matter how well intentioned it might be.

References

Bengtsson, M., & Kock, S. (2000). Co-opetition in business networks — to co-operate and compete simultaneously. *Industrial Marketing Management, 29,* 411–426.

Braithwaite, D., Greiner, R., & Walker, P. (1998). Success factors for tourism in regions of eastern Australia. *Rural Tourism Management: Sustainable Options — Conference Proceedings.* Auchincruive, Scotland (9–12 September) (pp. 69–96).

Christensen, D., Hall, C. M., & Mitchell, R. (2004). The 2003 New Zealand wineries survey, in *Creating Tourism Knowledge, 14th International Research Conference of the Council for Australian University Tourism and Hospitality Education,* 10–13 February, School of Tourism and Leisure Management, University of Queensland (pp. 144–149).

Cioccio, L., & Michael, E. J. (2006). Hazard or disaster: Tourism management for the inevitable in Northeast Victoria. *Tourism Management* (forthcoming: www.sciencedirect.com).

Clarke, H. (1997). Australian tourism industry policy: A new view. *Tourism Economics, 3*(4), 361–377.

Dixit, A. K., & Nalebuff, B. J. (1991). *Thinking strategically — the competitive edge in business, politics, and everyday life.* New York: W.W. Norton & Company.

Doeringer, B., & Terkla, D. G. (1995). Business strategy and cross-industry clusters. *Economic Development Quarterly, 9,* 225–237.

Enright, M., & Roberts, B. (2001). Regional clustering in Australia. *Australian Journal of Management, 26,* 65–86.

Faulkner, B. (2003). The role of research in tourism development. In: L. Fredline, L. Jago, & C. Cooper (Eds), *Progressing tourism research* (pp. 300–302). Clevedon: Channelview.

Fernández, J. (2002). The common agricultural policy and EU enlargement: Implications for agricultural production in the central and east European countries. *Eastern European Economics, 40*(3), 28–50.

Hall, C. M. (1999). Rethinking collaboration and partnership: A public policy perspective. *Journal of Sustainable Tourism, 7*(3/4), 274–289.

Hall, C. M. (2000). *Tourism planning: Policies, processes and relationships* (1st ed.). Harlow: Prentice Hall.

Hall, C. M. (2004a). Sports tourism and urban regeneration. In: B. Ritchie, & D. Adair (Eds), *Sports tourism: Interrelationships, impacts and issues* (pp. 192–206). Clevedon: Channelview.

Hall, C. M. (2004b). Small firms and wine and food tourism in New Zealand: Issues of collaboration, clusters and lifestyles. In: R. Thomas (Ed.), *Small firms in tourism: International perspectives* (pp. 167–181). Oxford: Elsevier.

Hall, C. M. (2005). *Tourism: Rethinking the social science of mobility.* Harlow: Prentice-Hall.

Hall, C. M. (2007). *Tourism planning* (2nd ed.). Harlow: Prentice-Hall.

Hall, C. M., Cambourne, B., Macionis, N., & Johnson, G. (1997a). Wine tourism and network development in Australia and New Zealand: Review, establishment and prospects. *International Journal of Wine Marketing, 9*(2/3), 5–31.

Hall, C. M., Jenkins, J., & Kearsley, G. (Eds). (1997b). *Tourism planning and policy in Australia and New Zealand: Cases, issues and practice.* Sydney: Irwin.

Hall, C. M., Mitchell, R., & Sharples, E. (2003). Consuming places: The role of food, wine and tourism in regional development. In: C.M. Hall, E. Sharples, R. Mitchell, B. Cambourne, & N. Macionis (Eds), *Food tourism around the world: Development, management and markets* (pp. 25–59). Oxford: Butterworth-Heinemann.

Henton, D., & Walesh, K. (1997). *Grassroots leaders for a new economy: How civic entrepreneurs are building prosperous communities.* San Francisco: Jossey-Bass.

Hughes, H. L. (1993). Olympic tourism and urban regeneration. *Festival Management and Event Tourism, 1*, 157–162.

Hugonnier, B. (1999). Regional development tendencies in OECD countries, *Regional Australia Summit, Keynote Presentation*, Canberra, 26–29 October 1999, 14pp.

Malecki, E. J. (2004). Jockeying for position: What it means and why it matters to regional development policy when places compete. *Regional Studies, 38*(9), 1101–1120.

McGee, J. E., Dowling, M. J., & Megginson, W. L. (1995). Cooperative strategy and new venture performance: The role of business strategy and management experience. *Strategic Management Journal, 16*, 565–580.

Michael, E. J. (2002). Antiques and tourism in Australia. *Tourism Management, 23*(2), 117–125.

Michael, E. J. (2003). Tourism micro-clusters. *Tourism Economics, 9*(2), 133–146.

Michael, E. J. (2006). *Public policy — the competitive framework.* Melbourne: Oxford University Press.

Porter, M. E. (1991). *The competitive advantage of nations.* London: Macmillan.

Porter, M. E. (1998). Clusters and the new economics of competition. *Harvard Business Review*, (6), 77–90.

Regional Australia Summit. (1999). See Hugonnier.

Rosenfeld, S. A. (1997). Bringing business clusters into the mainstream of economic development. *European Planning Studies, 5*(1), 3–23.

Sarris, A. H., Doucha, T., & Mathjis, E. (1999). Agricultural restructuring in central and eastern Europe: Implications for competitiveness and rural development. *European Review of Agricultural Economics, 26*(3), 305–329.

Saxenian, A. (1994). *Regional advantage: Culture and competition in silicon valley and route 128.* Boston: Harvard University Press.

Sloman, J., & Norris, K. (2002). *Economics* (2nd ed.). Sydney: Prentice-Hall.

Starr, J. A., & MacMillan, I. C. (1990). Resource cooptation and social contracting: Resource acquisition strategies for new ventures. *Strategic Management Journal, 11*, 79–92.

Tickell, A., & Peck, J. (2003). Making global rules: Globalization or neoliberalization., In: J. Peck, & H.W. Yeung (Eds), *Remaking the global economy* (pp. 163–181). London: Sage.

Tourism Victoria. (1997). *Strategic business plan 1997–2001 building partnerships.* Melbourne.

Tourism Tasmania. (1998). *Yield management — final report.* Hobart: Reed McKibben & Assocs.

Tourism Victoria. (2002). *Victoria's tourism industry strategic plan summary 2002—2006.* Melbourne.

Varian, H. R. (1990). *Intermediate microeconomics: A modern approach* (2nd ed.). New York: Norton.

Venkataraman, S., & Van de Ven, A. H. (1998). Hostile environmental jolts, transaction set, and new business. *Journal of Business Venturing, 13*, 231–255.

Waits, M. J. (2000). The added value of the industry cluster approach to economic analysis, strategy development, and service delivery. *Economic Development Quarterly, 14*, 35–50.

Ward, N., Lowe, P., & Bridges, T. (2003). Rural and regional development: The role of the regional development agencies in England. *Regional Studies, 37*(2), 201–214.

Chapter 10

The Contribution of the Micro-Cluster Approach

C. Michael Hall, Paul Lynch, Ewen J. Michael and Richard Mitchell

Objectives

- This chapter reviews the status of micro-clustering theory, to place it in a context that is relevant for social planners concerned with local economic development.
- It emphasises the integration between the economic forces that lead to the formation of a micro-cluster and the role that is played by its corresponding network to create the sense of trust that enables a community to share the gains from this form of economic development.
- The discussion serves as a reminder that the development of the domestic tourism industry in regional and rural environments is based on the actions of small businesses working co-operatively with their host communities, and that the formation of local social networks under these conditions will involve a complex mix of commercial and social criteria.
- The chapter is also concerned with the capacity to make use of micro-clustering concepts in the future, particularly in terms of the changing role for government in regional development.
- A number of issues are identified to help focus the attention of public sector planning agencies on effective cluster processes, but the conclusions imply that much of their activity needs to address the ways they use to support and address the needs of the supporting local networks.

Micro-Clusters and Networks: The Growth of Tourism
Copyright © 2007 by Elsevier Ltd.
All rights of reproduction in any form reserved.
ISBN: 0-08-045096-2

The extension to the traditional approach to clustering analysis developed throughout this book stems from the reconstruction of the theoretical premises for successful micro-clustering. This has been based on the new economics of complementarities and the integration of networking theory to provide a rationale for firms and communities to work together. This chapter, then, reviews the status of micro-clustering theory, and seeks to place it in a context that is relevant for social planners concerned with local economic development. It also considers some of the issues that planners and social analysts need to address or resolve in any action that seeks to put these concepts into practice. Nonetheless, the central focus remains on developing both the means and the mechanisms to enhance the development of rural communities that aim to build a tourism function to improve their economic and social well-being. The assumption, then, as it has been from the beginning, is that micro-clustering can enhance economic growth through the existing community structures — without overriding the values that inherently give a community its own sense of identity and purpose.

Integration: Micro-Clusters and Networking

The proposition that has been explored here is that small-scale, complementary business activities enhance their own capacity to form a successful tourism destination, particularly in a domestic market, when they operate in a cluster formation (Michael, 2003). While the micro-clustering approach seems to have a particular relevance for the tourism industry, because its activities are generally location based and the level of commerce is derived from travel and visitation, it is an approach that may also have applications for many other communities seeking to specialise at a micro scale in other forms of industrial output. While there are many approaches that can be considered to support and sponsor local economic development in rural areas, the micro-cluster model implies that business firms and communities can work co-operatively to exploit the dynamics of complementary activity to capture economies-of-scope to add value to both the cluster members' activities and to the local community's economic welfare. Needless to say, successful clustering is possible only where the basket of activities that makes up the local product has been improved and the efficiency gains are captured by the operators and shared within the community. If those benefits are forthcoming, then an understanding of the forces that promote this *clustering* effect will also serve to enhance the capacity of economic and social policy to contribute to improving living standards in the appropriate local circumstances.

Given the wealth of literature and analysis into the segmented structure of markets by public sector researchers and private organisations, and the extensive application of this knowledge within the tourism industry, it remains surprising that when policymakers turn to the issues that effect tourism development they often ignore its predominantly small-scale nature. In the rural and regional areas of many countries, small businesses and local operators are the mainstay of the domestic tourism product (Middleton, 2001; Hall, 2005; Hall & Rusher, 2005; Cioccio & Michael, 2006). These businesses deliver the tourism reality, often in the form of niche products based on the resources available in their particular locality (Hall, 2005). They provide the platform that makes a region attractive and accessible. How they choose to operate determines the local industry's level of cultural interaction with its host communities, and its sustainability over time (Seiragaki, 2006). In many rural areas, where economic opportunities are declining, it is these small tourism firms that provide one of the few sources for employment growth, and the potential for future innovation.

Australia's circumstances are similar to those in many other parts of the world, and so, just for this purpose, can be used to demonstrate the significance of the role played by small firms in sustaining the tourism industry. In data for the State of Victoria, for 2000–2001, the total level of tourism activity, both domestic and international, is identified as 54 million visitor nights and 42 million day trips (Tourism Victoria, 2002, p. 67), with two-thirds by either measure occurring in regional or rural areas. Apart from a small volume of packaged tour business, most of these *visitors* were identifiable as independent travellers consuming a vast range of products and services supplied by thousands of small businesses scattered across the State — and, of course, this picture remains the same for many regions in the world's more developed countries. It seems incongruous, then, that the issues that most concern these firms rarely form a focus for the business development strategies of public sector planning authorities.

While these issues have been of concern to municipal and regional authorities over the last decade in a number of countries, the reality is that there are very few examples of *national* governments that have set the development of rural tourism and the expansion of their domestic tourism markets as a critical priority for local economic development. On the other hand, a number of governments, such as those in Australia, Canada, Finland, Ireland, New Zealand, Scotland and Sweden, have at least recognised the significance of these issues but are only now demonstrating an increasing awareness of the role that domestic tourism development can play for their constituent local economies. This recognition is put quite eloquently in one of the planks in the Australian federal government's 'Tourism White Paper'

> "Domestic tourism contributes to the long term sustainability of communities and improves quality of life through promoting improvements in facilities and public amenities. Domestic tourism is, therefore, of greater importance to regional Australia than inbound tourism. A long term strategic view that promotes the benefits and contributions of domestic tourism will benefit regional and rural communities." (Australia, 2003, p. 18)

In Australia and elsewhere, however, there is little consensus about the ways and means that governments might deploy to foster this process, and little evidence of concrete actions to support local tourism development — at best, the changes to development policy might be described as incremental and *ad hoc*. Indeed, there appears to be little commonality in the approaches taken by different countries. Most provide little direct support for cluster formations in rural environments and, the few that do, deliver that support through entirely different mechanisms: Canada, for example, supports the emergence of clusters under the auspices of its agriculture department, while New Zealand sees it as part of its industry enterprise development programme. Nevertheless, it is within this rather confused context, where local administrations seek the means for enhancing their goals for regional economic development and where national governments seek competitive policy approaches that deliver efficiency gains for broad industry sectors that the micro-clusters model presents itself as an effective means to deliver a desired set of outcomes — social, economic, and perhaps most importantly, political!

Starting from first principles, the micro-clusters model is concerned with the enhancement or development of an industry at a community level, and with the distinct economic and social impacts, both positive and negative, that may arise from geographic clustering in the context of particular localities. While these circumstances can be envisaged in any metropolis, where distinct locational divisions and commercial precincts are almost always observable, the obvious applications for this form of development policy are in rural and regional areas. The micro-clusters model makes use of the presumptions of locational theory, which asserts the potential to enhance the flow-on effects from specialisation by building economies-of-scale from the co-location of like firms within an industry: either in the sense of horizontal integration (where firms are co-located to deliver outputs at the same stage in a value-chain) or vertical integration (where firms are integrated through different stages of a production process to deliver a final product), or through some combination of the two. This, however, is merely the first premise; for the micro-clustering model is about taking these principles into a specific context to optimise a co-operative process within a community framework to generate the dynamics that enhances both business performance and the growth of market size, with the clear intention of building and sustaining local economic welfare (Michael, 2003).

The micro-clustering approach, however, is quite distinctive — not so much in its intended outcome but rather in terms of how this is to be achieved. The traditional model envisages growth through specialisation, where the gains are apparent through economies-of-scale that lead to lower costs and, perhaps, some level of competitive advantage. The micro-clusters model integrates the concept of *diagonal* clustering (Poon, 1994), where the providers of *complementary* services (Brandenburger & Nalebuff, 1997) facilitate the development of baskets of products or services to create unique *segmented local markets*, which consumers enjoy as a single entity. In this sense, micro-clusters leverage not just the advantages of co-location, but generate further economies-of-scope that expand the breadth of the locality's product offerings and the opportunities for industrial output. Of course, it needs to be remembered that this model is about very small communities and the development of small business enterprises; hence, the gains in absolute terms that can be generated from this form of co-location are never going to be substantial and are limited by the potential to increase the local market's size over a period of time.

This argument, however, might also be perceived to contain the seeds for its own self-destruction, for because the rationale for membership of the cluster would be eliminated should any one firm within it seek to capture those gains to itself. What distinguishes the micro-cluster model for local development from any other is that it incorporates the mechanism that enables the firms and community groups that make up the cluster to co-operate, and postulates the economic and sociological reasons to explain why they will do so. In this way, the real gains from the cluster formation, small as they may be, will actually be shared among the membership and community well-being will actually be enhanced.

In this sense, it is the integration of the role of networks and the networking process that converts the micro-cluster model from an abstract explanation for one form of economic development into a functional schema for real-world applications. In effect, networks provide the social oil that allows the economic engine of a cluster formation to operate. In theory and in practice, the benefits from clustering stem from enhanced cost efficiencies for firms, the potential growth in the local market's size and their consequent multiplier effects, all of which in turn will add to local incomes and flow-on as improvements in community wealth and well-being. However, even if these gains are achieved in a successful cluster formation, they will not be distributed evenly. Some firms may reap substantial benefits, while others may see very little that they would regard as a positive commercial outcome. In the same way, within the local community, individuals and groups would anticipate the benefits from a cluster to flow in the form of externalities that enhance their standard of living, but, again, the distribution of these benefits will be uneven and the emergence of some potential negative externalities may impact more on some than on others. In short, the gains to be had from clustering will be asymmetric, for there is no reason to suppose that they would be distributed equitably. Given that this is the reality of the cluster environment, and given that the firms themselves operate in a competitive framework, there would appear to exist a fundamental impediment to the co-operative practices necessary for a cluster to operate successfully — unless some assurance exists for the range of cluster members to *trust* each other in the process of extracting the common gains.

The evolution of trust in this situation is the critical factor that facilitates the operation of a cluster (see Chapter 8). The networking process builds the social relationships between the various actors — individuals, firms and institutions — involved in the cluster's formation, allowing them to develop an understanding of common aims, values and intentions. Networks provide the social exchange that complements the economic activities of the cluster's members, drawing commerce and community values into a common alignment. Networks, however, exist in myriad forms, and each emerges according to the needs and values of the local participants that make them up. Despite their structural differences, they serve to enhance the communication process between the operators of firms and the community, to educate each other on matters that affect their common interests and to build the basis for sharing resources, ideas and the means to access the infrastructure that enhances their common market position (see Chapter 8, Table 8.2 for more detail).

The founding of a *network* does not in itself create an environment of trust and co-operation, but rather generates the social conditions necessary for individuals to explore the personal relationships that are amenable to co-operative processes. When networks are truly successful, they provide not just a framework to guide the interactions of its membership but also a context for resolving disputes and disagreements that permit those relationships to continue over time. Among the many consequences of network formations is the building of a collective understanding about the nature of the distribution of the gains from clustering, so that its members know not only why the gains accrue disproportionately, but are simultaneously assured that whatever level of benefit ought to accrue to them is actually being shared appropriately.

There is a role too for the public sector agencies responsible for local economic development and social planning in building successful clusters by fostering and supporting their associated networks. It is perhaps redundant to note, but local government agencies ought not to be concerned with those aspects of business development strategy that the firm itself controls, where the internal decision processes determine how a firm responds to its own environment and to opportunities that might optimise its outcomes through *alliances* and other forms of commercial arrangements that deliver benefits from integrated activities (see Dyer, Kale, Singh, 2001). Rather local authorities have a concern with the collective outcomes from the clustering effect, in terms of its consequences for economic well-being and managing the impacts from its externalities.

In this sense, local authorities can act as critical players in the network's success in a number of different ways. Most obviously, these agencies have better access to a range of information resources, and a better capacity to collate, process and disseminate that information to the network members. They can also serve a liaison function to connect the network with the different branches of administration as the need arises. This is not a one-way process, of course, for the agencies themselves need the input of the network members to inform the planning process and make it relevant for any particular locality. They also need this advice to guide the setting of the technical parameters for supporting the formation of a cluster of co-located firms to ensure that their actions will complement the existing economic resources and the existing social perceptions that the local community aspires to enhance.

Directions for Social Planning

If these observations on the role of cluster theory can contribute to the growth of economic opportunity in small communities, it will be because their practice is compatible with the contemporary role for government. As observed earlier in Chapter 2, past intervention policies have tended to promote one region or economic interest ahead of another, leading inevitably to electoral disharmony. The tenor of contemporary development policies now seeks to enhance the dynamics of competition, but this does not imply that intervention is precluded, rather that such actions are taken only to support the common needs of the market systems' participants (Michael, 2006).

New approaches to development now have a focus on governance to ensure that public administrators deliver a higher level of transparency and equity in their actions that is comparable for all regional interests, which was not necessarily part of common practice in the past. One option for the policy process, which matches democratic demands, is for governments and their attending agencies to devolve much of the decision making about the priorities for action, and the consequent choices about the use of limited public resources, to the affected communities. This approach does not absolve government from any responsibility for development, but instead imposes on them a need to support the unique nature of each community, perhaps with information and infrastructure, or common access and marketing, which helps them determine their own social *cost–benefit* outcomes.

Arguably, a development strategy that makes use of the micro-clusters model serves as one of the many possible approaches that fit within this emerging paradigm to make some contribution to the reconstruction of economic and social opportunity in regional communities. In the context of this discussion, of course, it is a model that has been drawn for those circumstances where growth is linked to the development of tourism, but there is no reason to suppose that it cannot be applied equally to other areas of economic specialisation. The inherent value of this model lies in its compatibility with the new policy framework because it is premised on the inclusion of community needs and its application is determined by local interests and values — but this assumes that local community groups and their various forms of networks or association have the capacity to express those democratic demands and that the responsible planning authorities are structured to receive them. If these conditions are operational, then micro-market clustering theory provides an explanation for at least one option to enhance a region's competitive advantage through specialisation.

The descriptions of the factors for successful clustering, which seem to drive the creation of a competitive advantage, are based on the co-operative and mutually supportive linkages among the cluster's members. However, these have only been tested in areas that are already regionally successful, as Porter (1998) has explained in the cases of Silicon Valley in California and in Boston Massachusetts. The micro-clusters approach has yet to be formalized for regional policy purposes, but the analysis here seeks to make use of a locality's existing market niche industries to identify the potential success factors that might apply in the specific local circumstance. This approach searches for a dynamic alignment of complementary firms (economic activities) that can be envisaged to add value to the total regional product. The desired outcome is a package of attributes delivered by a host of small businesses, which the intended target consumer will identify as the single entity they want to consume. While small scale, the synthesis and synergy between the co-located firms continues to extract economies-of-scale that service growth, but now adds a new dimension through economies-of-scope to increase opportunity and diversification. In combination, and with community co-operation, these two dimensions are presumed to generate a new pattern of accelerator effects, but the form that growth takes remains directed by the existing community.

For this approach to be made practical there still remain a number of issues to be resolved before policymakers could regard a micro-cluster model based on tourism and visitation as an appropriate tool to contribute to regional development; for in reality, it remains a hypothesis in need of still further empirical validation. Despite this constraint, the purpose of the micro-cluster approach is to actively support those communities in search of their own competitive advantage; but, almost inevitably, those same communities will lack the means to generate such information — hence, the significance of the role that public sector agencies can play in their development.

One direction for support stems from the capacity of local planning authorities to contribute to the *search* process at the local level, by servicing the information needs of communities. Local communities — their networks and their member firms — are best positioned to determine what they wish to achieve collectively, but how they choose to allocate their own resources is contingent on the information they have available and their capacity to interpret it, or to access the services that it might identify. Precisely what information is required varies in every case according to each community's unique circumstances, but municipal and regional administrative authorities by their very nature hold information and access to communication channels that is entirely relevant to those needs. As public institutions, they also hold the means to obtain still further information for collective purposes if it is needed. One obvious requirement for a cluster-building exercise is to identify the range of complementary activities suited to the delivery of a particular regional product. These complementarities will differ in every case, not only because each community seeks to deliver its own specialised and unique product, but also because the basis for visitation to each is different. The *search for complementarities* is not simply a matter of determining cross-elasticities (although these provide one type of indicator); but rather of identifying those synergies that actually add value to the total outcome for both producers and consumers. This implies a need in each environment for both a market analysis and an assessment of the psychology of consumption — as it relates to the potential visitor — for ultimately it is the consumer who determines the complementarity of what goes with what.

An avenue that emerges for public sector support stems from the capacity of government, at all levels, to contribute to this *search* process with outcomes that are useable by the community at the local level. While the cluster's individual members may well be able to make substantial contributions to this process, inevitably it will be a task beyond the resource constraints of small communities to generate such information, yet it is one that public sector development agencies are equipped to support. A priority for policy, then, is to service these information needs, allowing communities to make their own choices without superimposing an interventionist strategy by the central authorities. The evolution of the mechanisms to support the provision of information at this level will not occur without difficulty, but is essential for communities to identify and build their own competitive advantage. The task is compelling as the availability of these resources enables a community to assess the externalities of the choices it wishes to make.

A second issue for the emergence of new policy applications in this context concerns the mechanisms that public agencies can deploy to support the co-location of new firms into new clusters. Set within the broader prescriptions of a nation's economic policy and its interpretation of the competitive paradigm, this problem still has two dimensions of its own:

- servicing the needs of individual firms which might join the cluster; and
- servicing the collective needs of the association of firms that make up the cluster.

At the first level, the concern is with the location decision of the firm itself, for the growth of the cluster is contingent on the willingness of new firms to establish themselves within it. To make such a decision, the owners of a firm require the information that is necessary for them to devise their own business development strategy, and where locational choice is pertinent to the development of such a strategy, they need the information that enables them to assess both the benefits to be extracted from joining a cluster and the appropriate assurances for the sharing of co-operative gains. Local development policy, then, needs to contain guarantees that will ameliorate the risk of the location decision, not necessarily in financial terms — for the conduct of the business is the individual firm's responsibility — but in terms of institutional support to facilitate the firm's position within the cluster and the means to access its benefits. In part, this will require the provision of information that is specifically tailored to the firm's needs and its place in the network. Many municipal authorities in many different political jurisdictions already claim to carry out these functions to support new industrial development, but these actions are rarely integrated directly within the community setting and the commercial environment that the new firm will need to join.

Local development policy, of course, still needs to address the more traditional problems of providing public infrastructure, finance and collective marketing for development programmes. The issue for local planning agencies remains the lack of capital resources to initiate and maintain these activities — a problem that is made worse in small communities with limited funds by the consequences of national competition policies that seek to throw back the costs of industrial externalities to the private sector. Tourism developments tend to highlight and exacerbate these issues, because they often impose new demands on public infrastructure and new requirements for communication and marketing to regions well beyond the locality's environs. Seen in this light, and with due recognition for the need for transparency and accountability in the system of governance, effective development becomes possible only through a *whole-of-government* or multi-government approach to policy implementation. The old framework for policymaking sees national and regional government authorities equipped to deal with the broad collective demands of some industries, and leaves municipal authorities to deliver the physical needs for local development, but the mechanisms for implementation are slow and driven by common interventionist strategies that do not necessarily meet the specific needs of communities. Tourism, as an activity, calls for specific development in the destination (an internal locality issue), but also for a range of supporting actions to provide the infrastructure for travel and visitation (an external issue that may extend beyond a nation's borders); and, in these circumstances, development policies can only function when all of these interests operate from the same basis. Whole-of-government approaches seek to bring the range of public sector decision makers into single communication entities to ensure that community needs are dealt with in a timely manner and through a co-ordinated set of responses.

Issues in the Application of Micro-Cluster Theory

In essence, the principles of the micro-clustering approach have their origins in the traditional concepts of cluster theory. Many of these ideas were once taught as part and parcel of undergraduate Economic Geography subjects more than 40 years ago, but they have long since been revised and substantially recalibrated to fit with more contemporary interpretations of development, and more recently as a consequence of Porter's analyses (1991, 1998) over the last decade or so. However, microenvironments do not generate the same scale of activities that are often visible in larger regions, which for tourism includes a plethora of small communities, towns and villages with their own sense of place and identity; hence, the same assumptions about the dynamics that sustain cluster theory in broader regional applications may not necessarily be applicable. To illustrate the point, one of the core assumptions embedded in broader notions of clustering is that the benefits from a cluster formation of economic activities derive from either or both the *horizontal* or *vertical* integration of firms, because these formations have the potential to extract the economies-of-scale inherent in their *co-location*. On occasion, these benefits have been demonstrated to be significant in some larger regions or cities, but, in a microenvironment, the sum of these gains may often be too small to be detected as visible economic or social benefits at a micro level.

While this form of location analysis can be applied in some specific micro circumstances, it often does little more than illustrate the effects of economic specialisation. However, when the effects of *diagonal* clustering are added to the analytic framework, in the form of complementary activities that add value to an existing local specialisation, then the level of benefit is enhanced by increasing the economies-of-scope for firms operating in the locality. In this way, the potential is created to expand the market's size and new opportunities are generated for local wealth creation, even in small communities (see Michael, 2003). Micro-clusters based on tourism lend themselves to this hypothesis, if for no other reason than that any expansion of the complementary activities at a destination, which can be integrated into the local product, adds new attributes and new value to the basket of benefits available to consumers. The proposition that emerges, then, is that *micro-clusters* are different in both form and function to simple *co-locations* of like enterprises. What makes them different, however, is what makes the micro-clusters model a mechanism for growth.

In reality, however, there are myriad regional towns and communities with groups of co-located firms that display characteristics similar to clustering, but many (if not most) do not appear to deliver the anticipated outcomes. Often firms co-locate simply to exploit the advantages of a concentrated market, where customers are drawn to a pool of sellers on the assumption that they will offer a wider range of product choice in the particular segment that interests them. The simple act of co-location creates no other advantage than this. Rather than being a contradiction to the theoretical proposition, the principles of micro-clustering offer an explanation for these circumstances. In short, an integral part of the micro-cluster hypothesis is that the synergies generated by a cluster's formation must actually be *captured* and *shared* by the cluster's members. The implication being that the distinction between mere *co-location* and effective *clustering* in small economic communities is contingent on the mechanisms that enable the cost savings and welfare benefits from a cluster's formation to be transferred to the enterprises and to the community that makes up its membership. This does not imply that the distribution of benefits or economic gains will be equal, for as already noted it will be asymmetric, but rather that all the cluster's members understand and participate in the process.

For social planning purposes, there are a number of lessons inherent in these observations. First, the outcomes that an effective cluster can deliver are unlikely to occur without some level of social support. Indeed, the *clustering effect* arises not just from the dynamics of a particular form of economic association, but is actually determined by the extent of co-operation and trust that can arise between the cluster's members. Building trust between individuals and between individuals and organisations is not an economic process, no matter how convoluted the arguments might become about the exchange relationships involved, but necessarily must be seen as a social relationship based on shared expectations and common goals. The cluster effect emerges because the cluster members share these values and seek their implementation in their common territory. In this context, then, *networks* play a critical role in the successful formation and operation of the clustering process, and so the founding and maintenance of a functional network becomes a key target for social policy enhancement.

The evidence offered in Chapters 5, 7 and 8, makes it clear that network formation is not a simple task. Like the layers of an onion, the formation of a network consists of a series of constraints. First, a network is about the process that brings people together to deal with issues that are common to all of them. The *people*, in this context, comprise individuals with different interests and with disparate roles to play in the communal exchange that a network makes possible. Each person brings their own personality, with all the foibles that make up the human condition, and an agenda based on their particular focus — from business, community or local government — all of which adds complexity and vibrancy to the pursuit of the network's vision for local development. Second, the entrepreneurs and managers of the firms that contribute to this process have superimposed on them the reality of the constraints of commercial competition, where business survival forces them to accept only those choices that lead to cost reductions or revenue growth; hence their willingness to contribute to the network's goals is conditioned by the value of the outcomes it can achieve. Third, according to most of the case studies examined earlier, the success of a network appears to rest in the capacity of one, or a very few, individuals to play a leadership role — motivating other individuals, sharing a vision, convening meetings, building communication channels between the group and with those agencies that can provide assistance, etc. The leadership role is invariably voluntary, and almost always by self-selection, but it leaves the membership vulnerable to personality clashes, partisanship change and succession.

Nevertheless, the success of a cluster depends on the level of outcome that its corresponding network can deliver. This process, then, is often in need of more support than individual endeavour can provide. There is a role here for local government, or more precisely for the public administrative authorities and planning agencies that are responsible for community development. These bodies hold professional resources, including information and access pathways to link local community needs to a broader range of public services, and, as a function of their own core tasks in planning and development, they hold communication channels that can help co-ordinate the group's interests with the objectives of other aspects of a region's governance. Some of the case studies imply that support from the public sector is often absent, or is too slow to materialise, or is confused by agencies that are structured to pursue only commercial goals or only community goals, rather than seeking both in tandem. The lessons here suggest that the successful development of local destination networks would be enhanced by support agencies recognising the contribution they can make at this level and by adopting more proactive approaches to network support. One option, too, is for enhanced training among support agency staff to better understand how to work successfully with mixed organisations that blend community aspirations with commercial criteria, and which seek assistance rather than direction or arbitration.

Last, there are perhaps some lessons that can be learned regarding the support that is offered to relatively young networks. In order for local development agencies to maximise the potential contribution that a network formation can make to a local destination's development, first there is a need to recognise that tourism is a broad economic activity rather than a specific form of industrial production, and that it will consequently encompass a very much broader range of community interests than most other industries. The nature of tourism, with its interconnection of complementarities, provides a dynamic that both encourages network behaviour — because there are more common issues — and discourages it — because the market is highly segmented and those common issues are complex. In these circumstances, much is to be gained by actively supporting network formation, and network maintenance, at an early stage in a destination's development, for it will not necessarily occur organically. Some networks also require some modicum of financial support to become functional, but many local development agencies lack the capacity to identify new networks, or lack the political authority to contribute to them until they have become fully established and recognised as entities to be included in a budget cycle. Once beyond the start up phase, of course, public funding should be contingent upon the development of the same specific tangible performance measures that other community organisations are required to meet, perhaps in this situation addressing the potential contributions of networks in terms of learning and exchange, business activity and other desired community benefits.

Here, in this volume, clustering theory has been explored as a development framework that is amenable to public sector planning for applications within tourism micro-markets. While, it is only a beginning, it has established that there exists a theoretical basis for the evaluation of micro-clusters as a tool for regional economic development, and a rationale for public sector intervention. For the practice of policy, this approach is focussed on the creation of *opportunity*, potentially optimising the delivery of significant and sustainable economic and social benefits for regional communities. In the social context, it sees business and community development as inextricably linked, but carries with it the political advantage of devolving to a community's members the core choices affecting their economic direction and the use of those resources in ways that do not conflict with national strategies for development or with the principles of competition. The incorporation of community development and externality analysis with business strategy, perhaps, improves the capacity of public sector development agencies to enhance growth in specialised industries, such as tourism, in a manner that will prove consistent with local community ambitions.

References

Australia. (2003). *A medium to long term strategy for tourism (tourism white paper)*. Canberra, Dept. of Communications, Information Technology and the Arts.

Brandenburger, A. M., & Nalebuff, B. J. (1997). *Co-opetition* (foreword ed.). New York: Currency Doubleday.

Cioccio, L., & Michael, E. J. (2006). Hazard or disaster: Tourism management for the inevitable in northeast Victoria. *Tourism Management, 27* (forthcoming: available *www.sciencedirect.com*).

Dyer, J. H., Kale, P., & Singh, H. (2001). How to make strategic alliances work. *Sloan Management Review, 42*(1), 37–43.

Hall, C. M. (2005). Rural wine and food tourism cluster and network development. In: D. Hall, I. Kirkpatrick, & M. Mitchell (Eds), *Rural tourism and sustainable business* (pp. 149–164). Clevedon: Channelview.

Hall, C. M., & Rusher, K. (2005). Entrepreneurial characteristics and issues in the small-scale accommodation sector in New Zealand. In: E. Jones, & C. Haven (Eds), *Tourism SMEs, service quality and destination competitiveness: International perspectives* (pp. 143–154). Wallingford: CABI.

Michael, E.J. (2003). 'Tourism micro-clusters'. *Tourism Economics*, 9 (2), 133–146.

Michael, E. J. (2006). *Public policy – the competitive framework*. Melbourne: Oxford University Press.

Middleton, V. T. C. (2001). The importance of micro-businesses in European tourism. In: D. Lesley, & D. Hall (Eds), *Rural tourism and recreation* (pp. 197–201). Wallingford: CABI.

Poon, A. (1994). *Tourism, technology and competitive strategies*. CAB Wallingford: CABI.

Porter, M. E. (1991). *The competitive advantage of nations*. London: The Macmillan Press.

Porter, M. E. (1998). Clusters and the new economics of competition. *Harvard Business Review*, 6(November—December), 77–90.

Seiragaki, K. (2006). *Sustainable tourism revised: From partiality, conflict and compromise, to holism, synergy and integrated management*. Doctoral thesis, La Trobe University, Bundoora.

Tourism Victoria. (2002). *Victoria's tourism industry strategic plan summary 2002–2006*. Melbourne.

Glossary

This glossary has been prepared to assist readers with the terminology and jargon that is frequently used in discussions relating to economic development, clustering and networking. The more important terms have been identified within the text in bolded italics and are identified here with an asterisk (*). Other terms have been included to assist readers with concepts and related issues.

A

Absolute advantage
The advantage in the efficiency of production of a product enjoyed by one country over another when it uses fewer resources to produce that product than the other country does.
Accelerator effect*
The tendency for investment to increase or decrease more rapidly, when aggregate output increases or decreases, thus accelerating the growth or decline of output. Accelerator effects are different to multiplier effects. *See Multiplier.*
Actors*
Individuals, groups or institutions that play a role in making public decisions.
Aggregate demand*
The total amount that is spent on domestically produced final goods and services by all consumers, businesses, government agencies and foreigners at a given price level.
Aggregate demand curve
A graph used to depict the negative relationship between aggregate output [income] and the price level. Each point on the curve identifies the total expenditure on goods and services at a given price level.
Aggregate expenditure
The sum of all expenditure by private consumers, businesses and foreigners on domestically produced goods and services in an economy in a given time period.
Aggregate output
The total quantity of goods and services produced within an economy in a given period.
Aggregate supply
The total value of newly produced goods and services in an economy.
Aggregate supply curve
A graph used to depict the relationship between the aggregate quantity of output supplied by all firms in an economy and the overall price level.
Automatic stabilisers
Revenue and expenditure items in a national budget that automatically change with the economy to reinforce a move towards, or restrain a move away from, equilibrium GDP.
Autonomous variable
A variable that is assumed to be fixed in value, or not dependent on another function.

B

Balance of current account
A broader indicator of a nation's trading position with other countries; determined by the balance of trade plus net exports of services, net investment income and other transfer payments.

Balance of payments
A nation's record of its transactions in goods, services, assets and foreign exchange movements with the rest of the world.

Balance of trade
A nation's record of its trade in saleable goods and services; determined by the value of its merchandise exports minus its merchandise imports.

Barrier to entry*
A term used by economists to identify any cost factor or any regulatory restriction by governments that prevent or constrain a new firm from entering or competing in an industry.

Barter
The direct exchange of one good for another without the use of money.

Black economy or black market
The term used to describe the circumstances where economic activities or transactions occur, which generate outputs of value, and income for the participants, but which remain unidentified by government. The activities in black markets usually seek to avoid government regulations, and consequently remain unreported and therefore not included in any estimation of a nation's GDP.

Budget deficit/surplus
The difference between the total level of formal government spending and the total level of revenue it collects in taxes and the sale of government services in a given period. A budget deficit arises when expenditure exceeds revenue, while a surplus occurs when revenues exceed the level of spending.

Business cycle*
The term is used to refer to the theoretical notion that an economy continuously goes through a cycle — from growth, to excess demand, to inflation, to cutbacks in production, to recession and recovery through reinvestment in the economy.

C

Capital*
This term is used in two distinct contexts: first it refers to those goods produced within the economy as inputs for the production of future goods and services, such as plant, buildings and machinery; and, second, the term is used to refer to the level of funds available to support an economic activity.

Capital gain
An increase in the value of an asset over the price initially paid for it.

Capital market
The label given to the market in which households and other income earners supply their savings, for interest or for claims to future profits, to financial intermediaries to lend to firms that demand funds in order to purchase capital goods.

Capital stock
The current market value of all firms' plant, equipment, inventories, and intangible assets.

Capital-intensive industry
Those industries that use a technique of production requiring relatively large amounts of capital relative to their needs for labour or other factors.

Cartel
A group of firms acting together to manipulate either or both the market price or the volume of output in order to maximise joint profits.

Ceteris paribus [Latin]
Literally, 'all else being equal'. Used to analyse the relationship between two variables when the values for other variables are assumed to remain unchanged.

Circular flow
An economic model used to explain the relationships in a macro-economy between consumers' expenditure, the level of production or output and the income that is earned, which then becomes available for consumers to repeat the cycle.

Collective failure
A government's policy response to a perceived market failure that does not enhance the public good. *See government failure.*

Collusion*
The situation where firms act together to manipulate an economic outcome; this may involve the prices paid for resources, trading conditions, competition with other firms or the prices of final outputs. Most developed countries hold these actions to be illegal.

Co-location*
The location of firms in close geographic proximity to each other.

Comparative advantage*
The advantage in the production of a product enjoyed by one country over another when that product can be produced at lower costs, relative to the cost of other goods than can be done in the other country.

Competition policy*
A guiding framework for government policies designed to facilitate the operation of market forces within an economy.

Competitive tendering
A form of competitive practice by governments that allows private operators to bid to provide a service as defined by a public agency. *See contracting out.*

Complementarities*
A relationship between firms where the activities of one adds value to the activities of another.

Complements*
Goods and services which are different in their production process, but which are consumed together (bread and butter); hence, according to 'the law of demand', if the price of one increases the quantity demanded of both will fall.

Constant returns to scale
Where the increase in the quantity of output by a firm has no significant effect on the average cost per unit produced.

Contracting out
Where a firm or public agency lets contracts to another firm or public agency for the supply of goods or services, rather than producing them with that firm's own resources.

Consumer*
An individual or a household who consumes goods or services for their own benefit.

Consumer goods*
Goods produced for present consumption.

Consumer price index
A scaled measure of changes to consumer prices, usually computed from a bundle of consumer goods that represents the *market basket* purchased by the typical consumer.

Consumer sovereignty
A concept from contemporary economic theory which holds that consumers ultimately determine what will be produced, or not produced, by choosing what to purchase, or what not to purchase.

Consumer surplus
The difference between the maximum amount a person is willing to pay for a good and its current market price.

Consumption*
The expenditure by individuals and households on the purchase of goods and services.

Consumption function
The relationship between total consumer expenditure and total disposable income.

Contestable market
In the literature of economics, it is said to be a market in which entry and exit is costless to the producer, but in the broader management literature the term is used to identify a market in which it is possible for different firms to compete.

Cost-benefit*
A technique by which the benefits of an investment project over time are calculated and weighed against its costs.

Cost-push inflation
Inflation caused by an increase in inputs to production costs.

D

Decreasing cost industry
An industry that captures external economies-of-scale so that average costs decrease as the industry grows.

Decreasing returns to scale
Where the increase in the quantity of a firm's output leads to higher average costs per unit produced.

Deflation
A sustained decrease in the general price level.

Demand*
The quantity of a given product that an individual or a household would be willing to buy at different prices.

Demand schedule
A set of data showing how much of a given product a household would be willing to buy at different prices.

Demand-pull inflation
Inflation caused by a sustained increase in aggregate demand.

Demerit good
A product or service that generates some form of social harm.

Depreciation
The decline in the economic value of an asset over time.

Depression
A prolonged and deep recession, normally implying more than one year of declining GDP.

Deregulation*
The removal of regulatory constraints on the production or distribution of goods and services.

Derived demand
The demand for a good or service or for some other resource that arises as a consequence of the availability of some other economic activity or some other resource.

Destinations*
In the context of tourism, destinations are the places that tourists visit, where the experience is provided that the tourist is seeking.

Discretionary income
A concept from marketing theory that is being increasingly used in tourism analysis — it identifies the amount left over from a household's or an individual's budgeted expenses on essential items that can be used for the purchase of nonessential goods or services (not to be confused with disposable income, below).

Disposable income
National income minus taxes plus transfer payments by government to individuals; or the income available to households or individuals to spend or save.

Durable goods
Consumer goods that last a relatively long time, such as cars and household appliances.

Dyadic linkages*
Two organisations that find they can gain a mutual benefit from pursuing a common goal.

E

Economic cost
The full costs of production including a normal rate of return on investment, and the opportunity cost of each factor of production. Economic costs include normal long-run profits.

Economic development*
The process of creating the conditions that lead to economic growth (below).

Economic growth*
An increase in the total output of an economy (or the region that is under examination). It occurs when a society acquires new resources or when it learns to produce more by using existing resources.

Economics
The study of how individuals and societies allocate and use the scarce resources that nature and previous generations have provided.

Efficiency*
At the simplest level, efficiency refers to 'the absence of waste'. Economic analysts also regard it as the situation where all resources are allocated effectively so that it is not possible to improve the welfare of some members of society without making some others worse off. *See Pareto efficiency.*

Employment*
Any person aged 15 years to 65 years performing paid work. Some state's statistical definitions use different age ranges or nominate specific minimum hours of work per week.

Entrepreneur*
A person who bears the responsibility for organising, managing or assuming the risks for a firm: also, the person taking a new idea or a new product into the market.

Equilibrium [market]
Occurs when there is no tendency for change. It is the condition that exists when the quantity supplied is exactly matched to the quantity demanded.

Equilibrium price
The price determined at equilibrium in the market, where the quantity supplied matches the quantity demanded.

Equity*
Fairness.

Excess profit
Profits over and above the normal rate of return on investment; anything greater than the normal opportunity cost of capital.

Exchange rate*
The price of one country's currency in terms of another country's currency; the ratio at which two currencies are traded for each other.

Excise taxes
A form of tax set for the purchase of specific commodities.

Expansionary policy
An increase in government spending, or a reduction in taxation, that aims to stimulate both output and employment to increase the rate of economic growth and the level of national income.

Expected rate of return
The annual rate of return that a firm expects to obtain through a capital investment; the rate varies between industries to reflect risk and historic profit margins.

Externalities*
The costs or benefits resulting from some activity or transaction that is imposed or bestowed on individuals, households, or other organisations that are unrelated to that activity or transaction: also called *spillovers* or *neighbourhood effects*.

F

Factors of production
The inputs into the production process: land, labour, and capital.
Final goods and services
Newly produced goods that are not resold to someone else; that is they are the goods that are for use by consumers.
Financial intermediaries
Banks and other institutions that act as a link between lenders and borrowers.
Firm*
The smallest identifiable organisation that makes decisions about transforming resources (inputs) into products or services (outputs).
First mover advantage*
The situation where the first firm to move into a market (or locality) enjoys a series of commercial advantages that allow it to build a customer base in the absence of competing operators.
Fiscal policy
The spending and taxing policies used by the government to influence the direction of aggregate demand and aggregate supply.
Floating exchange rate
Exchange rates that are determined by the unregulated international forces of supply and demand.
Free entry
The absence of barriers to prevent new firms from commencing production in an industry.
Free exit
The absence of costs or conditions when firms cease production and leave a market.
Free market*
An economic environment in which the principal decisions concerning the production, allocation and distribution of resources are made by private individuals; hence, it will not normally be constrained by excessive regulation, and trade between counties will not be constrained by political barriers, tariffs, quotas, or other constraints on production and distribution.
Free rider*
The circumstance where individuals or organisations make use of a resource without contributing fairly to its cost: it is an issue commonly found in the analysis of public goods where people are able to access the benefits irrespective of their level of contribution; hence they often become unwilling to pay for them.

G

Game theory*
A mathematical approach to the analysis of the competing strategies of firms where the outcome depends on the assumptions made about the strategies chosen by the rival firm.

General Agreement on Tariffs and Trade [GATT]*
An international agreement, signed originally in 1947, to promote the liberalisation of foreign trade.

Globalisation*
The generic term used to describe the actions of states to liberalise trade and establish common rules for the free movement between them of goods and services, labour, and capital.

Government failure*
The circumstance where government decisions exacerbate a market failure, hence the allocation of resources is made even less efficient by this intervention. *See collective failure.*

Government purchases [of goods and services]
Expenditures by national [or federal], regional [or state], and local governments on final goods and services.

Greenfield [site]*
A development project that starts without any pre-existing restraints or conditions; an analogy to a new construction site where every aspect of the project has to be built for the first time.

Gross domestic product [GDP]*
The total market value of all final goods and services produced within the domestic economy in a given time period.

Gross national product [GNP]
The total market value of all final goods and services produced by factors of production owned by a country's citizens, regardless of where that output is produced.

H

Household*
The individual or group of individuals that makes up the smallest identifiable decision-making unit about consumption in an economy.

Household disposable income
The amount of money available to a household for consumption and savings after tax and transfer payments. Includes wages, salaries, dividends, interest, and rents.

Human capital
Human resources; as a form of intangible capital that includes the skills and knowledge of workers acquired through education and training.

Hyperinflation
A period of very rapid increases in the overall price level.

I

Imperfect competition
An industry in which single firms have some control over price and competition. Imperfectly competitive industries may give rise to an inefficient allocation of resources.

Imperfect information
The circumstance where either or both the consumer or the producer has insufficient knowledge of market conditions, regarding product, input characteristics, prices, etc., to make a rational decision about consumption or production.

Import substitution
An industrial trade strategy that favours developing local industries that can manufacture goods to replace imports.

Income*
The sum of all a household's wages, salaries, profits, interest payments, rents, and other forms of earnings in a given period of time.

Income effect
The presumption that if leisure is a normal good, when wages rise, people may decide to consume more of it and to work less. *See substitution effect.*

Increasing returns to scale
Where the increase in the quantity of a firm's outputs leads to lower average costs per unit produced.

Indirect taxes
Taxes on consumer goods and services that are hidden in the price, such as sales taxes, customs duties and license fees.

Industrial policy
Government involvement in the allocation of resources and other factors across industry sectors.

Industry*
The group of firms (one, few or many) that produce a similar product using similar inputs in the production process. An industry may be defined widely — *agriculture* — or, can be increasingly segmented — *dairy* — until it defines a unique activity — *cheese.*

Inflation
A sustained increase in the general price level.

Inflation rate
The percentage change in the price level over a given time period.

Infrastructure*
The supporting industries, services and resources that are necessary to enable other forms of production to take place, for example: water supply, roads, power, education, etc.

Innovation*
The use of new knowledge to produce new products or produce existing products more efficiently.

Inputs*
The factors (labour skills, capital, technology, goods and services, and other resources) that firms purchase and turn into outputs.

Interest
The opportunity cost of borrowing money, often expressed as a fee that a borrower pays to a lender for the use of their funds.

Interest groups*
An identifiable group of people who share common goals and values, who come together in a formal or informal organisation to influence the outcome of particular economic or social processes to deliver decisions in their favour.

Intermediate goods
Goods that are produced by one firm for use in further processing by another firm.
Investment*
Planned expenditure on new capital, plant, equipment, and technology to create new goods and services for consumption in the future.

L

Labour force
The number of people in work or actively seeking employment and able to work. This includes the number of people unemployed.
Labour market*
The input, or resource market, where individuals supply work to firms that demand labour in return for wages.
Labour-intensive industry
Those industries that use techniques of production requiring a relatively high usage of labour relative to the need for capital or other factors.
Lag
The time that it takes to put a desired policy into effect.
Laissez-faire economy
Literally from the French: 'allow [you] to do'. An economy in which individual people and firms pursue their own self — interests without any central direction or regulation.
Law of demand
The negative relationship between price and quantity demanded: as price rises, quantity demanded decreases, and as price falls, quantity demanded increases.
Law of diminishing returns
When additional units of a variable input are added to fixed inputs after a certain point, the marginal product of the variable input declines.
Law of supply
The positive relationship between price and quantity of a good supplied: an increase in market price will lead producers to increase the quantity supplied, while a decrease in market price will lead producers to decrease the quantity supplied.
Long run
The period of time for a firm in which there are no fixed production costs; that is all costs can be varied. Firms can increase or decrease the scale of operation, and new firms can enter or existing firms can exit the industry.
Luxury goods
Goods which are not necessary for normal living, sometimes observable as goods where the income elasticity is positive and greater than one. Many economists argue that most forms of tourism can be categorised this way.

M

Macroeconomics
The branch of economics that deals with the aggregate economy. Macroeconomics focuses on the determinants of national income, aggregate expenditure, aggregate production, and the overall level of prices.

Marginal product
The additional quantity of output that can be produced by adding one more unit of a specific input.

Marginal propensity to consume
The proportion of a change in income that a household spends on consumption.

Marginal propensity to import
The proportion of a change in income that is spent on imports.

Marginal propensity to save
The proportion of a change in income that a household allocates to savings.

Marginal social cost
The additional cost to society of producing an additional unit of a good or service. It is the sum of the marginal costs of producing the product and the correctly measured *social costs* incurred in the process of production. *See social costs.*

Marginal utility
The additional satisfaction gained by the consumption or use of one more unit of a good or service.

*Markets**
Institutions, which may be formal or informal, through which buyers and sellers interact and engage in the process of exchange.

Market demand
The sum of all the quantities of a good or service demanded by all households per period of time: often used in the context of one type of product or one industry.

Market failure
The circumstance where resources are misallocated, or allocated inefficiently to the production process, resulting in waste or loss of value.

Market power
The capacity to alter an efficient market outcome for the benefit of an individual firm or consumer.

Means of production
The resources required to produce any given good or service.

Merit good
A product that generates some form of social benefit.

Microeconomics
The branch of economics that deals with the functioning of individual industries and the behaviour of individual decision-making units: firms and households.

*Mixed economy**
An economy that combines government and private ownership to control resource allocation in the production of goods and services.

Model*
A formal statement of a theory — usually an abstraction from reality based on an observable relationship between two or more variables.

Monetary policy
The decisions of a state's central bank regarding the money supply and interest rates.

Money market
The market in which money is made available at an interest rate in return for guarantees of repayment.

Monopoly
An industry structure (or market organisation) in which there is only one firm that produces a product for which there are no close substitutes. Monopolists can set prices and control output levels.

Moral hazard
A circumstance that may arise when it becomes possible for one party to a contract to pass the cost or the risk of their behaviour on to the other party to the contract.

Multiplier*
The ratio of the change in the equilibrium level of output to a change in some autonomous variable.

N

National debt
The total amount of outstanding government securities held by the domestic public and by foreigners.

National income accounts
Data collected and published by a government describing the various components of the national economy.

Natural monopoly
A description for an industry that uses techniques of production that continue to deliver increasing economies-of-scale in producing its output, given the limits to the market's size; hence production of the goods or services by a single firm is the most efficient outcome in that industry.

Negative externality*
Costs of an economic activity that are imposed on a third party who is unrelated to the production or consumption of the good or service being produced; where the social costs of production or consumption exceed the social benefit.

Neoliberalism*
A generic label used to describe the set of ideologies that seeks to constrain the role of government to favour actions that focus largely on enhancing the development of a free market economy and the benefits from global trade.

Net trade flow
The difference in value between all exports and all imports — the result can be positive or negative.

Networking*
The process and activities involved in building and sustaining a network.

Networks*
An association of individuals seeking a common purpose; these associations are usually relatively small and confined to a particular locality or to a particular kind of activity pursued in common by the members. Networks consist of ties or relationships between one actor and a set of other actors — firms, government agencies, organisations, or individuals. The term 'network' is often used as a descriptor for the interactions between a firm and the people who make up its external environment.

Niche markets*
A market comprising a very specialized product that appeals to a small segment of consumers; often referred to in tourism analysis as 'special interest tourism'.

Nominal GDP
Gross domestic product measured in current prices.

Nondurable goods
Where the value of a good is used up quickly by the consumer, as with food or clothing.

Normal goods
Goods for which the quantity demanded goes up as income rises, and for which the quantity demanded will fall as income declines.

Normal rate of profit [return]
A rate of profit that is just sufficient to keep entrepreneurs and investors satisfied, sufficient for firms to stay in the industry rather than seek to exit.

North–south trade*
A term used originally to describe the disparity in trade between Europe and Africa (north/south) but now used generally to apply to the disparity in trade flows between rich, developed nations and poor, underdeveloped ones.

O

Oligopoly
A form of industry or market structure dominated by the existence of only a few firms, each large enough to influence the market price of the industry's output.

Opportunity cost*
The value of the option that is given up when another choice or decision is made: that is the value of the next best alternative foregone.

Optimal method of production
The production method that minimises economic costs.

Outputs*
Useable products; identifiable as actual goods and services.

Outsourcing
The use of an external supplier under contract to supply or carry out some function for and on behalf of a principal.

P

Pareto efficiency [Pareto optimality]
The situation where all resources are allocated efficiently, such that it is not possible to improve the welfare of some members of society without making some others worse off.

Per capita GDP
A country's GDP divided by its population.

Perfect knowledge
The assumption that all households and economic decision makers possess a knowledge of market conditions, including the quality and price of alternatives goods and services, inputs and resources.

Personal income
The net income received by households before paying personal income taxes.

Physical capital
Material things used as inputs in the production of future goods and services: includes non-residential and residential structures, durable equipment and inventories.

Political business cycle
A business cycle that has been manipulated by elected office-bearers so that periods of strong growth coincide with scheduled elections, for the obvious purpose of maximising their chances for reelection.

Positive externality*
Benefits that derive from an economic activity that are bestowed on a third party who is unrelated to the production or consumption of the good or service being produced; where the social benefits of production or consumption exceed the social cost.

Potential GDP
The level of aggregate output that can be sustained in the long run without inflation: often referred to as maximum efficient output for the aggregate economy, or as full-employment GDP.

Poverty cycle
The concept that poverty is self-perpetuating because poor nations are unable to save and invest enough to accumulate the capital stock to stimulate economic growth.

Present [discounted] value
The present discounted value of a given number (*X)* dollars at some point of time in the future (*t* years) is the sum of the amount you need to pay today multiplied by the current interest rate.

Price*
The money amount that a product sells for per unit. It reflects what individuals are willing to pay.

Price ceiling
A maximum price that sellers may charge for a good: this can be set by government as a method to limit increases in prices.

Price index
A scaled measurement showing how the average price of a bundle of goods changes over time.

Principle of increasing costs
When the production of a good is increased, generally the opportunity cost of producing another unit of that good also increases.

Private consumption expenditure
A major component of GDP: it comprises the total expenditure by consumers [households] on goods and services.

Private investment
A major component of GDP: it comprises the total investment by the private [or non-government] sector on the purchase of new housing, plants, equipment, and inventory.

Private goods
Products produced by firms for sale [and ownership] to individual households.

Private sector
Includes all independently owned profit-making firms, nonprofit organisations, and households; all the decision-making units in the economy that are not part of the government.

Privatization*
The transfer of the ownership of government businesses and resources to the private sector.

Producers*
Those people or groups of people, whether private or public, who transform resources into useable products or output.

Production function
A mathematical expression of a relationship between inputs and outputs: shows units of total product as a function of units of inputs.

Production*
The process by which inputs are combined, transformed and turned into outputs.

Production possibilities*
The maximum combination of goods and services that can be produced when the available productive resources are used efficiently.

Productivity*
The change in the value of outputs from a given value of inputs.

Productivity of labour
Output per worker hour, the amount of output produced by an average worker in one hour.

Productivity of an input
The amount of output produced per unit of the input.

Profit*
The difference between total revenues and total costs: not to be confused with *economic profit*.

Property rights*
The recognition through the legal process to the right of ownership of physical and intellectual property, including the rights to ownership in the future.

Protection
The practice of shielding a sector of the economy from foreign competition.

Public-choice theory
An economic approach to the analysis of public decision making. It assumes that the same motivations that are used to explain private decision making are equally applicable to explanations of public decision making.

Public debt
The debt of government to private sector lenders.
Public goods*
Goods or services that bestow collective benefits on members of society. Such goods are both non-rival in consumption and their benefits are nonexcludable. Also called *social* or *collective* goods.
Public sector*
Includes all agencies at all levels of government: national [federal], regional [state], and local.
Public welfare*
Government transfer programs that provide cash or other benefits to low income earners to maintain basic levels of consumption.

Q

Quantity demanded
The amount (number of units) of a product that a household would buy in a given period of time at a given price.
Quantity supplied
The amount of a particular product that a firm would be willing and able to offer for sale at a given price during a given time period.
Quotas*
A prescribed limit set by government on the quantity available of a product; for example, it may be in the form of a limit on output or a limit on the volume that can be imported.

R

Rational expectations hypothesis
A theory that people have reasonable information to forecast events in the economy and that they use it to form their expectations of the future.
Real gross domestic product*
Gross domestic product measured in the prices of a fixed or base year.
Real interest rate
The difference between the interest rate and the inflation rate.
Recession
A period in which real GDP declines for at least two consecutive quarters; usually accompanied by falling output and rising unemployment.
Recognition lag
The time it takes for policy makers to recognise the need for a change of economic policy.
Regional equalisation*
Policies practiced by governments that aim to provide the same level of fiscal support to the regions within a state, irrespective of those region capacity to enhance economic output.

Resources*
Anything provided by nature or by human effort that can be used directly or indirectly in the production process.

Response lag
The time taken for the economy to adjust to the new conditions after a new policy is implemented.

Revenue
Receipts from the sale of products.

S

Savings*
The part of income that a household does not consume in a given period of time.

Services*
Nonphysical or intangible things consumers buy that are not storable, e.g. hospitality, legal or medical services and education.

Shift of demand
The change in demand that occurs when a factor determining demand alters and a new relationship between quantity demanded for the product and its price is established.

Short run
The period of time for which two conditions hold: first, the firm is operating with costs that are fixed for at least one factor of production, and as a consequence that firm can neither enter nor exit the industry in which they operate.

Social capital*
This term is used in two distinct applications. In Economics it refers to the capital that provides services to the public, usually in the form of public works [such as roads and bridges] and public services [such as public health or fire protection]. In social theory the term refers to those resources embedded in the character of the relationships between individuals, communities, networks and societies, and realized through members' ability to participate in collective goals and the propensity to trust another party.

Social choice
The problem of deciding what society wants. From a political perspective, it might be seen as the process of adding up all the preferences of individuals to make a choice for society as a whole.

Social contracts
Agreements between communities and government, also applied to industrial agreements between workers and firms.

Social embeddedness*
A term used in network analysis to refer to the level of engagement and participation in day-to-day activities of the community in which an individual or an organisation is located.

Social networks*
Networks that are based on the personal or cultural ties or relationships between the individuals and their families, their friends and acquaintances that makes up the network's membership.

Social costs*
The costs that a society incurs as a consequence of maintaining its production processes which are not recovered by the private producers of goods and services and must be met by the communities themselves.

Speculation
An expectation that the purchase of high-risk assets will deliver a price rise above normal market prices to make a windfall profit: gambling.

Spillover effects*
See externalities.

Stabilization policy
A term used to describe the use of both monetary and fiscal policy, where the goals are to smooth out fluctuations in output and employment and to keep prices as stable as possible.

Subsidies*
Government payments made to domestic firms and other public sector producers to lower prices or increase outputs.

Substitutes*
Goods that can serve as replacements for another; when the price of one increases, demand for the other rises.

Sunk costs
Costs that cannot be avoided or recovered, regardless of what is done in the future, because they have already been incurred.

Supply-side policies
Government policies that focus on aggregate supply and increasing production capacity.

Sustainable*
A term that is much used in tourism analysis, but which appears to have a variety of meanings in different applications — but where the general intention is to imply that the resources needed to produce the desired economic and social outputs continue to be available over protracted periods of time.

T

Tariff
A tax on imports.

Technological change*
The introduction of new methods of production or new products intended to increase the productivity of existing inputs or to raise marginal product.

Terms of trade
The ratio at which a country can trade domestic products for imported products.

Three economic tasks
The economic questions that all societies must answer:
(1) What will be produced?
(2) How will it be produced?
(3) Who will get what is produced?

Time lags
See *lags.*
Trade deficit
Occurs when a country's exports of goods are less in value than its imports of goods in a given period.
Trade surplus
Occurs when a country exports more goods in value than it imports in a given period.
Transaction economics*
The costs for producers and consumers that are inherent in the process of conducting transactions or exchanges.
Transfer payments
Cash payments made by government to people who do not supply goods, services, or labour in exchange for these payments: includes various social security benefits, veterans' benefits, and welfare payments, etc.

U

Unemployment*
A person aged 15 years to 65 years who is not working, but who is able to work and actively seeking employment. The employment age range may differ between states.
Unemployment rate
The ratio of the number of people unemployed to the total number of people in the labour force; i.e. the percentage of the labour force that is unemployed.
Utility
A term used in economics to identify how a consumer makes a choice, based on the satisfaction, or reward, that a product or service is perceived to yield to the individual consumer of it.

V

Value added
The difference between the value of goods as they leave a stage of production and the cost of the goods when they entered that stage.
Value chain*
A description of the production process where raw materials are converted through a series of steps into a final product, where each step adds additional value.
Variable
A measure that can change from time to time or from observation to observation.

W

Wealth* (net worth)
The total value of what a household owns minus what it owes. It is a measure of stocks, assets and liabilities.

Wealth effect
The change in consumption brought about by a change in real wealth that results from a change to the price level.

World Bank
An international agency that lends money to individual countries for projects that promotes economic development.

XYZ

Youth unemployment*
The level of unemployment of young workers, usually described as those seeking their first job or as under 21 years of age.

Zoning
A term used in land use planning to designate certain areas for development, recreation, industry, commerce, residential housing, etc.

Author Index

Subject Index